It's all about
thinking

It's all about thinking

Creating Pathways for All Learners
in the Middle Years

LEYTON SCHNELLERT, LINDA WATSON,
AND NICOLE WIDDESS

FOREWORD BY FAYE BROWNLIE

PORTAGE & MAIN PRESS

Portage & Main Press gratefully acknowledges the financial support of the Province of Manitoba through the Department of Sport, Culture & Heritage and the Book Publishing Tax Credit, and the Government of Canada through the Canada Book Fund (CBF) for our publishing activities.

Printed and bound in Canada by Friesens
Cover and interior design by Relish New Brand Experience Inc.

Library and Archives Canada Cataloguing in Publication

Schnellert, Leyton, author
    It's all about thinking middle years : creating pathways for all learners in middle years / Leyton Schnellert, Nicole Widdess, Linda Watson.

Issued in print and electronic formats.
ISBN 978-1-55379-509-4 (pbk.).--ISBN 978-1-55379-528-5 (pdf)

    1. Middle school teaching. 2. Middle school education.
I. Widdess, Nicole, 1976-, author II. Watson, Linda, 1958-, author III. Title.

LB1623.S35 2014   373.1102   C2014-905122-0

                                          C2014-905123-9

21 20 19 18   2 3 4 5 6

PORTAGE & MAIN PRESS

www.portageandmainpress.com
Winnipeg, MB
Treaty 1 Territory and homeland of the Métis Nation

FSC
www.fsc.org
MIX
Paper from
responsible sources
FSC® C016245

Dedication
To teachers who extend every effort and stretch their reach to embrace and learn from diversity.

Acknowledgments

This book—and our learning—would not have come to fruition without the support of our families. Thank you Mike, Kate, Megan-Riley, Jim, Sarah, and Trevor for your love, support, and wisdom.

Our thinking and practices continue to develop through our collaborations with teachers and students in classrooms. This book came together because colleagues accepted our invitation to collaborate with us and publicly share their learning journeys. At the beginning of each chapter, we acknowledge the colleagues whose voice and work you will encounter.

Most of all, we thank Faye Brownlie for generously sharing her work and passion with us and encouraging us to develop and share our practice.

Table of Contents

tenet — an opinion, principle, belief
— held to be true

Foreword

①Collaborating. ②Uncovering potential. ③Extending who we are. ④Building relationships. ⑤Developing thinkers and thinking. ⑥Celebrating diversity.

With these as foundational tenets, we are invited into the opening chapter "Teaching and Learning in the Middle Years: Diversity as Strength." Authors Leyton, Nicole, and Linda focus their first chapters on the why behind their practice. They are passionate about working in fully inclusive classrooms, about seeing the strengths in each and every middle years learner, about the power of teachers working together with common goals, sharing their expertise and continuing to build this expertise as they take risks in their own learning, fueled by personal inquiry questions. In their classrooms, they:

- start the year getting to know their learners by using (in)formative assessment.
- integrate their curriculum by uncovering the big ideas and essential questions, guided always by who the learners are, what strengths they bring, and what will stretch them.
- focus on deep learning, the learning that will last a lifetime, learning that connects to individuals and enables each to become more capable and self-reliant as a learner.
- use big ideas, backward design, collaboration, choice, cross-curricular integration, assessment for learning, and universal design for learning.
- continually turn to research for guidance and support.

The heart of the book and my favourite sections follow. Each chapter offers a pathway, a way to put into practice the authors' beliefs, to build on the energy and excitement of middle years learners. There are multiple pathways—integrating the arts, using inquiry and project-based learning, through social-emotional learning to self-regulated learning, using diverse texts, through writing, and through technology and new literacies.

Within each chapter, we visit middle years teachers throughout British Columbia as they share a lesson or a unit exemplifying a pathway that they have explored with their learners. The lessons are clear and easy to follow in the familiar three-stage pattern:

- *connect* with the learners and their background knowledge to build motivation and enthusiasm for the upcoming learning
- *process* new information in active and different ways
- *transform* new learning into knowledge, a process that has been transformed by the learner

Key point ✱

They also all follow a guided "release of responsibility" framework—model, provide guided practice with partners and give feedback, independent practice and feedback, and finally independent application. Although we have known for many years that this is the backbone of teaching, the necessity of pacing ourselves to implement all these stages in classrooms filled with diversity continues to pose challenges. Now we have more examples to follow.

I always find it exciting to see the multiple ways that teachers have to reach their students. Even more exciting is when these multiple ways are made accessible to me so that I can springboard from their expertise and stretch my practice. That excitement permeates this text. As an example, Matt Rosati presents his journey into project-based and inquiry learning. He walks us through how he manages the class, beginning with a co-inquiry and a focus question and moving to personal inquiry. Noting that his learners need to develop specific reading skills, Matt presents a sequence of lessons to help them decode texts and construct meaning. Yes! In middle school, explicitly teaching reading in an inquiry PBL class, it's possible even with high diversity—and absolutely necessary! I await the start of school so I can grab a class and try the focus question, image, and reading skills sequence.

For many years, I have been passionate about Literature Circles with text sets, no roles, changing groups, and no limits on reading. It thrilled me to learn about so many extensions: Marna Macmillan and Jacquie Moniot with Information Circles investigating persecution and compassion; Nicole, Leyton, and Lynn Wainwright investigating multiple perspectives on the issues of residential schools through Poetry Circles; Ken Wayne, Tammy Orthner, and Sheri Gurney moving with Numeracy Circles; Kristi Johnston's use of graphic novels; Andrea Hart using diverse texts and online tools for her students to explore the urinary system; Tammy Renyard exploring the concepts of courage and strength from within in a "Stop cyberbullying" unit. How about exploring issues of homelessness in the community with Julie Hearn? Or using drama to learn about the French Revolution with Linda and Leyton?

I do a disservice by not mentioning all the teachers who contribute in this book. For that, I apologize. The stories and examples are rich and wonderful. They will enrich your practice and the lives of your students. Find your pathway and enjoy!

Faye Brownlie
Author and Staff Development Consultant

Chapter 1

Teaching and Learning in the Middle Years: Diversity as Strength

What is essential is not always visible to the eye. *The Little Prince*

(L'essentiel est invisible pour les yeux. *Le petit prince,* Antoine de Saint-Exupéry)

Picture this. You walk into a classroom of 13- and 14-year-olds who are so engrossed in their work that they do not notice your entrance. One pair of boys are sitting on the floor with a stack of books and a pad of pop-up notes. They are writing two-sentence summaries to be added to their mind map. A trio—two girls and a boy—are sketching out the rough draft of a design they have been planning for several days. The pencil moves slowly, and the two observers offer ideas to their peer. After scanning the room for a while, you spot the teacher conferencing with a student about his work. The teacher nods as the boy, an English language learner new to Canada, describes his 3-D model. Over on the far side of the room, a group of students sit in a Literature Circle debating the plausibility of a historical novel they have all chosen to read. Through the classroom window, you can see two groups of students making tableaux to represent scenes from a revolution. It's active. It's dynamic. Students seem genuinely engaged, and they are directing their own learning. You wonder why and how this classroom is so positive and productive. What's essential here may not, at first, be visible to the eye.

In this classroom, the teacher and students share ownership of the approaches and principles in place. It took time and patience to create this classroom environment and to develop the approaches and practices in place. But the pay-off is evident: the students and the teacher are thriving as learners.

Developing and Sharing Our Practice

Teaching is a learning profession. Teaching is a practice of uncovering potential and extending who we are, what we know, and what we do. The learning and personal growth that we are so privileged to experience as teachers is parallel to what we wish for all our students.

We are three experienced educators who have taught middle years learners in a variety of school configurations—elementary, middle, junior high, and secondary schools. We are passionate about creating classrooms that nurture critical thinking, creativity, collaboration, social responsibility, and self-regulated learning. In this book, we pull together current philosophy and practice about middle years education with examples from our own classrooms and those of colleagues we deeply respect. Our professional development has come from identifying areas in our practice that we want to improve, getting ideas and examples from resources like this one, and inquiring together. Our goal is to inspire and support you, our colleagues, in taking up leading edge ideas and practices.

The approaches we describe in this book demonstrate characteristics of effective middle grades education. This chapter draws from *This We Believe: Keys to Educating Young Adolescents* (Lounsbury, AMLE 2010) to introduce research-based philosophy and practices that you will encounter throughout this book (Figure 1.1).

Middle Years Philosophy and Practice

Educators value young adolescents and are prepared to teach them.

Effective middle grades educators make a conscious choice to work with young adolescents and advocate for them. They understand the developmental uniqueness of this age group, the appropriate curriculum, effective learning and assessment strategies, and their importance as models. (Lounsbury, AMLE 2010)

All students deserve to have learning experiences that recognize them as individuals who have untapped potential, unique to them. Middle years learners are in developmentally different places and will grow and develop in remarkable ways if we meet them where they are. Teaching and learning in the middle years is a relational endeavour. Making a difference in the lives of young adolescent students is the foundation of our work as teachers. We are guided by the knowledge that relationships are at the centre of all successful classrooms. We need to learn about each student's strengths, stretches, interests, and background to effectively design learning in the content areas.

Because relationships are central to middle years teaching and learning, we must recognize that our teaching practice is a reflection of who *we* are as people. Middle years learners look at us as models. They need to see and hear about the choices we make and how we see ourselves as learners. We agree

Figure 1.1 Middle Years Philosophy and Practice

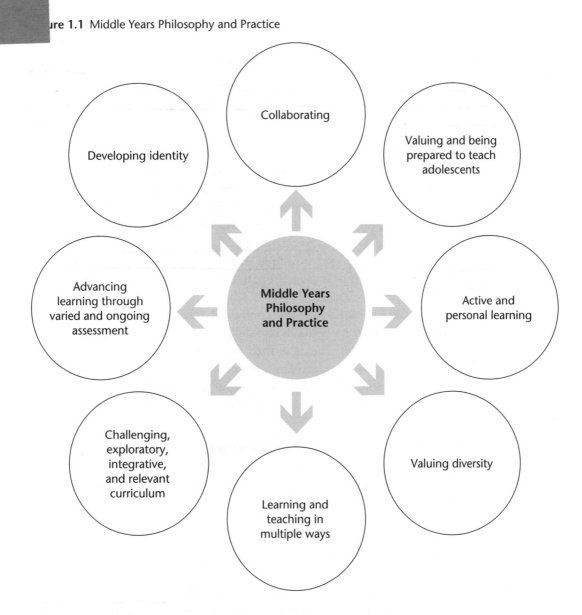

with Parker Palmer (2007) who writes in *The Courage to Teach*: "We teach who we are." Accepting the challenge of teaching in the middle years means finding appropriate, professional ways to engage authentically as a role model. Rich learning for teachers and students comes from exploring and coming to understand *our* needs, interests, backgrounds, strengths, and challenges. Linda Watson, through reflecting on her life experience and teaching, models that she is dramatic, funny, strict about proper behaviour, self-aware of how her actions affect others, and sensitive to emotions around her. She reveals these elements of herself throughout her teaching. We purposefully create a safe space for learning by sharing who we are and asking students: "Who are you?"

We can tailor learning opportunities to meet the needs of our students when we work from principles and frameworks that are developmentally appropriate, research-based, and philosophically sound (Figure 1.1). Teaching and learning in the middle years means drawing together the experiences of our diverse students, the big ideas of the curriculum content, and related issues. Both teachers and students have roles to play in creating and participating in challenging, responsive, and relevant curriculum.

Active, purposeful learning involves teachers helping students see the world in new ways, engage in investigations, and connect what they are learning from curriculum content to themselves and to the world. The nature of what each student might bring to the class is not always "visible to the eye," yet each student has a role to play in the classroom community, a role that no one else can play. We need to actively build a learning community where each student is acknowledged as unique and as having something valuable to contribute. Framing differences as strengths helps middle years students as they develop their identity.

Building the foundation for this community requires numerous activities designed specifically for students to investigate their own history and to draw conclusions about how key events in their lives have shaped who they are. We use community-building activities, performance-based assessments, our Who am I? Profile, class reviews, transition meetings, field-book writing, collecting artifacts, inquiry processes, and many more classroom activities to encourage this.

See Ch. 3

Students and teachers are engaged in active, purposeful learning.

As they develop the ability to hypothesize, to organize information into useful and meaningful constructs, and to grasp long-term cause and effect relationships, students are ready and able to play a major role in their own learning and education. (Lounsbury, AMLE 2010)

Students have to be at the centre of their own learning. Student self-assessment and reflection on what is working and what needs improving have been shown to increase students' transfer of learning to new settings and events (Donovan, Bransford, and Pellegrino 1999). We design learning experiences that offer them opportunities to think and communicate critically, creatively, collaboratively, and with growing awareness of their own thinking processes, that is, with metacognition. Research highlights the critical role that teachers play in helping students take control of their own learning (Butler and Schnellert 2012; Willms, Friesen, and Milton 2009). Because *understanding* is central to meaning making and purposeful learning, students have to develop their capacity to determine what they understand and what they have to figure out by seeking new information to clarify and extend their meaning making. Such active, purposeful learning leads to students' self-regulating their learning.

Individuals who engage reflectively and deliberately in self-regulation are more likely to be successful (Zimmerman and Schunk 2011). Teachers can help students self-regulate their learning. Some questions we must ask ourselves are:

Do my students get choice in the creation of this learning task?

Do they get to decide how they will represent their learning?

Am I challenging students to use thinking skills like synthesizing in this task?

When will I build in opportunities for self-assessment and reflection?

Throughout this book, we describe how we design lessons and units of study that require students to actively refine their beliefs, perceptions, and thinking processes. Within our design of learning opportunities, we ask students to access their prior knowledge and experiences related to tasks and concepts, but we also extend their experience and their understanding of the content, of themselves, and of the world.

There is so much content we *could* cover, but we know that teaching to cover content is not how students' purposeful and deep learning happens. Because we want our students to develop as creative, critical, collaborative thinkers, we design learning experiences that are purposeful and oriented to "big ideas." Our focus must be on developing thinking and thinkers—we do this through explorations of content-area concepts. The development of competencies and thinking skills (e.g., making connections, determining importance warranting a conclusion with evidence) is central to the design of middle years experiences. Our learning tasks should require students to plan, to draw from multiple resources, to focus on key concepts, and to use them in generative ways, which will help them develop related thinking strategies. In chapters 3 through 11, we explicitly teach and develop these skills within the study of big ideas and tasks that extend over several days.

Challenging, exploratory, integrative, and relevant curriculum

Curriculum embraces every planned aspect of a school's educational program. An effective middle level curriculum is distinguished by learning activities that appeal to young adolescents, is exploratory and challenging, and incorporates student-generated questions and concerns. (Lounsbury, AMLE 2010)

We must use the curriculum to design teaching units that are issue-based and inquiry-oriented. Classroom events should engage students in cooperative learning and be interdisciplinary. Our learning outcomes in the content disciplines should be more concept-based than detail-based. Content area concepts and processes are interdependent. Each can be developed through relevant, integrative, and challenging learning tasks. For instance, we ask—and help—students to develop open-ended questions and hypotheses that require them to explore content-area concepts (e.g., *What is fair?*). At the centre of our design for curriculum and instruction, we place the development of students' capacity to be collaborative and creative—as well as being critical thinkers and learners who are more personally and socially conscious. We want students to find the relationships between these competencies and the concepts that they explore.

Using approaches like inquiry, project-based learning, and service learning—which increase challenge and relevance for students—requires that teachers identify their learning goals for students. When students have a role in defining a learning task, they engage more deeply (see chapters 6, 7, and 8). In Kim Ondrik's grade 6/7 classroom, students create their own projects through which they explore and demonstrate these outcomes in a variety of ways.

See Ch. 7

Educators use multiple learning and teaching approaches

Teaching and learning approaches should accommodate the diverse skills, abilities, and prior knowledge of young adolescents, cultivate multiple intelligences, draw upon students' individual learning styles, and utilize digital tools. When learning experiences capitalize on students' cultural, experiential, and personal backgrounds, new concepts are built on knowledge students already possess. (Lounsbury, AMLE 2010)

Today's classrooms are diverse, yet students have *always* had different learning styles and different rates of learning (Brownlie, Fullerton, and Schnellert 2011). We believe that all students belong in inclusive classrooms, engaged in high-quality, thoughtful learning experiences with their peers while pursuing a complex, meaningful curriculum. We begin our planning with all students in mind and with the conviction that planning for a full range of learner strengths and styles means that more students will have opportunities to be successful more of the time. Such planning means that fewer adaptations and modifications are required for students with special needs. This is the essence of "universal design for learning" (UDL) (Brownlie and Schnellert 2009).

See Ch. 4

Teachers and students must welcome and interact with one another in ways that recognize and celebrate diversity. We invite all students to share and develop themselves within a community that values diversity.

We use multiple teaching and learning approaches in the middle years. Approaches such as Project-Based Learning, Inquiry, Literature Circles, Information Circles, Numeracy Circles, Writing Workshop, New Literacies, Formative Assessment, Self-Regulated Learning, and Arts Integration all include differentiation and choice. Throughout this book, we provide examples of these approaches to show how they offer students different pathways to engage in, explore, and express their learning.

However, offering different pathways is not enough. We need to empower and support students as they choose and determine how they go about and communicate their learning.

Varied and ongoing assessment advances learning

Continuous, authentic, and appropriate assessment measures, including both formative and summative ones, provide evidence about every student's learning progress. Such information helps students, teachers, and family members select immediate learning goals and plan further education. (Lounsbury, AMLE 2010)

A key aspect of teaching and learning in the middle years is formative assessment. In chapters 3 and 9, we describe how formative assessment helps teachers and students reflect on their efforts and adjust what they are doing in relation to the evaluation criteria. It is important to use different kinds of assessment—our students must have the opportunity to show us what they have learned in a variety of ways so that we get a good sense of how they express their learning and what they can do.

Formative assessment (assessment for learning) is a hot topic in teaching and learning. Over the past decade, we have placed less emphasis on reporting out summative information in percentages and grades and placed greater emphasis on offering students and parents information while the learning is still in process so that they can use our feedback to refocus their efforts. Perhaps the most important shift is that teachers do not "mark" everything a student does. Students need an opportunity to build their knowledge and skills before having their work evaluated. Growth takes time, and formative assessment propels this growth.

To align our formative and summative assessment, we use rubrics that help us to give descriptive feedback, engage in criterion-referenced decision making, and think of development as a continuum. One rubric should be used over time so that students can see where their performance registers on the continuum and determine where they want to improve. We use positive, learning-oriented language when giving feedback, by using phrases like:

- *"I noticed that… ."*
- *"You successfully…now try… ."*
- *"How can you stretch yourself in this area… ?"*
- *"I find… powerful… ."*
- *"More of this, please!"*

When we support students by giving descriptive feedback early—and often—during a unit, we can help them understand what they are aiming for. The process of working with students to create the criteria for levels of expectations in a rubric is also powerful for learners. It builds investment and ownership—it is time well spent.

Identity Development in the Middle Years

A major goal for middle level educators is to help students become fully functioning, self-actualized people. This is a long-term life goal that begins with being aware of and accepting yourself and recognizing that you have a place in the world. For students in the middle years, change and growth can be overwhelming and confusing. In fact, early adolescence is an ideal time for students to develop self-awareness. We can help them when we, as teachers, draw in their perspectives, feelings, opinions, and experiences for consideration. Each year, we must remind ourselves that it takes time for students to engage with us and their peers as collaborative and metacognitive learners.

We have to win students over and build their trust in us. It takes time for them to believe in themselves and to accept that we believe in them. We can have a significant impact on their life journey. To help students become more self-actualized, we have to connect with them as authentic individuals *and* as learners. When a learning community is one where students feel welcomed for who they are and valued for what they bring, we can help them engage in deep self-investigation within explorations of curriculum content. We want students who come to realize that they can make a difference in their own learning and the learning of others—and in their communities. Our role is to help each student shape their own life. At the beginning of the year, Julie Hearn hangs a banner in her room that says *We are creating ourselves.* We all need to make this goal explicit, and we can do so with approaches such as memoir writing, cooperative learning, class meetings, and researching issue-based topics as we help students become self-reflective learners. In the chapters that follow, we have two underlying goals.

See Ch. 7

1. Active Awareness

We want to help students become actively aware of the larger world, asking significant and relevant questions about that world, and wrestling with big ideas and questions for which there may not be one right answer.

Students in the middle years need meaningful and thoughtful topics, curriculum, and teaching that helps them see how they are connected to the larger world. For instance, Nicole Widdess organizes her English language arts and social studies around issues like displacement. Displacement is important in the lives of Nicole and her students, many of whom were born in other countries. They have experienced emigration from "home" to Canada and, while many have taken Anglo names, they are still very connected to their home country, their mother tongue, and the beliefs and values of their culture. Displacement occurs in many ways around the world—living things are forced out of their native ecosystems, families have to move for work, some want to escape bullying by other social groups, and some to escape changing political climates. Issues like displacement are connected to real life, to real-world issues. Investigating issues helps students acquire experience and insight.

See Ch. 6

Middle years students respond to the emotional impact of real-world issues and examples. A few years ago, Leyton Schnellert and Linda started using *Iqbal* (D'Adamo 2003) in their Humanities classes. Suddenly, the issue of child slavery—an issue during the Industrial Revolution—had a modern-day example. As students learn how to work with issues and to explore points of view, we develop their self-awareness. Our planning includes topics that range from local issues to broader global issues. Collaborative inquiry into issues such as residential schools, financial literacy, and child slavery can shed light on them but also require that students use multiple sources to become familiar with different perspectives.

In chapter 4, we walk through our unit-planning process. We plan with the goal of helping students become actively aware of the larger world by wrestling with big ideas and asking questions for which there may not be clear answers. As we plan, we ask ourselves: *"How do the themes from our curriculum content link to the world today?"*

When we use issue-based, real-world examples and topics in our classrooms, students can be coached to pose powerful questions that are open-ended and engaging. We strive to help students develop their own questioning skills. Many of our students have noted that learning to improve their questioning skills has been a challenge, but very worthwhile.

See Ch. 6

Part of our role as teachers is to help students make connections between curriculum content areas. To be successful at integrating content areas, we must be specific about what we are teaching and why. We approach Language Arts, Social Studies, and Science through major themes. Our first task is to reduce and amalgamate the outcomes by identifying the major themes in each and the links between them; during this process, we identify relevant "big ideas" and "essential questions" that middle grade students can explore. When we integrate content areas we can create rich opportunities for deeper learning.

2. Acceptance and Appreciation

We must accept and appreciate students for who they are and what they can give.

Accepting one's abilities as part of a learning community is essential if diversity is to be understood and practised. Not all students arrive in our classes with this understanding; therefore, it must become an explicit part of our unit- and lesson-planning. The objective is to develop students' understanding of the critical role of diversity—diversity as strength. We must nurture students' ability to see themselves and how they fit into the human spectrum. Students learn to accept their own contribution and recognize the contributions of others. We view our classrooms as learning communities and sometimes as a big community jigsaw puzzle with each student being a piece of the puzzle.

In classrooms where the focus is on learners and learning, students are accountable for their participation as individual members of the learning community. Our objective is to figure out how each student learns—and the ways we can help each one take part in the learning journey in their own best way. This is preferable to expecting all students to be in the same learning place, at the same time, and competing with each other. A classroom community works best when every type of learner can be honoured. This book offers examples of ways that you can adjust your practice to better meet the needs of your learners. In chapter 7, for example, Marna Macmillan and Kim Ondrik discuss how they explicitly develop students' social-emotional and metacognitive capacities. We must accept students for who they are and what they can give, then build from these strengths to extend and personalize their learning.

Conclusion

As you read the chapters of this book, we hope you will build your toolkit so that you can support your students to build their capacities. We invite you to expand your professional teaching practice to incorporate some of these pathways into learning. We are deeply committed to middle years learning theory, philosophy, and methods that appreciate, respond to, and support our diverse learners. As educators, we have an immense opportunity to develop students' strengths, skills, talents, and interests. Through our practices, we can nurture students' potential to contribute to society, and personal fulfillment.

Middle level educators support students as they:

- make responsible, ethical decisions concerning their own health and wellness.
- respect and value the diverse ways people look, speak, think, and act within the immediate community and around the world.
- assume responsibility for their actions and be aware of and ready to accept obligations for the welfare of others.
- think rationally and critically and express their thoughts clearly.
- read deeply and, independently, gather, assess, and interpret information from a variety of sources.
- read avidly for enjoyment and lifelong learning.
- use digital tools to explore, communicate, and collaborate with the world, and to learn from rich and varied resources.
- become stewards of Earth and its resources and wise and intelligent consumers of a wide array of goods and services available to them.
- recognize how the pathways of arts integration can effectively develop personal growth, emotional health, and interpersonal and social skills.

While our responsibility is great, we need to start small. Teaching is a learning profession. We are developing our skills just as we are helping students do the same. In this book, we offer many examples of frameworks, units, and lessons to help you explore pathways to learning and, perhaps, see what is not easily "visible to the eye." We hope you find something in these pages to support your journey as a teacher.

Key point

Chapter 2

Pathways to Professional Learning: Inquiry, Collaboration, and Professional Reading

Educators Involved

Skye Herrman: Integration Support Teacher, SD 63, Saanich, BC

Del Morgan: Classroom Teacher, SD 63, Saanich, BC

Jean Bowman: Classroom Teacher, SD 63, Saanich, BC

Jean-Ann Stene: Classroom Teacher, SD 38, Richmond, BC

Lorraine Minosky: Classroom Teacher, SD 38, Richmond, BC

Carole Fullerton: District Curriculum Coordinator, SD 38, Richmond, BC

Catriona Misfeldt: Classroom and Resource Teacher/Literacy Leader, SD 38, Richmond, BC

In order to develop our practice and get better at meeting the needs of our students, we have to look for ways to inquire and learn together. The report entitled *What Makes Middle Schools Work* describes the research by a team led by Kristen Campbell Wilcox with Janet I. Angelis (2007) that studied ten of New York state's higher performing schools to get a better understanding of the factors that predict their success, and to learn how those commonalities might be developed in other schools. They found that, in order to support their focus on academics, the ten schools consistently nurture a culture of trust that is shared among administrators, teachers, students, and parents, as follows:

Higher-performing middle schools build a culture of success by maintaining these five common elements:

1. Trusting and respectful relationships

Relationships based on mutual trust and respect among administrators, teachers, students and parents are fundamental to all of the common elements in the findings. Nurturing these relationships provides the backbone for successful learning.

2. Students' social and emotional well-being

Higher-performing schools recognize that creating a sense of security for middle school students provides them with a support network and a connection to their school, removing significant barriers to learning.

3. Teamwork

Higher-performing schools establish a collaborative environment and organizational structure that support teamwork between and among teachers, school leaders and administrators. Groups of teachers, administrators, and specialists meet frequently and focus on specific instructional strategies and student performance within and across grades.

4. Evidence-based decision making

Sharing and using data from a variety of sources to make decisions is critical to helping schools achieve success. Data are frequently gathered, analyzed and used in decision making regarding the impacts of new programs, instructional practices and interventions.

5. Shared vision of mission and goals

When teachers and administrators build a vision of success and share goals, this leads to better communications, mutually agreed-upon expectations and more long-term success.

When teachers work together with shared goals in mind, students are able to develop understandings and practices that are celebrated, reinforced, and applied in various settings. When we work together to understand our students' strengths and challenges, then develop approaches that help students connect to, process, transform, and personalize important concepts and thinking skills, *schools* become learning communities—and the most important unit of change. The many ways that teachers can learn collaboratively include:

- participating in grade level teams
- working with teachers of different subject areas who teach the same students
- participating in professional study groups
- planning Lesson Study activities
- collaborating on preparation of unit plans
- co-teaching

All Teachers, All Subjects

Every classroom should be a *thinking* classroom—a place where students get to access and use their prior knowledge, process and make connections between ideas, and personalize and transform what they have learned. We want engaged, meaning-making, critical, and self-regulating thinkers. We see schools and classrooms as places where students are *apprenticed* into this way of being in the world. We want to nurture these thinking skills and build on what students already bring us, rather than thwart their creativity and individuality. Thus, we want our students to participate in authentic learning activities that contribute to their future choices and potential to participate in the world.

To create authentic and coherent learning opportunities for diverse classrooms, teachers benefit from planning lessons and units of study together. By doing so, they can align formative assessment, instruction, learning activities, and summative assessment. When we use our combined knowledge and expertise, we can better engage and support our diverse learners as they learn key concepts and develop learning strategies simultaneously (Brownlie and Schnellert 2009; Wilhelm 2007).

Working Together for All Learners

When we work together to integrate planning, assessment, and instruction, we can use our shared expertise to create learning activities for students, plan how to engage students' thinking abilities, and develop them over the course of a unit.

Ongoing professional development (PD) can significantly help teachers reflect on their students' learning profiles while they learn about and incorporate new approaches that build student engagement in active, strategic, self-regulated learning. Effective PD must continue over time for teachers to develop, explore, and integrate the ideas and practices that support the development of their students' competencies.

Individual schools and school districts that want to make a difference in student learning should organize frequent and serial PD activities for teachers to learn collaboratively. They benefit from sessions in which they can use what they know about their students, the curriculum content, and recent research in order to plan, try out, and reflect on the instructional/learning approaches that they choose, create, and/or adapt. Offering research-based methods and approaches that teachers can explore is more effective than suggesting to them that one approach or instructional strategy alone will lead to success in any classroom. Instead, teachers need opportunities to look at formative assessment information from their students, set goals together, and select, plan, or adapt relevant ideas and approaches. Subsequent PD sessions should offer them the opportunity to reflect with their colleagues on how the plan worked out and see more clearly how to make the curriculum more accessible with approaches that engage their students' thinking skills (Butler and Schnellert 2008).

Ongoing Formative and Summative Assessment

When we link our formative and summative assessment activities to the content and strategies we teach, we can clearly see the progress our students have made—and see whether or not our teaching is making a difference for our students. Without the specific results from activities that call upon students' key thinking skills, it is difficult to devise supports for student learning or to review the success or failure of particular approaches. When we see that our students are successfully applying the thinking strategies that we have been working on, we can target *new* thinking skills. If their work or assessment results show that things are *not* progressing as expected, we can then plan and teach in new ways. By paying careful attention to our students' work, we can be very specific in the next stage of goal-setting to help us focus our planning and teaching on ways to help all our students.

See: Ch. 3

Schools and teaching teams must engage in repeated cycles of assessing, planning, goal-setting, doing, assessing, reflecting, and adjusting. The formative assessment data at the school level might include performance-based assessments of reading, writing, or numeracy in the fall. We can use this information to set specific grade-wide or school-wide goals for the year. Often the teaching team for a grade might set one shared learning goal such as "determining importance"; individual teachers might then set a related class-specific goal such as "supporting responses with relevant details." Schools can also use the formative assessment information to plan specific professional reading and collaborative activities for upcoming PD.

When summative data are related to the formative assessment data, both teachers and students can track individual progress and set new goals. The key, of course, is that formative and summative assessments are parallel—that they require students to do similar things. Such assessments are meaningful at multiple levels and can be used to assess progress toward class-, grade-,and school-wide learning-centred goals and interventions. From locally developed summative assessments we see what our students have internalized and can now do independently because they go beyond both formative and large-scale assessments, providing a snapshot of student progress in achieving specific school, grade, and classroom goals. Summative assessments that are grade-

or school-wide usually take place in the early spring. Teacher teams and schools can use these results as evidence of overall progress toward school goals; classroom teachers can use the same data to inform their lesson plans and to provide descriptive feedback to individual students.

Assessments are meaningful and useful when teachers and students are fully involved, when they have time to reflect on the results, continue the cycle, and make meaningful classroom and school decisions.

Teacher Teams

To avoid having students experience school as confusing, schools should support coordinated instruction across the curriculum with interdisciplinary teaching teams. Collaboration takes flexibility and planning to develop community-minded classrooms, where all kinds of minds are welcome and celebrated.

In classrooms where teachers work together — learning resource teachers and classroom teachers co-teaching, literacy coaches and classroom teachers, two classroom teachers combining their classes — we see more students getting support when they need it. In collaborative classrooms, the emphasis is on designing learning experiences so that more students have more success. As professionals we should constantly examine and refine our practice. By working together, we discover what does and does not work and can adapt our instruction in real time. When collaborative teaching is ongoing, that is, the co-teachers work together weekly, we always build in 5 to 15 minutes to debrief, to determine how a lesson went, and to plan ahead. We have found that collaborative teaching and problem-solving bring in new ideas, new or better units, and a feeling of connection with colleagues—and that our lessons and activities reach more learners. Most importantly, we design learning sequences that better engage our students while we apply more strategies in our teaching.

Grade-wide teams can make a significant difference in student learning. Teacher teams that meet regularly increase coherence for students moving from class to class and help them to make connections across subject areas. By using formative assessment information and looking for links between curricular areas, teachers can develop and reinforce the same thinking skills in all subject areas.

Administrative Leadership and Team Leadership

Many an initiative lives or dies based on a principal's or superintendent's support, that is, whether or not these administrators fulfill the key responsibilities of "instructional leader." Their participation in the school community is crucial. By collaborating with teachers in their classrooms, or covering a class so that the teacher can co-teach or co-plan with a colleague, or by sitting in on grade-wide planning meetings, administrators help teachers as they work together to improve student learning. An educational leader must keep up to date with research and practice. Principals who teach or co-teach a class can support the development of a school as a learning community by publicly sharing their own process of revising and integrating planning, instruction, and formative and summative assessment.

Similarly, teacher leaders must also take a collaborative, learning-centred approach to PD and curriculum innovation. When librarians, coaches, consultants, and grade team leaders take a side-by-side and collegial approach, they model and contribute to a culture of professional learning. Working in this way honours a range of teacher philosophies and styles. We recommend that leaders openly share what they learn and how they are developing their own practice; within this context, they can collaboratively establish instructional goals with colleagues, allowing for each professional to have input.

A Collaborative Model of Support

Change often drives innovation. This is exactly what happened at Royal Oak Middle School in Saanich, British Columbia. When the staff faced the necessity of changing to the integration support model, they saw an opportunity to create a new approach overall. "I want to have a more active role in your classes," said Skye Herrmann, an integration support teacher (IST), to classroom teachers Del Morgan and Jean Bowman. This statement began the transformation in the school's IST-support model. Today, if you walk into Del's or Jean's classroom when Skye is in there, you will find two teachers simultaneously and effectively using a variety of different strategies within a single class. The students consider it a bonus to have two teachers with complementary approaches in their class. The two teachers know their curriculum, know the students, know how to meet their needs and how to push each of them to their potential, whether the students have an individual education plan (IEP) or not—and they all know what is happening in the class.

Having a teaching team that is willing to learn, to try, and to reflect *together* is crucial. They check their egos at the door and look at a team member's proposal as an opportunity to learn from and to build upon. In their model starting from day one, they introduce their students to the IST as one of the teaching team—all of whom are there to help with everyone's learning.

All the teachers involved have to be flexible in the classroom. The IST has to be comfortable and knowledgeable enough to take the lead in the classroom, while the classroom teacher has to be comfortable and have enough trust in the IST to relinquish control. Each member of the team has strengths, such as curriculum creation, technology integration, or knowledge of diverse strategies to meet different student needs. They blend these skills to make effective lessons for all the students while simultaneously learning from each other to constantly improve the ways they help students learn.

The number of teachers within the team, in this case three, seems to matter less than their openness and willingness to try strategies to meet the diversity of needs for all students. What works in one classroom may look very different in another classroom. This team found they could share and transfer teaching skills in a fluid and continuous manner that enhanced their practice. Their flexibility allowed them to combine six blocks of IST time, assigning it each week to where it was needed most. Sometimes they split the time equally between the classes and sometimes not. Sometimes the need was dealing with learning challenges, at other times about the teaching challenge. These two multi-age, inquiry-based classes worked on parallel projects, because having the same starting point in both classrooms provided continuity for the IST who is integral to the planning process.

The school administration arranged the timetable so that all three members of the team had common preparation time each week for collaboration. Before beginning a unit, they plan together and decide what approaches they will use. They use the common prep time subsequently for planning lessons for the following week. Sometimes the session is as simple as reviewing the original plan; other times it involves taking the original plan and changing it to suit unanticipated developments in the classroom. The team also collaborates by brainstorming to create assignments, graphic organizers, and assessments. Being able to do this within their regular workday instead of outside the school day is important.

Encouraging Diverse Learning Styles

Together Del, Skye, and Jean work to build students' self-regulation skills. In each classroom, the students are encouraged to make decisions for their own learning. The teachers help the students understand how they are learning. By letting them have a say in an assignment and by allowing them choices in how to demonstrate their learning, they help them self-regulate and develop autonomy.

Students can choose a task that meets their needs and are encouraged to evaluate their own schedules and decide what they can accomplish. The teachers work to help the students build a good school-life balance. They give students a broad choice in the ways they can show what they have learned—by writing or oral presentation, visual representation, dramatic performance, web design, or a technological format. Some students use such technology as voice-to-text, text-to-voice, mind map creation, book creation, video and other multimedia devices as part of these choices.

Students with significant learning difficulties have access to these tools in the regular classroom. Justin, for example, has difficulty completing his work to meet deadlines, so the team implemented the strategy of having him photograph the assignments on the white board at the end of the day. Now, half the class uses this strategy effectively. The team's goal is to provide such opportunities for any student, whether or not their learning need meets specified criteria for an officially-recognized learning disability.

The students themselves offer their expertise with technology. No one looks twice at a student who whips out his iPod to dictate his assignment, or another who grabs his laptop, or still others who head over to the classroom computers. When a technical issue comes up, it is often a student who helps solve the problem. Usually one of the teachers is responsible for introducing a new technology tool, but then the students figure out how to make it work effectively, sometimes for completely different and novel purposes unforeseen by the teachers. The goal of collaboration involves not just the teachers but also every student in the room.

Diversity of learners

Through this collaborative model, Del, Jean, and Skye have found that the culture of learning and support is changing. Students understand that asking for help is okay for everyone, so working with a specialist teacher loses the former stigma. The culture also teaches that there are as many ways to learn and to show learning as there are students. Moreover, this team found that the students' contributions to their own and others' learning have been significant. In this model, the students are put in charge of their learning, and they rise to the occasion. The students who require assistive technology because of their learning challenges get their equipment out and get to work without much teacher help. Although these students still need guidance, the teachers' explanations and clarifications are directed to all students equally. Students ask one another for clarification and support. Some days the model works better than others, but the team looks at it as a much more effective way to support the needs of their learners. Every day is a new learning experience for both the students and the teachers.

Collaborating to Teach Math to Combined Grades

Research tells us that young adolescents thrive in learning environments that promote and sustain relationships. Students in middle grades need both the support of their peers and their teachers' consistent role-modelling more than at any other time in their education. Combined grades in one classroom ensure that learning relationships can be nurtured. Yet, when it comes to teaching mathematics, teachers tend to revert to grouping same-grade students—perhaps because teaching just one section of the math curriculum is more manageable. However, several issues crop up for teachers: the time wasted in the transition between classrooms—moving students, resources, and learning materials; the feeling of being trapped in a rigid sequential schedule for math lessons; their inability to access prior knowledge; the time constraints that mean students have less time to consolidate their understanding and that teachers are less likely to spontaneously explore the math ideas that crop up daily. Students also feel the pull and tend to see math as separate and distinct from all other subjects: they learn that math is age-specific and linear—that some math is appropriate for grade 6 while other math is reserved for grade 7. Instead, they should become aware of the broad concepts of mathematics and the connections between them.

A team of grade 6/7 teachers (Nicole, Jean-Ann, and Lorraine) at Ferris Elementary School in Richmond, BC, faced that pedagogical struggle. They were confident in identifying core ideas in other disciplines and adapting the content and instruction for their grades 6s and 7s—and they wanted the same for their math instruction. They recognized, however, that they also had to deepen their background knowledge of mathematics in order to produce effective lesson sequences. So they approached Carole Fullerton, the Numeracy Consultant for the school district, to help them teach math to their combined grades 6/7 students in one class by adapting their instruction as they did in other subject areas.

The teachers met three times to deepen their own understanding of algebraic thinking. Carole supported them by designing a combined-grades unit and six demonstration lessons. By the end of October, they had observed and debriefed those lessons as a collaborative team, focusing on the big ideas in math—concepts common to both grades—and how to develop these ideas with both grade 6 and grade 7 students.

For the teachers, Carole devised a three-part lesson model. In part one, she connected the topic of the algebra lesson to background knowledge, a reminder of the important learning from the previous day's lesson. Carole based her suggested approach for students on the picture book *Two of Everything* by Lily Toy Hong (1993) in order to introduce the terms *relation* and *variable*. The characters in the story, Mr. and Mrs. Haktak, have a magic pot that increases the number of items they place in it. The readers have to figure out what's happening in the magic pot and how to describe the process. As the story progresses, the teacher can break at each stage, ask questions for students to discuss/brainstorm what's happening with the magic pot, and introduce the mathematical terms *relation* and *variable* to describe how to make generalizations that help them reach a solution. They start by using a T-chart with IN and OUT columns. From there, the teacher can pose a question or open-ended problem to students. Students work together on the problems, showing what they know with numbers, pictures, words, and manipulatives. The debriefing conversations allow for a description of the essential concept.

To assess what students learn, the teacher can issue an exit slip, that is, a ticket-out-the-door question. These exit slips are invaluable for teachers to track progress as students work through the lesson sequence, but they also hold each student accountable for their learning. Guided practice, games, and mini-lessons follow to consolidate the learning.

Co-Planning the Next Unit

Following this guided experience, the school-based administrative team covered the grades 6/7 classes, which allowed Nicole, Jean-Ann, and Lorraine to co-plan the next unit with Carole. Having the time to focus on pedagogical content knowledge was invaluable. It allowed them to continue to differentiate their instruction and keep their grade 6 and 7 learners together. They focused on ratio, proportion, fractions, decimals, and percent—and on connections between these important concepts at their grade levels. Designing lessons with pedagogical support helped them to identify and highlight the big math ideas and to see how these concepts are interwoven.

As the unit went on, they noticed that their students needed reminders of how to convert between fractions, decimals, and percents. Using the format they established for a combined grades lesson, they added a "daily practice" component to make sure that students were revisiting concepts and getting computational practice with fractions, decimals, and percents. Each morning, they put between 3 and 5 questions on the board to explore together. Each set of questions focused on a connection or reminded students of an important mental math strategy. This short daily practice helped students consolidate their thinking.

Deepening Algebraic Thinking

The last unit of the year involved *integers* and *operations on integers* as well as solving equations, still keeping the two classes together. They expected the grade 6 students to engage with each lesson, but assessed them only on the concepts and outcomes of their grade level. The grade 7 students benefited from the review of grade 6 concepts, but the teachers expected them to also master the grade 7 learning outcomes.

For this unit, the teachers had them use algebra tiles and a 4-pan algebra balance to model how to preserve equality while solving for unknowns. Several students had ah-ha! moments while they experimented with the scale. Watching the action of the balance and the manipulation of the algebra tiles with the abstract algebraic notation was powerful for students.

At the end of the unit, students were asked how they felt about learning math in this way, and what lessons they enjoyed most. One student responded:

> I think the "Two of Everything" lesson went well because I didn't get algebra at all before it. With the pictures there to help, I learned a lot about algebra and that it wasn't that hard. I learned that a generalization is an equation that contains a variable like n or x. This is important to know because it applies to real-life situations. It really helped me as a learner, and it taught me how to find the generalization and how to look at algebra problems.

The teachers developed their collaborative practice throughout the year, after which Lorraine wrote this reflection:

Participating in the collaborative planning sessions has been of great benefit to my math program this year. Because of the time spent getting a broader and deeper understanding of the math concepts, I've been able to be more selective of the lessons I'm teaching and I'm being less dependent upon the math text. The text no longer drives the sequence of lessons and I'm feeling much more in the driver's seat these days.

But the biggest benefit has been my ability to weave the math concepts into the other subjects, often spontaneously. For example, while we were studying ratio and proportion in math, we were exploring ecosystems in science. I was able to see the connections and I guided the students in applying their knowledge and skills in ratio and proportion when examining the balance of consumers and producers in sustainable ecosystems. And just recently, after a conversation about math with a colleague, I decided to postpone teaching finding volume as part of the math measurement unit and will instead teach it in the context of the chemistry unit focusing on mass and density.

Jean-Ann, too, reflected on the year: "Overall, teaching a combined grades 6/7 math class has been the source of great learning for me. I am seeing and understanding the big math ideas much more than ever before. I have always known the benefits of teaching the whole class rather than platooning. But I never thought I could manage the complexity of evaluating using two different IRPs. I am still learning and sometimes I revert back to my old ways ("segregate and conquer"), but I am beginning to see the many benefits of teaching a combined grades 6/7 class as I focus more on the big ideas of math. I am very grateful for the opportunity and look forward to future epiphanies."

Lesson Study: A Powerful Approach to Teacher Teams

One approach that we have explored with success is Lesson Study which offers teams of teachers a chance to work and learn together by developing and carrying out an inquiry lesson. Team members plan the lesson based on a class profile, the unit of study, and the goals set by the teacher. The team incorporates key instructional components that they want to observe in action so that they can deepen and refine their own teaching. Debriefing is a key stage in the Lesson Study process as team members discuss their observations of the teachers and students, how what they observed relates to student learning, and the success of their collaborative instructional plan. When possible after the debriefing, they revise the lesson based on their reflections and carry out the revised lesson with another class. After observing, they again discuss what and how they can incorporate their observations in their own teaching.

Linda and her colleague Catriona Misfeldt were part of a team that planned and carried out a Lesson Study in their school. An interdisciplinary team of teachers were invited to take part in the Lesson Study. The success of any collaborative approach requires administrative support, release time, and resources for teachers to work with each other. As Literacy Leader, Catriona had responsibility for supporting staff in meeting the school's literacy goals and for raising awareness of how to improve their instructional practice. As a resource teacher, she knew the benefits of co-teaching in helping teachers to better meet the diverse needs of their students. Lesson Study provided a platform for building collegial teams, created a culture of inquiry among the staff, and illuminated the value of co-teaching. When she invited interested teachers to participate, Linda volunteered her class. Any time a teacher invites colleagues into their classroom, they are taking professional risks, but when we open ourselves and our practice up to scrutiny, we can gain unexpected insights. Linda saw the benefits of having a supportive teacher like Catriona in her classroom and how they could strengthen each other's practice by working together.

Lesson Study in Three Phases

Lesson Study has three phases: planning for the lesson; conducting the lesson; follow-up debriefing on the lesson.

Planning for the lesson
1. *Understanding the students*

See Ch. 3

Linda had created a class profile that identified the strengths, stretches, and interests of her class. The lesson study session made her turn again to her class profile to guide her instructional decision making. Linda knew many of the students because they were involved in her drama class and productions, but they were not transferring their experience of risk-taking, sharing opinions, and working together in performance into their behaviour in her Humanities class. She was surprised at how reluctant the students were to think and share their ideas in class discussions when the class had no underlying social dynamic preventing them from participating. Lesson Study became her vehicle for purposefully planning the instruction that would address the profile of her class.

2. *Setting the context for the lesson*

See Ch. 3.

Linda had just completed a read-aloud on child labour and had been working on reading comprehension strategies that would support her students' reading for information. From the results of her previous fall performance-based assessment, her students did not efficiently use text features to preview and support understanding or to locate information. Using text features became the main instructional focus for the lesson. As Linda shared her observations and concerns about her students' engagement and social skills, Catriona jotted down key themes in the conversation to help focus the lesson goals. Linda wanted to know more about the quality and length of students' conversations, the types of questions they were asking (e.g., powerful or superficial), the kinds of connections they were making, and whether or not they were able to provide supporting evidence.

3. Designing the lesson

They based the lesson design on a current article, rich with text features, about child labour in Africa. Using a template adapted from *Powerful Designs for Professional Learning* (Easton 2008*)*, Catriona and Linda planned the lesson sequence. Their overarching question (research theme) was:

> *Can students use prior knowledge, text features, and selected text to make a variety of rich connections that will extend their understanding of the issues related to child labour?*

They wanted to model research-based practice. Their teaching objectives included:

- Scaffolding for diversity: e.g., strategy selection, student grouping and activities, use of visuals
- Creating a lesson sequence that flows
- Using the gradual release of responsibility to build success and confidence
- Observing and documenting student thinking to better understand the quality of their conversations

After developing their overarching question and stating their teaching objectives, the next step was to define the sequence for the lesson, which they designed in four stages:

> Stage 1: What the teachers are doing
>
> Stage 2: What the students are doing, and what we want them to be thinking about
>
> Stage 3: What we want the observing teachers to notice and assess
>
> Stage 4: What materials and strategies we need for teachers and for students

After setting out the steps in each stage, they compiled their lesson plan.

4. Selecting the focus for observation and data collection

An important component of Lesson Study is the participation of colleagues in the data collection. Their feedback enables the teacher to see how students' learning progressed over the lesson, and how each element of the experience (e.g., lesson design, materials, prior knowledge, students' characteristics, social dynamics) supported or interfered with the students' learning.

Conducting the lesson

1. Introducing the research lesson

On the morning of the Lesson Study, Linda and Catriona met with several interested and invested colleagues who taught the same students, were exploring similar strategies, or were curious about co-teaching or lesson study. They shared the lesson design and focus for observation and data collection. It is at this point in the process that the ownership of the lesson shifted to the entire team.

2. Teaching the research lesson

Catriona and Linda co-taught the lesson while the other teachers observed and recorded student thinking, learning, engagement, and behaviour; they also gathered the data outlined in the Lesson Study sequence. Linda asked teachers positioned around the room to watch specific students. At the end of the lesson, Linda asked each teacher/observer to write a narrative of everything their designated student said and did, including any non-verbal behaviour.

3. Conducting the lesson colloquium

After the lesson, all the teachers gathered for the colloquium facilitated by Catriona, who also took notes. The colloquium is the final stage in the Lesson Study protocol and follows a specific structure. Linda began by sharing her observations, thoughts, and feelings about her lesson. Then the observing teachers discussed the data they collected with its specific focus on how student thinking progressed as they reflected on the overarching question.

Following the lesson

1. Consolidating the learning

To help the team move forward in their reflection, Catriona synthesized the team's reflections by noting the successes, challenges, learning, questions, and next steps. The themes emerging from the data allowed the team to reflect on the extent to which the lesson sequence met the objectives. Using this information, the team adapted the lesson to revise and strengthen it.

2. Repeating the cycle

Linda and Catriona taught the revised lesson to a new group of students, with the team observing. Because the colloquium focuses on student engagement and learning, the teachers/observers watched to determine the effects of the changes in the lesson. In the colloquium debriefing, teachers described their observations of the impact of the revised lesson on student learning, and described how they could use particular approaches with their own classes in other subject areas. All teachers then planned and shared how they would use these ideas in their practice within the next week.

Teacher-Leaders as Facilitators and Co-Learners

When Leyton took on the role of Teacher Consultant for the district, his job was to consult with school teams and teachers as they supported students within the autism spectrum and others with challenging behaviour and, in addition, to facilitate the professional development of learning resource teachers. Tagged onto the end of the job posting (after the list of special-education-related qualifications) was the sentence "An interest in literacy would be an asset."

Attending student-specific meetings on individual education plans (IEPs), Leyton found that teachers were most interested in adaptations or modifications that benefited more than one student in the class. The best meetings were those that focused on the entire classroom community. Although Leyton turned to professional journals and books and asked questions of his colleagues, he found that he wanted—and needed—more. Working as a consultant, or helping teacher, he was missing what had made a difference for him in his own teaching and learning. He needed opportunities to try out new ideas and approaches with students and to learn together with other colleagues.

Leyton began working with school staffs and embarking on follow-up action research projects with small groups of teachers. After a workshop with a school staff, Leyton had a critical conversation with one isolated colleague, Jonina Campbell. She suggested forming a study group for the whole district. By doing so, they found that the expertise was no longer based in Leyton alone trying to fit all of the district's teachers into his schedule—the ownership of ideas and learning and inquiry was distributed across the group.

Twenty-two grades 4 to 10 teachers gathered for the first sharing session that June. The synergy of that one meeting led to a full school year of monthly meetings where teachers shared lessons and used student samples as a springboard to discuss their successes and challenges and to problem-solve together. During the school year, the group used Nancie Atwell's *Lessons that Change Writers* (2002) as a common resource. Careful to respect the style and strengths of one another, teachers also brainstormed several intersecting questions for inquiry that year (Birchak et al. 1998). Teachers who had avoided or abandoned Writing Workshop were sharing examples of effective memoirs and class-generated criteria.

In the spring, the group decided to hold a Share-In evening and invited teachers from across the district to attend mini-sessions where they shared powerful discoveries from their classroom inquiries. This professional learning community had become strong and safe enough for neophyte presenters to offer sessions and share their thinking. At the end of the evening, group members marvelled at the power of sustained inquiry within the community.

The next year, they adopted the format of Information Circles and added Linda Christensen's *Reading, Writing and Rising Up* (2000), Jeffrey Wilhelm's *Action Strategies for Deepening Comprehension* (2002), and Harvey Daniels' *Subjects Matter* (2004). Of course, they had to hold the Share-In again. The more expertise and ownership grew within the group, the more targeted Leyton's search became for inspiring, research-based resources. This group continued for eight years with as many as 75 members at times. By meeting monthly in Information Circles (i.e., reading different book choices), the group size was manageable because small groups shared and discussed ideas and approaches with their individual, diverse classroom communities in mind.

Another exciting development was that some Information Circles explored books and ideas that connected literacy and science: Campbell and Fulton's *Science Notebooks: Writing about Inquiry* (2003) and Chancer and Rester-Zodrow's *Moon Journals: Writing, Art, and Inquiry through Focused Nature Study* (1997) and literacy and mathematics Bay-Williams and Martinie's *Math and Literature: Grades 6–8* (2004), and *Reading and Writing to Learn Mathematics* by Martinez and Martinez (2001).

For Leyton, the cycle of inquiry came full circle. The longer the group met together, the more they started to wonder about and address students with the most complex needs within the context of classroom teaching. Perhaps what was most important to group members was the sense of community. Teachers who had felt isolated in their schools found colleagues who were taking risks and trying out ideas.

Conclusion

Whether in a district study group, a grade level team, or with a co-teaching partner, the support of our colleagues can help us grow in new and unexpected directions. Experts agree that by working together with shared goals, teachers, cross-curricular teams, and schools can make a significant difference. Using information from formative assessments, schools, teams, and groups must establish shared goals:

- that focus on developing students as active, independent learners
- that can be embedded in content teaching
- that are shared by teachers across classes and subjects
- that are shared and reflected on by students
- that are maintained and sustained across one or more years
- that are assessed (summative assessment) and used to reflect on and refine efforts and set new goals

The richest examples of successful implementation of shared goals involve collaborative teaching, whether between classroom teachers or between classroom teachers and support teachers, that is, a resource teacher, a librarian, or a literacy coach. Such co-teaching and shared ownership of goals for improving student learning lead to richer professional learning for the teachers involved.

Chapter 3

Responsive Teaching: Connecting Assessment, Planning, and Instruction

We think of responsive teaching as honouring students' interests and adjusting our content and practice based on what our students need. Responsive teaching is not clinical; it is based on careful attention and deep listening—both to ourselves and to our students. So often, as teachers, we create a great lesson and follow it without being attentive to how our students are receiving the lesson. Being willing to adjust our plan is as important as the plan itself. Responsive teaching means that we listen to our students' voices and share with them the responsibility for creating and adjusting the curriculum. For us, responsive teaching is *ethical* practice. Ethical in this context means morally good, constantly working to align our actions with our values.

Responsive teaching means that we use language that invites our students to engage with the content and with other students. We are often unaware that we use judgmental or limiting language that takes away students' confidence in and ownership of their learning. Instead, we should frame our communication with students in descriptive and inquiring language, in ways that enable two-way interactions (*I notice that…, What would you like to share? What do you think is the most powerful part of your piece? What would you like to conference about? Good use of…, Have you thought of…?, Good start with…, What else do you wonder about this?*). Ethical, learning-oriented teachers constantly adjust how they interact with students, based on events and relationships in the classroom. It's important that we pay attention to whether and how our language is nurturing and extends the learning.

(In)formative Assessment: Getting Started

A cornerstone of responsive teaching is (in)formative assessment. We have modified the term formative assessment to (in)formative assessment to imply this type of assessment informs our planning and practice—the process through which we gain insight into our students as individuals and as learners, both initially and throughout the school year.

At September start-up with our new classes, our primary goal is to build a community of learners where all students can develop a sense of belonging and experience success. With that goal in mind, we begin to learn more about each individual—what interests them, what concerns them, what makes them tick as learners. We must discover who our students are as learners before we make too many plans.

The purpose of getting to know students through (in)formative assessment is to guide our instruction, so we start by building a class profile, as a tool to provide an overview of the class while also paying attention to individual students. The process can reveal commonalities and differences in students' strengths, passions, and areas of skill and talent. Many approaches to formative assessment focus on student's individual challenges and what can be done to fix them. We work instead from the mindset that each learner is a capable, but unique, individual. When our goal is for all students to develop as thoughtful, self-regulating learners, we have to scaffold this process from the beginning of the year, and communicate that goal to our students. Teachers can use many activities and assessments to build a class profile. Our approaches include the Who am I? Profile, a performance-based reading assessment, observations, artifacts that students collect and create, and students' reflective writing. These sources reveal students' strengths, stretches, concerns, and goals. The subsequent Class Profile guides our decisions about how to design our classrooms and activities, but it also provides another step in building relationships with students.

Who am I? Profile

In her grade 6/7 classroom, Nicole Widdess begins the year working interactively with her students to complete their copy of the graphic organizer Who am I? Profile (Figure 3.1). She models how to brainstorm and jot down personal qualities, moving from section to section in this graphic organizer while giving students the choice to use words, images, or diagrams to show or explain who they are. Nicole shares by describing herself as *emotional*, *giving*, and *determined*, then by drawing a picture beside each word—a tear for *emotional*, a present for *giving*, and a stick figure trying to climb to the top of a mountain for *determined*. She then invites her students to describe themselves in that section of their graphic organizer. As the modelling continues, she reminds her students that what they share must be kept confidential among themselves, the classroom teacher, and the resource

Figure 3.1 Who am I? Profile

Who am I? Profile

Some words that describe me are….		
My favourite books/stories are…	Some things I like to do with my friend are…	My favourite activities that I do on my own are…
My favourite activities I do with my family are…	I am very good at/ or interested in…	Some hopes and dreams that I have for myself are…
Some important things that you should/ or need to know about me are…	The easiest way for me to show what I know is…	Something I would like to get better at this year is…
Some of my greatest fears are…		

© Portage & Main Press, 2014, *It's All About Thinking: Creating Pathways for All Learning in the Middle Years*, BLM, ISBN 978-1-55379-509-4

teacher. We have found the most revealing prompt is "Some important things that you should know / or need to know about me are…". This prompt allows students to share things that they might not otherwise share if they feel unsafe or if they feel obligated to share with everyone.

For Linda Watson and Leyton Schnellert, getting to know the students as individual learners helps engage them as partners. When devising relevant questions and tasks for formative assessment, teachers use the knowledge they gain from the "profile process" to honour their students' prior experiences, abilities, and knowledge. Students are more able to engage in a unit of study when they feel welcome, when they have opportunities to use what they know to make connections between prior knowledge and course content, when they are encouraged to use the skills they already have, and share more of what they know about topics, issues, ideas, and themselves as learners. As well, they are more likely to take risks in their learning, and to develop as independent and confident learners.

Key point ✳ (handwritten margin note)

Lesson Sequence

Linda begins each school year with a new class by following this lesson sequence and modelling each step for her students.

Connecting

Ask the class "*What do you need to know about me/us that will help you to learn this year?*"

- Be prepared with responses to field all kinds of questions, including about teaching styles, about what students have heard about the class from others, about what counts for grades, and so on.
- They will not remember all your responses, but the process sets a tone of openness and exploration, becoming an interactive "conversation." Students can see teachers modelling how a person's interests and passions, and the ways we think and do things relate to the kind of learners we are. This process also sets up modelling as a key instructional approach.
- It's important to think ahead and prepare thoroughly, even rehearsing possible responses—so that the process leads to a light-hearted and fun class. What you share sets the stage for drawing out a diversity of honest questions and responses from students.

Processing

- Project the graphic organizer Who am I? Profile (Figure 3.1) on the overhead projector. Model responses to the first two boxes as students watch ("Some words that describe me are…." "My favourite books/stories are…"). Provide a wide range of possible answers and explanations. Linda, for example, talks about her passion for teaching, her love of horses, her need to talk out her thinking processes when she is learning something new, and about how she learns best when she's active and moving about, and about how drama has been part of her life. When possible, Leyton also takes a turn at the overhead projector, offering up examples. We find this to be a powerful way for students to see support teachers as a member of the classroom community and to reinforce the idea that we are all different, and that there are no "right answers" to these questions.

- Once students have their own copy of Figure 3.1, explain to them that their answers give you a chance to learn something about them, about what they think they need (in terms of instruction) to be successful as a learner/student. Be sure to emphasize that what they share is between you and them, but also that the information will guide your decisions on how to plan and teach in ways that can best help them learn.
- Using the projector, fill out the first two sections as you discuss them with your students. Then, have students fill out those two boxes on their own copy, jotting down all the ideas that come to mind—just to get them down on paper. Using this routine, go through the rest of the boxes, and keep encouraging students to be reflective.
- At the bottom of the page, model a response to the prompt "Some of my greatest fears are…". Emphasize the importance of this sentence stem, pointing out that it's not meant for listing "spiders, falling down, or bad hair days" but rather for noting their fears about the class, or about their learning issues, about success in school, or about not realizing their hopes in life. At times, a response here becomes a lead-in to a conversation with a student when a challenge in class is related to what the student has shared. The more sensitive we are to our students and their profiles, the more we find that they engage and take risks in their learning.

Transforming/Personalizing

- Ask students to pick one important idea from their profile to share with the class. This request marks the first time you ask them to determine relative importance and to justify the reason for their choice—a thinking skill that can become the basis of all units of study during the school year, as it does in Linda's class.
- Suggest to students that they mentally rehearse what they want to say by mumbling it at their desk. This idea of mental rehearsal before expressing one's thought will also become a basis of class discussion that will support students' learning during the year.
- Before collecting the profiles encourage students to share their response with a partner. Sharing with a partner and using strategies to encourage talking and conversation provide the cornerstone of Linda's teaching practice. Observing how our students work together and support each other through their own unique and

diverse styles of learning is an important influence on our teaching strategies. We encourage our students to share and build on each other's thinking as ways of developing self-confidence and good relationships.

- Collect students' profile pages at the end of the class. Tally their responses, looking for patterns, and add the data on your Class Profile summary page (see Figure 3.2, adapted from Brownlie and King 2011, p. 117).

Using a Performance-Based Assessment to Guide Your Teaching

We value the data we get from implementing a criterion-referenced performance-based assessment (PBA). We use an assessment of informational reading that requires students to use and demonstrate their use of meaning-making reading strategies based on short excerpts of content from their subject curriculums. Most ministries of education offer rubrics concisely describing four progressive levels of content knowledge and skill development (learning expectations) in reading informational text. Such documents allow teachers to select or customize an initial assessment, administer it, and record the results to take a snapshot of the current levels of their students' reading abilities. The PBA results are added to the Class Profile from which teachers set specific goals for the next units of study or apply the data across content areas for a cohort of students (Brownlie and Schnellert 2009; Brownlie, Fullerton, and Schnellert 2011). The results of a fall performance-based assessment administered not for marks, but rather to inform our teaching provides baseline data for making instructional decisions. With this assessment we want to see what students can do independently with minimal prompts.

Assessment Process

Select a grade-level piece of informational text (e.g., newspaper article, 2 or 3 pages from a textbook, or a short persuasive essay). The piece should also include text features such as images, graphs, maps, charts, or boxed sidebars. Distribute a copy to each of your students; ask them to quickly scan the text and record their predictions about the text on their copy of the response sheet (Figure 3.3; see also Brownlie and Schnellert 2009).

Then, invite them to read the complete text and respond to the rest of the prompts on their response sheet. For students who struggle significantly with grade-level text, invite them to circle the words they do know and draw or mind map what they think the main ideas are. We prefer that all students engage with the same text initially so that the class results show the full range of performance on grade-level text.

Figure 3.2

Class Profile summary

Adapted from Brownlie and King 2001

© Portage & Main Press, 2014, *It's All About Thinking: Creating Pathways for All Learnings in the Middle Years*, BLM, ISBN 978-1-55379-509-4

Classroom Strengths

- Attentive
- Good listeners
- Ask for help
- Like real life examples
- Visual and hands-on learners
- Good with text features
- Positive toward each other

Classroom Stretches

- Generating their own strategies
- Determining importance
- Discussion
- Self-monitoring
- Accessing prior knowledge

Classroom Interests

- Socializing, sports, performing arts (dance and drama), social networking, reading

Classroom Goals

- Making connections
- Determining importance
- Applying their learning across the curriculum
- Developing planning and self-monitoring strategies
- Writing a persuasive piece using research skills

Classroom Decisions

- Connecting, processing, transforming/personalizing lesson structure
- Targeted, extended strategy instruction
- Multimodal representation opportunities (differentiation)
- Metacognitive steps in lessons

Individual Concerns

Medical	Language	Learning	Social-emotional	Challenge
Nate (ADHD)	Peter (ESL 2) Cory, Doug & Allie (ESL 3) 6 others (ESL 4/5)	Nate, Jason, Lars	Nate	Izzy, Keisha, Glen

Performance-Based Assessment Response Sheet

1. **Predicting:** What do you think the text will be about? Why?

   _____

   _____

   _____

2. **Summarizing:** Show that you can clearly identify the key ideas and details from this passage, using a web, words, diagrams, and/or drawings. (Use the back of this page.)

3. **Connecting:** How does what you read connect with what you already know?

   _____

   _____

   _____

4. **Strategies:** Give a brief definition for the words underlined in the article:

   a. _____

   b. _____

   c. _____

5. **Inferencing:** Read between the lines to find something you believe to be true but that is not actually written. Explain your thinking.

   _____

   _____

   _____

6. **What strategies** did you use to determine the meaning of the words in question #4?

   _____

   _____

   _____

7. **Reflecting:** Was this piece easy or hard for you? How did you help yourself understand? (If this piece was easy, how do you help yourself understand something more difficult?)

   _____

   _____

   _____

© Portage & Main Press, 2014, *It's All About Thinking: Creating Pathways for All Learnings in the Middle Years*, BLM, ISBN 978-1-55379-509-4

Oral Conference

While the students are reading and responding, conference with each individual student, asking them to read aloud while you listen and record on a teacher/student conference sheet, noting their reading behaviours on a blank copy of the text. Assure students that they don't have to read aloud in front of their peers. Some might prefer to read aloud at your desk or in the hall—so let them know these options. We also have called upon other helping teachers in the school (librarians, learning resource teachers) to help with this process. Complete a running record noting omissions, repetitions, substitutions, insertions, reversals, unknown words (teacher gives word), and self-corrections (Brownlie, Feniak, and Schnellert 2006). Ask the four conferencing questions and jot down students' responses (Figure 3.4). When complete, give each student some positive feedback about their oral reading. If students need more time to respond, we do our best to accommodate. If students finish early, they can read quietly.

After all your students have read to you orally and all have completed their response sheet, collect the responses and code them using your rubric.

Assessing Student Work

Upon completion of the assessment, the teacher codes the assessment using a rubric. We use the *BC Performance Standards for Reading for Information:* <www.bced.gov.bc.ca/perf_stands/reading.htm>. Some schools use group coding as a way to better develop their understanding of what criteria mean and how they can be applied. When possible, code with a partner until you reach a shared standard for coding. We have found that group coding (that is, a group of teachers of the same grade who work together on the assessment and debrief and discuss their combined results) is the most powerful approach. By working collaboratively, teachers have the opportunity to plan common strategies and language for groups of students.

Assessment tool

Group Coding and Planning

Initially, it can be challenging for groups of teachers to focus on learning about and from a performance-based assessment during the debriefing stage. Too often we use data to beat ourselves up or compare ourselves to others. This is not the intention—if our goal is to be responsive teachers, we should keep the focus on who our students are, what we see as positive trends in the data (even if these are relative strengths), and to set goals. A cohort of students benefit greatly when they have a small collegial team of teachers who teach them for more than one subject (e.g., Math/Science; English/Social Studies; all core subjects; or other combinations) and share assessment data to plan future lessons.

Figure 3.4 Assessment questions about reading strategies for vocabulary and for meaning

Conference Questions for Performance-Based Reading Assessment

1. When you come to a challenging word, how do you figure it out? Check the strategies you use.

✓	Word Strategies
	Reread it.
	Ask someone.
	Look it up in the dictionary or on my phone.
	Skip it.
	Sound it out.
	Try and figure out what makes sense in the sentence.
	Look at the picture.
	Break the word into syllables.
	Chunk the word.
	Cover the ending or look for smaller words within.
Other:	

2. If your reading does not make sense, what do you do? Check the strategies you use.

✓	Sense Strategies
	Reread it.
	Skip it.
	Try another book.
	Make a picture in my mind.
	Make notes on what I've read.
	Make a connection between the text, myself, the world, another text.
	Look in the paragraph for words I do know.
	Look at the pictures and the captions.
	Try to make it make sense.
Other:	

3. What is this selection mainly about?

4. What is something about this text that surpris

   Surprise:

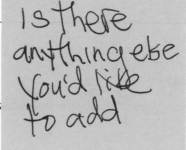

Is there anything else you'd like to add

As a professional learning activity, coding the Assessment for Learning, collating the data, and then planning subsequent instruction takes time. As a classroom level assessment process, teachers who are experienced at coding student responses based on the Performance Standards can complete their work within 90 minutes per class.

Materials required

- Completed student responses and oral conference sheets
- Copy of your Rating Scale (We use the *BC Performance Standards* www.bced.gov.bc.ca/perf_stands/reading.htm>.)
- One extra copy of the Rating Scale as master
- One highlighter

Organization of the Assessment

Procedure for coding student responses

preparation for assessment

Read the response sheet and conference sheet at the beginning of the coding process so that teachers have a collaborative starting point. As a group, match the questions to the bulleted criteria on the Performance Standards, and make a coding key for the team. For example:

- The first question focuses on predicting and text features, which match with the 2nd bullet.
- The second question focuses on inference, which corresponds with…
- The third question focuses on details, inferences, and evaluation/ reflections, which match up with several…
- The fourth question involves note-making, main ideas, and details, which offer information about…
- The fifth question involves word skills, which relate to…
- The sixth question involves checking for understanding, which corresponds with…

Coding Together

Read the passage that the students read.

- With a partner, answer the questions.
- It is easier to recognize a powerful answer when partners construct an answer together.
- Partners should familiarize themselves with the scale that will be used.
- Read all of each student's answers before scoring the response.
- Look on the scale for bullets that describe what has been read and observed. Code the various bullets first and then the overall snapshot last.
- Although each question is designed to elicit a specific type of thinking, a student may demonstrate one kind of thinking in response to another one of the questions. For example, in a student's sketch, coding partners might find an example of inferential thinking.

- Code each student's work on their own rubric, using a highlighter. (You can use this scale during the year to chart each student's progress.)
- Think back over the samples coded and discussed.
  - Look for skills that many students may need to learn, as well as a group of students who have a particular need. From these observations, pick no more than three skills to focus on over the next term.

The Cycle of Assessing, Planning, and Teaching

Use the initial assessment for learning as a springboard for planning and teaching. You will want to reassess the targeted skills in 6 to 8 weeks to check whether what you're teaching is making a difference.

Check-in to monitor progress

As part of our teaching and assessment cycle, we carry out a performance-based assessment in September for baseline data, then repeat in February and late May to assess individual growth. Teachers can track reading development over the year by using a different colour of highlighter pen on the same rubric for each assessment. The patterns that emerge from this coding data become the focus for discussion between teachers, parents, and students and for subsequent instruction.

We find it helpful to choose two or three specific aspects (from the rubric) to focus on instructionally class-wide (e.g., inferencing). This is a great opportunity to ask colleagues for ideas and approaches that they have used to develop these areas of students' reading. These then become a focus in the following month or so. If no change is noted, the strategies are changed, but the instructional focus remains the same. If growth is noted, new areas of focus are chosen.

One effective way to improve student performance — and develop students' understanding of what powerful readers do — is to develop criteria for responses with the students. To do this, choose 4 or 5 responses that demonstrate different kinds of strengths from a wide range of students. Have the students work either as a whole class or in groups of conversation partners. Introduce the task:

> "I've chosen specific response samples because of something in them that really worked. I'd like you to read what is written (or drawn) and, as a class, we will decide what strikes us as powerful in the response."

- As students describe what they find powerful and why, the teacher records the points on the board or an overhead. It is important to have students share their reasons for each powerful idea. With these notes, the class can begin framing the criteria.
- After analyzing several responses, the students can use the criteria to self-assess and to set a personal reading response goal for the next month.

- Once teacher and students have clarified the bulleted list of criteria, they select samples and post them for reference during other response events in the class.

Over time, invite students to revisit the criteria when conversations about reading or writing responses come up again. The teacher can add or delete items that will better match the different genre or response task. After these conversations, invite students to note which of the criteria they have achieved and to set a new goal.

Making a Class Profile

The goal of the class profile process is to reveal the uniqueness of every student. We combine the results from the Who am I? Profile, performance-based assessments, and other classroom observations and artifacts, and we look for patterns and commonalities.

The Class Profile summary synthesizes class strengths, stretches (areas that need further development), interests, goals, decisions, and individual concerns. Teachers can use a variety of classroom activities to learn about their students. For instance, Linda asks her Humanities students to bring in an artifact that represents an important event in their life and says something special about them.

See Ch.5 in Brownlie and Schnellert 2009 for Linda's detailed lesson sequences.

Compiling the Data

- Look for patterns in the information from the "Who am I? Profile"
- Summarize the data from the Performance-Based Assessment
- Include observations from class activities

Planning to Use Formative Assessment Information

When planning Science units, Nicole and Leyton target the related reading/thinking skills for students to develop over the course of the unit. The baseline data from the assessment helps direct their initial planning. Working within the assessment-to-instruction cycle, they complete a parallel performance-based reading assessment as a summative assessment at the end of the unit so that they can see whether and to what degree students are more successful in using the target reading/thinking strategies. For example, in this unit they wanted students to be better at:

- determining importance
- applying their learning across the curriculum
- planning and self-monitoring what strategies to use
- using their thinking strategies and content knowledge when engaging in an authentic task
- transforming what they learned into a persuasive piece using their research skills

When looking at the theme "Diversity of Life" and the learning outcomes in the provincial curriculum, they decided to focus on three big ideas:

1. Living things have similarities and differences.
2. Classifying things helps us understand the diversity of life.
3. Living things adapt to their environment.

With the big ideas, the Class Profile, and their targeted reading/thinking skills, they developed a unit that included:

- a connecting, processing, and transforming/personalizing lesson structure (open-ended strategies)
- targeted, extended strategy instruction (gradual release)
- multimodal representation opportunities (differentiation)
- opportunities for students to plan and reflect on learning activities (self-regulation)
- inquiry questions

Building a Class Profile School-Wide

The Class Profile can be used school-wide. Nicole (at WD Ferris Elementary) facilitated a PD afternoon on the topic with her staff in an effort to coordinate instructional goals and teaching approaches, and to consider how non-enrolling teachers could use their time in a more targeted and consistent manner.

Prior to that afternoon, Nicole asked staff to begin thinking about their classes and to come prepared with some thoughts about their students as learners. She provided the Who am I? Profile learning questionnaire as well as other learning inventories for teachers to use. Nicole was careful to let teachers know that it was okay to come with whatever information they had—even if it was just in their heads—so as not to overwhelm teachers before beginning the process.

Their meeting went from 12:45 p.m. to 2:30 p.m., not a lot of time, but a great opportunity for the entire staff to work together as a team and see the benefits of developing a school-wide profile. The professional development committee sent the following invitation to staff prior to their afternoon together:

> Before our learning support teachers create their schedules this year, we are going to spend an afternoon using our formative assessment information to build a Class Profile and identify goals for our classes. As a staff, we will use this information to decide where and how we can work together to best support our students this year. Here's what to expect:
>
> Goal: To work together to identify and plan based on the needs of all learners
>
> Rationale: By working collaboratively to meet the needs of all learners, we can tap into one another's areas of expertise, knowledge, and experience

Process: Build a class and school profile of learners that is positive and proactive

Class Profile includes *class* strengths, stretches, interests and *individual* medical, language, learning, and social-emotional needs

Goals: Set goals for your class, based on this information

Decisions: Discuss what's next in terms of how to meet these goals by working with other educators in the school

Nicole modelled completing the Class Profile section by section, and teachers completed each section in parallel. On an 11" x 17" graphic organizer, teachers used their formative assessment information and knowledge of their students to describe class strengths, stretches, and interests. She provided time during each section for teachers to brainstorm and share their ideas with a colleague who was teaching the same or similar grades.

After discussion with a colleague, teachers recorded three strengths and two stretches on their class charts, also noting particular students with special needs that all teachers should know. When they had completed and posted all charts, staff circulated around the room, then shared their impressions within the whole.

During this process and based on assessment information, they planned activities across classes and the school as a whole. At later class review meetings (scheduled during school time), teachers brought their charts to discuss with their school-based resource teacher and teacher-librarian (Brownlie and King 2011). Teachers felt ownership of their classes, had a vision for moving forward, and created opportunities for co-planning and co-teaching.

From Assessment to Instruction

The artistry of teaching includes refining your ability to adjust to the learning needs of your students. Some students need explicit instruction, some need space to take risks and explore, but all students need clear goals, expectations, and feedback. To support students' learning, we build the strategies of gradual release of responsibility, open-ended questions, co-operative learning, and differentiation into our teaching.

Modelling

Teacher modelling is a key instructional approach. When we forget to model, assuming that students get the point, the sea of confused faces reminds us how essential it is. Two effective modelling approaches are "think-alouds" (Wilhelm 2001) and "gradual release of responsibility" (Pearson and Gallagher 1983) (Figure 3.5).

Figure 3.5 Gradual release of responsibility

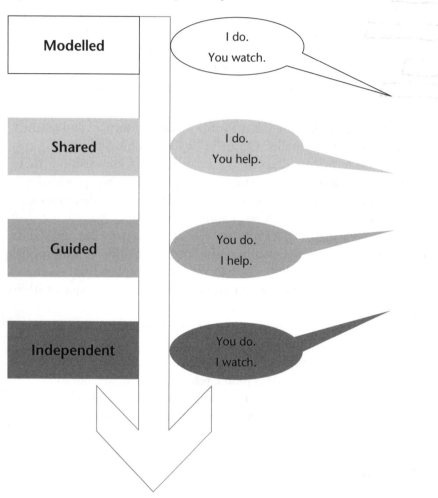

Using a think-aloud takes the mystery out of what goes on in a learner's brain as they make sense of a situation, task, or text. Modelling using a think-aloud lets students see our "thinking moves" as we access our background knowledge, make connections between recent and new concepts, and apply analytical skills that we have been developing. The gradual release of responsibility helps ensure that students have support during meaning-making and problem-solving activities with coaching from teachers and peers. For maximum effect—and to ensure that we do not limit the quality of students' thinking — we combine modelling with open-ended strategies.

Open-Ended Strategies to Support the Learning of ALL Students

Teachers must not underestimate the importance of designing their lessons for ALL learners. When lessons include connecting, processing, transforming/personalizing phases, all students gain access to the curriculum.

Using teaching strategies with these phases in mind helps students engage with the content while developing their thinking skills (Figure 3.6) (Brownlie, Close, and Wingren 1988; Brownlie, Feniak, and Schnellert 2006).

We use open-ended strategies that are collaborative to capitalize on the social aspect of learning. We want all students to connect what they and others already know to the new ideas and concepts emerging in our lessons throughout the unit of study. We start a learning sequence by asking students to predict, to link to prior knowledge, and to compare key words, ideas, images, artifacts, or relationships before engaging with new content. Connecting strategies help students build from what they know, which might involve a simple quick-write in which students record, draw, web, or give examples of what they know about the topic of the day's work. A simple strategy that,

Figure 3.6 Open-ended strategies

Connect	Activate prior knowledge, helping students connect what they are learning to what they already know	
	Activities could include:	
	• 3-2-1	• Anticipation Guide
	• 3 Pieces of Tape	• Think-Aloud or Thought Bubble
	• Inside Circles / Outside Circles	• Think of a time…
	• Should I stay or should I go?	• Partner Interview
Process	Help students process new content, building their repertoire of meaning-making strategies.	
	Activities could include:	
	• Magnet notes	• Venn Diagrams
	• Quick-Write	• Reciprocal Teaching
	• Partner Talk	• Carousel
	• Listen-Sketch-Draw	• Four Quadrants
		• Say Something
Transform/ Personalize	Provide opportunities for students to personalize and transform their learning.	
	Activities could include:	
	• Tableau	• Critical Timeline
	• What? So what? Now what?	• Comic Strip
	• Ideagram	• Storyboard
	• Mind Map	• Learning Journey
Metacognition	Create opportunities for students to self-assess, set goals, and take action to manage and improve their learning.	
	Activities could include:	
	• Three things I want you to notice about my work…	• Next time steps…
		• What I still wonder…
		• I am proud of…

nonetheless, activates students' prior knowledge, allowing openings for teacher prompts that help students make predictions about the lesson's big idea.

Next we use processing strategies to help students build thinking and interaction skills to successfully use, link, and compare key information from new content with what they knew previously. In Science, we might ask students to record key information and observations for an investigation they are engaged in. Processing strategies are useful with all kinds of "texts"—print, media, visual, and oral—as well as experiments, mathematical problems, learning situations, and applications of big ideas.

Finally, we use transforming and personalizing strategies. We want our students to be able to synthesize information and represent it in ways that show that they have understood important, relevant ideas well enough to interpret and transform them in their own way. Students' reflective writing that uses a range of graphic organizers and conceptual frameworks also provides valuable artifacts of students' growth and their deepening conceptual understanding. Creating dramatic or visual representations or using analogies and metaphors are other ways that students might demonstrate that they have personalized and synthesized their understandings. Linda and Leyton ask students to create their own reading logs based on criteria that the class generates from a variety of reading experiences. Nicole offers students choices in how they can represent their understanding of cell reproduction. She offers them two examples and has the students brainstorm two additional possibilities.

We develop and choose open-ended and collaborative strategies with all learners in mind. As opposed to worksheets, graphic organizers we create do not ask students to find the "right" answer, but rather ask them to make connections, process information, and transform information in a variety of ways, to solve problems with more than one answer—and/or show more than one way to arrive at that answer. Working with open-ended strategies leaves room for us to scaffold learning based on the strengths and needs of the individual students within the class. The strategies are collaborative in that they require students to share their thinking with others at several points along the way—both teaching and learning from one another—and we welcome all ideas as students refine their understandings over time.

By designing and carrying out our instruction this way, we find that we need to make fewer adaptations and modifications for the diverse learners in our class. This frees up more time for whole-class teaching, small-group coaching, and individual conferencing. We can include more students as members of the learning community where they are exposed to quality teaching while also learning from their age-group. Diverse students learn more from participation in the classroom than from working on separate material even if designed for them or from being removed from the classroom learning context. For us, a supportive classroom is one that welcomes and celebrates all learners and that develops all of its community members as strategic thinkers.

As teachers create sequences of "instructional activities that start with students' current needs, interests and abilities and build from there to develop needed expertise" (Smith and Wilhelm 2006), we must keep Class Profile results in mind. Leyton and Nicole share the following example of what they planned together. At the time, Leyton was a teacher-consultant and Nicole was teaching a grades 7/8 Humanities class in a middle school.

Leyton and Nicole built the course in a way that honoured each student in the class. Students had completed the Who am I? Profile organizer and a Performance-Based Reading Assessment. From such valuable data, Nicole and Leyton were able to construct a responsive approach to allow for student success by identifying three target areas: using text features, making connections, and determining importance.

Nicole began the course by focusing on helping students build an understanding of how making connections is a cognitive skill crucial for success in learning across subject areas. Many of the students were not aware of the role that background knowledge plays in meaning making, whether in school or in the world. She worked with students to practise making connections by relating what they learned from fiction and nonfiction texts (including web-based media) to the question *"How do bullying and peer pressure affect me and my world?"* Nicole helped to scaffold students' use of these cognitive strategies through read-alouds, shared reading activities, and independent reading tasks by providing engaging and appropriate texts at or near the students' reading level. Most of the reading materials they chose to model and teach with were short, nonfiction excerpts, from the Nelson's BoldPrint series.

To help students make connections between literature, themselves, and the world, Nicole used *Inventing Elliot* as a read-aloud text and the lyrics of "Where Is the Love?" by the Black-Eyed Peas, complemented by "Friends" and "I Fit In" from the *Nelson Friends Magazine*. Nonfiction texts included articles from the newspaper and articles from *Time for Kids* <timeforkids. com>. After introducing and modelling reading strategies through think-alouds, two-column notes, and coding text (text-to-self, text-to-text, text-to-world), Nicole and Leyton found that students were getting lost in the activities without being able to see how well they were doing with the strategy. They wanted to help students see their own progress over time, so they developed a graphic organizer to use across texts.

"Showing My Thinking" Lesson

The graphic organizer (Figure 3.7) supported students as they worked with a new target strategy, but it required a lot of modelling and practice before the teacher could step away to let the students respond independently to show their understanding.

Figure 3.7 Graphic organizer

Showing My Thinking

Connect	**Text feature:**
Process	**Chunk 1** Paragraph Heading
	Chunk 2 Paragraph Heading
	Chunk 3 Paragraph Heading
Personalize/ Transform	What I want you to notice about my thinking...
	Next time, I plan to... (goal-setting)

Nicole and Leyton created this lesson sequence to address the learning goals they had set for the class. Students were working with passages and articles 1 to 3 pages in length. Groups of 3 or 4 students each had a different article that they were responsible for investigating as part of research into a topic of interest to them. Topics spanned video games, sports, and beauty myths. During the connecting phase of the strategy, students debated and chose what they believed to be a significant text feature from the reading and used it to *make predictions* about the content of the article. For example, one group chose a photo, examined it and suggested that the text might be about the impact of dehydration when playing field sports, and recorded their thoughts in the Connect section of the organizer.

In their inquiry groups, students divided the text into 3 chunks. As a team they received three sticky notes. They then read through the chunk of text, looking for a *magnet word,* the most important word of the chunk, and recorded it in the centre of their sticky note. Then students reread the chunk looking for 4 to 5 key words that attracted to the magnet word and, after discussion, recorded them in the corners of the sticky around the magnet word (Buehl 2014). Students did this for all 3 chunks. Then students closed the text and quizzed one another about what they had read with reference to only their sticky notes. When finished, they individually looked in the text for one quote to share in the following day's discussion.

In the next class, students shared their quotes and discussed why they chose them by asking each other follow-up questions and making connections between the various quotes and what they had already learned about their inquiry topic. Students reviewed their magnet notes and discussed with their group what a good paragraph heading would be to capture the main idea of the chunk read, and recorded it on their Showing My Thinking graphic organizer. After discussion, the students (sometimes with support from the teacher) took the paragraph headings and wrote a summary together in the space provided. Students then completed the metacognitive step that required them to reflect on their thinking and on the activity's processes to personalize and transform their learning.

Leyton and Nicole provided a lot of modelling, coaching, and facilitating so that students could see and hear their thinking. As student teams continued with their inquiries they now had a strategy for note-making that they used and adapted successfully on their own.

Open-ended strategies require students to use key thinking skills to find information related to the essential question or big idea of the day or week. By using or devising graphic organizers, teachers can be more explicit with their students about the phases of strategic reading: connecting, processing, and transforming/personalizing their learning.

Cooperative Learning

Talk and collaboration are central to learning. Learning does not happen in isolation. In fact, students (and adults) can become stuck in the "scripts" they know, and they struggle to integrate new information with what they already know. We believe that thinking and learning happen through talk. We want students to take risks and share their background knowledge, ideas, and impressions aloud so that they can clarify and extend their understanding with input from others. Collaborative meaning-making supports one's ability to build an understanding. It is not easy, but it is critical and requires a safe environment to be successful. Today's knowledge society requires that we all develop and maintain strong communication skills and collaboration techniques.

Cooperative learning plays a key role in classroom learning communities. The teacher's job is to facilitate the process for all students, building their social and communications skills along with their thinking and learning skills. Karen Ngeow (1998) outlines the common attributes of any group-learning approach:

1. A group-learning task is designed based on shared learning goals and outcomes.
2. Small-group learning takes place in groups of 3–5 students.
3. Cooperative behaviour involves trust-building activities, joint planning, and an understanding of team support (e.g., building on each others' ideas, taking turns, asking questions).
4. Positive interdependence is developed through setting and reflecting on mutual goals.
5. Individual accountability and task commitment are expected of students.

While each of these factors is important, we agree with Duffy and Cunningham (1996) who have shown that it's the combination of these factors that can lead to critical thinking, communication, creative thinking, and increased personal and social responsibility. In cooperative groups that are scaffolded by teachers (often through partner work), students should be supported and encouraged to share alternative viewpoints, support each other's inquiry processes, and develop critical thinking skills that include the ability to reflect and improve on their own learning.

Ngeow's article offers five phases for designing instruction for collaborative learning (Figure 3.8), rather like the Learning Cycle Model 5E science lesson: engage, explore, explain, elaborate, evaluate (Bybee 1997, 2006).

Grouping Students for Optimal Learning

Classrooms are diverse, and their diversity plays an important role in grouping students. In Linda's Humanities class, she rarely allows students to pick where they sit in class or who they work with, because they choose friends

Figure 3.8 Ngeow's five phases for designing instruction for collaborative learning

Phase	Instructional Design
Engagement	Teachers set the stage by providing the class with a collaborative activity that is authentic and brings home a sense of ownership to its learners.
Exploration	Students work on the initial exploration of ideas and information. Teachers have to decide how much input to give the students for their learning task, and how much to leave to the students' resourcefulness.
Transformation	Students in their learning groups engage in activities to "reshape" the information by organizing, clarifying, elaborating, or synthesizing the learning concepts. It is crucial for this stage of learning that the tasks set will require discussion and contribution from all group members. The learning activity should, therefore, be designed as complex enough to provide many opportunities for knowledge transformation at different levels or in various subtasks, thereby involving as many group members as possible.
Presentation	Student groups have the opportunity to present their findings to an interested and critical audience.
Reflection	Students analyze what they have learned, identify strengths and weaknesses in the learning processes they went through, and offer constructive ideas on how their learning can be improved. Student reflection should be done both individually and collaboratively, and they need to analyze individual as well as group learning processes.

who are not always a good choice. Because our work involves students learning, interacting, thinking, and sharing together, the long-term goal is to provide opportunities for the class to form a supportive learning community. This requires careful consideration of how to group the students. We use our Class Profile to make decisions for partnering. We set up our students' expectation that, in our classrooms, everyone will work with everyone else and will eventually form a learning community that is supportive as well as collaborative. In these ways, too, we nurture students' acceptance of all learners in the classroom, including themselves.

The question of organizing diverse groups or homogeneous groups will arise as the arrangements of the groups develop. Does it make sense to put all the gifted learners together? Should the students who struggle cognitively be together? What about the students with poor work habits? Perhaps they should all be mixed up to become a group of learners, struggling to accept their strengths and their challenges? This is a question Linda has been wrestling with for a long time. It is not always possible to organize groups in ways that will satisfy everyone. We have to really know our students and what they can tolerate. Some students become frustrated when they are expected to be the leader of the group. What about the group where everyone is so quiet or shy that no one can share their thinking? These are difficult questions. The best answer so far has been to balance all groups with a range of strengths

Figure 3.9 Four ways of differentiation in the classroom

Content/Topic	We think of this as stopping to assess where students are at — with their knowledge, skills, and attitudes about what we want them to learn. For example, if we are teaching math and notice from pre-assessment that a student already has mastered the knowledge and skills required, then we as teachers should allow that student to move on with their learning in the way that best addresses their own learning needs and learning style.
Process	Being able to vary the learning activity or strategy means that we as teachers should look for ways to support the learners with several pathways or methods so that they can best explore and understand the concept. If, when teaching students in math how to find a growing pattern in images by using input and output machines or T-charts, we find that a student is struggling with the concept, we must find another way to support their learning. One way to change the lesson is by using manipulatives and allowing the student to use a hands-on approach. Other ways are using graphic organizers to support student learning as well as "partner talk time" or even a roleplay.
Product	Allowing learners a choice in how they might show their thinking and understanding is crucial. However, as teachers, we must also remember that we have students who are working at different levels. For example, a student working above grade expectations will require an assignment that challenges them and takes their thinking further. In contrast, a student who is working below grade expectations will benefit from an assignment with reduced learning tasks that allow time for understanding the concept, which leads to feeling successful in their learning. For example, when teaching math, we might ask students to complete 4 questions to show that they have mastered the concept taught that day in class. Students who have mastered the concept might need a challenge question or an activity that will allow them to become an expert. Students who are struggling with the concept might be assigned to answer only one question.
Classroom Environment	Dealing with concerns about the environment might include: Change seating arrangements; eliminate overstimulation, whether caused by visuals, light, or sound. Change or alter learning strategies based on students' needs, which can sometimes include learning styles and talents as well as personality or experiences.

and stretches. We believe that by balancing groups, we provide the best opportunity for students to see who they are and how valuable others are in supporting not only their challenges but also their strengths. Linda's Class Profiles inform her choices and become the necessary tool for making these decisions and changes.

When creating groups for the day, Linda places a student's name card on their desk for the day. Linda's students soon get used to looking for their name tag when they arrive in class. By the time they reach early spring, both the students and Linda have a good idea of who will work well together in a group. Linda explains to her students that she is working toward this goal, basing her decisions on what she thinks is best for them as learners. She is open to input and once a month asks students to confidentially share the names of up to 5 students that they would like to work with over the next few weeks. At some point over the next month, they get a chance to work with these partners.

It's particularly important for teachers to recognize or acknowledge the positive contributions each student makes to group work. For example, Tristan is an extremely humorous and talkative student with many creative ideas; he is also extremely pleasant and positive to his peers. However, his challenge is organization, time management, and written output. Tristan needs a group where his strengths can shine and he can receive support for his challenges. The real success for Tristan comes when he shares this about himself, accepts it in a positive way, offers support to others using his strengths, and asks for support from others in a proactive manner.

Differentiation

Differentiation is a way to nurture a community of learners without judgment. We don't want students to feel odd or different; we want them to understand their role in a learning community. Everyone has a part to play. Without their part, the community doesn't work. For us, differentiation means we do not have to use labels; rather, we can offer multiple pathways to learning. Our ultimate goal is for our students to create "differentiation opportunities" for themselves and each other.

Key Concept

Learning has greater depth and richness when the learner can show understanding in a variety of ways. In his research, Robert Marzano (2010) has shown how students who show their understanding with non-linguistic representations tend to have internalized concepts deeply. Differentiation also allows students to work in modes that may not be the teacher's strength. Differentiation is responsive teaching when the Class Profile guides teachers and students to create opportunities to learn and extend themselves.

Conclusion

Responsive teaching is at the heart of our philosophy and practice. It is what grounds us as ethical educators and keeps us learning along with our students. We set goals and develop our plans based on what we learn from and with our students. The decisions we make and the actions we take are emergent and ongoing. One underlying theme in the middle years is that formative assessment, instructional strategies, and classroom management are all based in relationships. Students are at the centre of our assessment, planning, and instruction. This holistic approach to teaching and learning connects theory, research, and practice.

Chapter 4

Deep Learning: Integrating Content, Process, and Product

Educators Involved

Shelley Moore: District Inclusion Teacher Consultant, SD 38, BC

Lenore Clarke: Classroom Teacher/Curriculum Support Leader, SD 62, Sooke, BC

May Crompton: Teacher-Librarian/Technology Teacher, SD 62, Sooke, BC

Justine Durrant: Aboriginal Education Teacher, SD 62, Sooke, BC

Barb Kersch: Classroom Teacher, SD 62, Sooke, BC

Jen Nixon: Classroom Teacher, SD 62, Sooke, BC

Regan Rasmussen: Visual Arts Teacher, SD 62, Sooke, BC

Linda's Experience: Learning to Leap

Ten years ago, I learned how to jump horses. Although I had had a lot of riding experience growing up, I had not actually been on a horse for over twenty-five years.

I started taking lessons and realized that, to be a good rider, I was going to have to invest time and money. My learning began in earnest and now, ten years later, I can say I understand better what it means to learn something deeply.

In the beginning, I made a lot of mistakes and I fell off numerous times. Being "launched like a lawn dart" was a necessary component of learning—the feedback was instant. Horses are strong, unpredictable animals. Soon enough, however, I improved my physical and emotional strength. My stamina grew, and I started to tackle small jump courses.

Several experiences supported my learning. I had to repeat the actions numerous times to arrive at any understanding. I had to visualize myself doing it the correct way. I watched myself on video and I talked in detail with my trainer about what I was trying to accomplish. My trainer was patient and kind, and gave me personalized feedback, pointing out what I did well and what I needed to improve on. My horse was also patient, but continued to throw me off when I did something wrong.

My trainer and I went over every detail after a jump course, a lesson, or a competition. I read books about good riding techniques and subscribed to magazines with pictures, riding exercises, and training tips. The support from my husband and daughter was strong even though committing to riding also meant sacrificing time away from them. Still, it took me a long time to feel successful. Despite many setbacks and lost confidence along the way, my motivation was high and I kept at it.

Now after competing in many horse shows, I have a drawer full of ribbons to prove my accomplishments. These symbols are more meaningful to me as an educator because learning to leap has made me a better teacher and learner. I often share this learning story with my own students as I encourage them to pose questions, to co-construct curriculum, and to stretch themselves as learners and people.

The Curriculum We Need

When considering how teaching and schools must evolve for the 21st century, we wanted to overcome the fragmented expectations of "covering" curriculum. We think our students deserve to be engaged in meaningful and relevant learning, even if it requires more time—learning that requires them to question, to wrestle with issues, to get inside an experience, and deepen their knowledge and skills. We want our students to engage with the big ideas of a discipline and to develop their knowledge and competencies over time.

Deep learning needs to be *about something*. We need to learn about ideas that are important, that we will remember, that relate to the world, and that are at the heart of subject areas. Such ideas connect the past, the present, and the future with our own individual and unique lives and experiences. When we work with big ideas, we can utilize our connections and deepen our understandings with prior knowledge, even though we all follow different paths to this shared moment. Constructing understanding with our students, who hold such a rich diversity of experience, creates the foundation for this deep learning. Just following scripted routines and curricular outcomes leads to a one-size-fits-all classroom, which is not what we want from our classroom explorations during our unit of study.

To us, a successful unit is one that provides an immersive and shared experience for our students; one that requires them to question their beliefs and attitudes. Education must offer students opportunities to build their understanding by wrestling with the big questions that relate to our lives and the world. When we began to write this chapter, Leyton posed two questions:

What is the importance of deep learning?

Why is teaching with the big idea in mind important?

As we thought about these questions around the table, Linda wrote a narrative and Nicole drew a web to show how she connects the big ideas. Our different paths into the conversation reminded us that deep learning is also about having multiple access points and pathways to a shared understanding.

The Bigger Picture

Working with big ideas allows teacher and students to inquire and explore within a domain. Projects, activities, and mini-lessons pull together knowledge, skills, and experiences that together construct a new big picture. The curriculum in each discipline can be daunting and the number of learning outcomes for the content may seem overwhelming. By identifying and developing the big ideas, we give ourselves permission, as educators and learners, to not just cover, but to uncover, the subject content.

Backward Design

The first two books of the *It's All About Thinking* series (Brownlie and Schnellert 2009, 2011) introduced backward design as a framework that focuses on one big idea as a critical aspect of planning. We can use that big idea, a foundational concept, to develop an essential question for a unit of study, and frame an inquiry project that helps us tease out enduring understandings. Planning and teaching this way helps to develop powerful topics of inquiry and engages learners in a quest, repeatedly tapping into background knowledge, making connections, and seeking diverse resources, information, and perspectives.

Over the years, the process of devising essential questions has changed as we learn more about a topic, as the world changes, and as we interact with different groups of students. We ask what concepts in the past, present, and future of the topic will resonate with our students, and what should they seek to understand. We want questions that require our students to engage in the human quest for knowledge. We have often planned an essential question for a unit, but happily found that our students were identifying their own profound questions.

Collaboration

We find that more possibilities emerge when we work with colleagues to plan a unit of study focused on big ideas. Different people have different perspectives, and these differences are resources for strengthening our collective work , rather than sources of conflict. We—Leyton, Linda, and Nicole—have grown immeasurably through co-planning, co-teaching, and co-reflecting. Our collaboration has offered significant professional development to the benefit of our students. By working through the challenges of melding different perspectives, we ensure that our students have diverse opportunities for pursuing their tentative answers to essential questions, revising those questions, and sharing resources and ideas.

Choice

Through our collaboration and cooperation, we do not assume consensus. We instead confirm our belief that we must allow for diversity and individualized pathways for learning and build them into the design of our units.

Choice is a big motivator for students that allows them to both share their voice and take ownership of their learning—choice in student texts, choice in ways to organize and present information, choice in ways to investigate questions; choice in showing what they have learned. Open-ended instructional strategies like those outlined in chapter 3 engage students with choice through diverse pathways that support personal engagement. In addition, when we offer choice, we offer our students opportunities to guide their own learning and simultaneously facilitate students' self-regulated learning.

Cross-Curricular Integration

In chapter 2, we discussed how students benefit when we identify and focus on learning across curricular areas. When we coordinate our unit plans and collaboratively target particular thinking skills, our students become more aware and begin using and applying these skills in various contexts. Similarly, when we integrate curricular areas to explore a big idea or theme, our students have more opportunities to make connections from one subject area to another, as well as connecting themselves to society, technology, science—and to the disciplinary knowledge and communication skills required for lifelong learning.

Assessment for Learning

To determine the thinking skills necessary for our specific class profile, we rely on assessment. Assessment for learning occurs early in the school year and at the beginning of each subsequent unit of study. Assessment results provide insight into our students' needs and strengths, insights that help focus our teaching throughout the unit. In addition, assessment allows us to differentiate learning sequences, so that all kinds of learners can be included. Assessment is one of the key tenets of "universal design for learning" (UDL).

Universal Design for Learning

When we consider diversity in each of our classes, we see the important relationship between big ideas and UDL. Rather than take the perspective that we should "fix" a child because he or she does not learn in a particular way, UDL takes a student-centred approach by redesigning the curriculum. This means designing many ways to engage students, many ways for them to access and process information, and many ways for them to express what they know and learn. We achieve this by using curricular materials and activities that provide multiple paths for students with differing strengths, interests, and abilities. These alternatives are *built into* the instructional design of educational materials; they are not added on after the fact.

There are three guiding principles of universal design. We might focus on one more than another within a unit of instruction based on the needs of our students. The principles of universal design challenge us to plan and use:

1. Multiple means to tap into learners' interests and background knowledge to activate prior knowledge and increase engagement and motivation.
2. Multiple means for students to acquire information and knowledge that helps them process new ideas and information
3. Multiple means for students to express what they know

We use UDL because it acknowledges and accepts diversity as a reality, and it helps us to plan and organize for teaching and learning with diversity in mind. In our approach to UDL we start from the concepts at the heart of the content, but we connect them to the heart of our class and the individual students in it. Teachers who differentiate learning sequences so that all kinds of learners can be included honour their students' strengths, stretches, and interests. By providing to all students a way of accessing the big ideas, we encourage them to learn from each other, and create a community of learners who rely on the strengths of everyone, while continuing to grow in their own areas of need. Many factors are involved in the promotion of deep learning in our students. Once activated, however, the classroom becomes a learning community in which questions are posed, thinking is extended, and ideas are provoked while everyone learns from each other.

Integrating Backward Design and Universal Design for Learning

As we use UDL to guide our teaching, backward design becomes the framework that supports us along the way. We find the backward design approach of Wiggins and McTighe (2005) to be a helpful framework to focus our planning, assessment, and instruction so that we build both the thinking strategies and content knowledge of all students. Backward design involves four key elements:

1. identify key concepts from learning outcomes and organize lessons and learning sequences around the enduring understandings we want students to develop by the end of a unit of study
2. identify what thinking strategies students need to develop and use to complete learning tasks and, in particular, summative assessment(s)
3. align formative and summative assessments so that students know what is expected of them
4. explicitly teach and assess thinking strategies as part of a unit of study so that students become increasing successful learners.

Combining these two frameworks helps us meet the needs of all our learners. By believing in every student's ability, we see "inclusion" as learning-focused instead of just the physical proximity of students in the same classroom. One way we do this is by ensuring that the curriculum is accessible. When we plan with the end in mind, we achieve accessibility by anticipating the choices and learning paths of our students and how they address the big ideas and outcomes. This framework helps us construct units based on the specific learning profiles of our class, including students with the most significant learning challenges.

Including Students with Significant Learning Challenges

Bridging the cognitive gaps between regular students and those with special needs means that teachers must develop appropriate literacy skills in *all* our students. The difficultly usually arises when trying to find age-appropriate resources for the range of students whose literacy levels are different from that of their peers. Professional collaboration is essential when including students with special needs fully in the content lessons. When two or more educators co-create unit plans and resources, they can draw on one another's expertise and experience to meet the range of abilities in one integrated classroom.

For a Humanities 9 unit, Linda wanted her unit plan to include particular ways for Evan, a student with a developmental disability, to access the content and to demonstrate what he learned in the assessment. She asked Shelley Moore, a district resource teacher, to assist her because Shelley had extensive experience working with and planning for students with significant learning challenges. Linda and Shelley co-constructed a unit by modifying the learning outcomes and offering multiple pathways to accommodate all learners. Another of their goals was to make the learning tasks meaningful and appropriate so that no student would have to be pulled out of the learning community in that classroom and be segregated to work on different and less-than-challenging activities.

Big Ideas and Essential Questions

Linda and Shelley met early to discuss the enduring understandings and essential questions related to the curriculum content in a unit they called "Let's go to Canada!" about early settlers and settlements. Together they looked for the big ideas that would be the basis of the lessons. They adopted a planning template to help them think about learners with the most significant learning needs (Figure 4.1). Both Linda and Shelley knew this research-based structure and design would help all learners in the class, including Evan.

Setting Goals and Designing Summative Assessment

Consistent with UDL and BD, Shelley and Linda first set down what they wanted their students to know (the goals), then considered how students could show what they had learned (summative assessment). They decided that the unit's summative assessment project would ask students to create a picture book telling, and illustrating with pictures, the story of an early group of settlers in Canada. Although they expected all students would develop their summative assessment project in the same format, they gave the students choice in selecting the group or explorer whose story they would tell and the format they would use to tell it—graphic novel, picture book, pop-up book, comic, or other creation.

After Shelley and Linda had designed the unit goals and the summative assessment, they focused on how they would develop the lessons. For this stage of their co-planning, they described what the students needed to "know" and what they needed to "do" to achieve the goals. It was clear, too, that students would also need to know the main elements of picture book design, which would necessitate revisiting the elements of a story. Students would also need to research information for their chosen explorer or settlers whose story would make up the content of their picture book.

To tie in the thinking and literacy skills that their students would need to use and develop, the teachers referred to their Class Profile. They saw that it would be best to focus on two skills:

1. determining main ideas and detail
2. making notes

To do so, they decided to include a lesson sequence specifically on the note-making strategy of building a mind map. Such a strategy would support the students in determining the relevant information about key players in the early settlement of Canada, and to find the information needed to develop the illustrated story—the summative assessment.

Figure 4.1 Co-planning for Humanities 9 unit "Let's go to Canada"

Subject Area: Humanities	Unit: Let's go to Canada!	Grade: 9
Planning Team: Linda Watson (CT), Shelley Moore (DST), Educational Assistant		

Essential Questions	
• Who came to settle Canada? Why did they leave their home country? Where in Canada did they go?	
• What happened when they got there? How was the conflict handled? What happened next?	

Summative Assessment	
Goals/Outcomes (What is important to know?)	**Modified Goals**
• Identify important events in the early stages of European exploration and colonization of Canada. • Explain the meaning of **colonialism** and **mercantilism**. • Tell/represent the story of the early settlement of Canada, and all its elements.	• Identify different groups that settled Canada: • When given a verbal cue, select 3 of the following names/words to identify by a visual or symbol: • France, Catholic, Jesuit, Acadian, England, English, • Native, Viking, fishermen, fish, first, fight • Answer the question "Who came to Canada?" verbally. • Identify 3 story elements.
Skills/Processes (What is important to do?)	**Modified Goals**
• Identify main ideas and details. • Determine importance while reading and researching information. • Tell a story orally.	• Identify the main idea of each settler group, and two details that make them unique. • Share an adapted story with a small group of peers.
Performance Task for Summative Assessment	**Modified Performance Task**
• Prepare a picture book answering the essential questions of the unit: • Who came to Canada? (characters) • Why did they leave? (rising action) • Where did they go? (setting) • What happened when they got there? (problem) • How was it handled? (results/consequences) • What happened next? (closure/ending)	• Interact by reading aloud and sharing an adapted picture book that answers the essential question: • Who came to Canada? (characters)
Texts	**Extended texts**
Oma's Quilt, Pink and Say, Bully	Modified: *Let's go to Canada*

© Portage & Main Press, 2014, *It's All About Thinking: Creating Pathways for All Learning in the Middle Years*, BLM, ISBN 978-1-55379-509-4

Considering Diverse Texts

Linda and Shelley next considered how students would access the information needed for their stories. Recognizing how essential it would be to have access to diverse informational texts and resources for both the lessons and their project, Linda went on the hunt for existing materials appropriate for a range of abilities and also collected texts from colleagues. Evan was still at an emergent literacy level, and they realized that no books on settlers of that era existed at that level, so Shelley started writing. Her ability to write levelled, but appropriate, texts was a critical skill in creating the resources that Evan needed to access the curriculum.

The Lesson Sequence

Linda and Shelley worked with students, first to construct a rubric of the criteria that they would use for assessing the students' projects (Figure 4.2). While doing so, they referred to exemplar picture books (e.g., *Oma's Quilt, Pink and Say, Bully*) to describe the progressive levels of the criteria by which they would assess the project that each student would research and develop. They read and examined a wide range of publication formats that describe and combine text, text features, and different types and styles of illustrations that students might use to communicate the story of the settler they choose for their project.

For the remaining lessons in the unit, the students used the various informational texts the teachers had collected to research their chosen settler or group and to build mind maps for their picture book. For Evan, Shelley created a picture book with the key content, but with more illustrations and text at his literacy level. She developed the book at two levels, one that Evan could read independently, and another that others could read to or with him. Using this text, although modified, still offered the benefit of rich, content-oriented material that other students could access if they, too, needed additional support in understanding the big ideas in the curriculum.

Figure 4.2 Summative assessment rubric for Picture Book project "Arrival in Canada"

Aspects	Minimal expectations Good start. Spend more time. You can do it.	Meets expectations Nice! You are there!	Exceeds expectations Wow! This would knock anyone's socks off!!
Cover	• The cover includes a title and image.	• The cover includes a title and image that relates to the story.	• The cover includes a title and image that relates to the story and entices the reader to pick up the book.
Images	• Images relate to the story. • You have images throughout your story.	• Images clearly relate to the story and reflect all major elements of the plot to the reader/viewer. • The images are visually pleasing and incorporate important details.	• Images clearly relate to the story and reflect all the elements of the plot to the reader/viewer. • The images are visually pleasing and evoke an emotional response.
Story	• The text includes some story elements (characters, conflict, setting, plot, and so on). • The plot is historically accurate and considers some elements of plot (rising actions, falling action, resolution, message). • The story addresses some of the essential questions presented in the unit (who, what, where, when, why).	• The text includes major story elements to illustrate a viewpoint (characters, conflict, setting, plot, and so on). • The plot is historically accurate and considers elements of plot (rising actions, falling action, resolution, message). • The story addresses the essential questions presented in the unit (who, what, where, when, why).	• The text includes all major story elements to convincingly illustrate a viewpoint (characters, conflict, setting, plot, and so on). • The plot is historically accurate and considers all elements of plot and includes more than one perspective (rising actions, falling action, resolution, message). • The story addresses essential questions presented in the unit and raises new issues and questions (who, what, where, when, why).
Style and Presentation	• Style and elements of the chosen form are mostly consistent. • Text is written, but needs to be edited.	• Style and elements of the chosen form are consistent and honour the individual unique characteristics of each medium (e.g., graphics for a comic, illustrations for a story book, 3D for a pop-up book). • Text has been edited and revised, with care taken to consider grammar and spelling.	• Style and elements of the chosen form are consistent and honour the individual characteristics unique to the medium. Student uses format to powerfully communicate their knowledge. • Text has been edited and revised. Spelling and grammar are accurate.
Teacher Comments			

© Portage & Main Press, 2014, *It's All About Thinking: Creating Pathways for All Learning in the Middle Years*, BLM, ISBN 978-1-55379-509-4

Including Students with IEPs

Evan was included in the planning for every part of the unit and lesson, from enacting and assessing to building the performance criteria, from researching to sharing his story. The final part of the unit assessment invited students to share their final picture book project, and Evan shared his book in a group with his peers. Linda's grade for Evan was based on the content-specific goals on a one-page IEP (Figure 4.3), a component often overlooked for such students in high school.

Figure 4.3 Individual Education Plan (IEP) for Evan

Student: Evan T. **Teacher(s):** Linda Watson **Educational Assistant:** various **Resource Support:** Shelley Moore		**Grade:** 9		**Course:** Humanities 9 **Term:** 2 **Block:** 3			
Goal Area/Topic: Social Studies Content							
Goal	Evan will identify the various groups that settled Canada by:		NYM	MM	FM	EE	NA
Objective	Identifying a symbol to represent words of the unit: France, Jesuit, Catholic, Acadian, England, English, Native, Viking, fishermen, fish, first, fight						
Objective	Building a mind map of major players and details about each one.						
Goal Area/Topic: Processes and thinking skills from English Language Arts							
Goal	Evan will identify main idea and details by:		NYM	MM	FM	EE	NA
Objective	Identifying the characters and one or two details about them						
Goal	Evan will increase his reading fluency by:		NYM	MM	FM	EE	NA
Objective	Practising an oral reading of a given text						
Objective	Reading aloud a given text to a group of peers						
Teacher Comments:	Totals						
	Weighting		x 1	x 2	x 3	x 4	x 1
	Goal scores		+	+	+		
	Total scores		# of goals x 4				
	Divide goal by total		/				
	Percentage		x 100				
	Term Reporting Mark		Letter Grade				

Figure 4.3 cont'd

Assessment Rubric for IEP Goals

Note: Use N/A when student has not yet been instructed in this area or when goal is not appropriate for this student.

Goals	Not Yet Meeting Expectations NYM	Minimally Meeting Expectations MM	Fully Meeting Expectations FM	Exceeding Expectations EE
Support Level What level of support is given?	• Student needs support to meet this goal.	• Student can meet this goal, with assistance and prompting.	• Student can meet this goal, without assistance within the context of the class; or • With some assistance, student can meet this goal within another context or with example.	• Student can meet this goal, without assistance outside the context of the classroom, and can generalize or make connections to other contexts or examples.
Independence Level Is student independent in responding?	• Student does not initiate a response.	• Student initiates responses sometimes.	• Student initiates responses most times.	• Student initiates responses every time.
Participation Level What does the student need in order to participate?	• Student can participate when provided with direct one-to-one matches (objects, pictures, or words).	• Student can participate when provided with 2 or 3 choices to select from (objects, pictures, or words).	• Student can participate when given more than 3 choices to select from (objects, pictures, or words).	• Student can participate without being given any choices to select from; or student uses AAC device independently to participate.

The lesson sequence plan (Figure 4.4) for the "Let's go to Canada" unit shows how the collaboration between Linda and Shelley resulted in a rich unit that addressed the needs of all the learners in the classroom. The plan includes the classroom lessons and the background support that Shelley provided by creating modified materials specific to the class and to Evan's IEP.

Figure 4.4 Plan of lesson sequence for "Let's go to Canada" unit

Lesson 1: Introduction			
Phase	**Lesson Activity**	**Modifications**	**Materials Needed**
Connect	• Read aloud a picture book of the history of Canada	• While searching through books, Evan is given a page filled with visual symbols (and some distractors) of story elements.	• Picture communication symbol (PCS) board with story elements
Process	• Students look through a collection of picture books to find common features and create categories; they develop criteria to distinguish historical picture books from traditional students' picture books (use of visuals, emotion, detail, perspective of characters).	• With a bingo dabber, he identifies the correct responses to the question: What makes a good story? • Using the prompt "Storybooks have _____," Evan writes sentences creating the criteria for his book.	• Sentence strips
Transform/ Personalize	• Introduce the "working rubric," which they will add on to during each class. This will become a working document over the course of the next few lessons and will then become the rubric used to assess their final performance task. • Students begin to add categories and criteria to a blank rubric.		

Lesson 2: The Mind Map			
Phase	**Lesson Activity**	**Modifications**	**Materials needed**
Connect	• Introduce mind mapping by making mini mind maps of a familiar topic, e.g., your house, cars, a colour and so on.	• Student uses a magazine (interest-specific, e.g., cats) to help make a picture mind map that focuses on 3 elements: topic, 3 main ideas, plus 1 detail for each idea.	• Cat magazine • Scissors, glue • Picture mind map template • Black marker
Process	• Students are given a piece of text and follow the teacher modelling, being guided through the strategy of "magnet notes" that build mini mind maps of chunks of texts. • Student continues through text selection until all chunks have been mapped.	• Teacher scribes words to label pictures, once completed.	
Transform/ Personalize	• Students independently move on to create categories and compile their mini mind maps of the individual text chunks, into a larger mind map giving " the big picture" of the reading selection.		

© Portage & Main Press, 2014, *It's All About Thinking: Creating Pathways for All Learnings in the Middle Years*, BLM, ISBN 978-1-55379-509-4

Figure 4.4 cont'd.

Lesson 3: The Who and the What			
Phase	**Lesson Activity**	**Modifications**	**Materials needed**
Connect	• Introduce unit vocabulary with a word game.	• First reading of adapted text, "Let's go to Canada."	• Adapted book • PCS symbols of major characters
Process	• Given various texts, students use the mind map strategy using the content vocabulary (Vikings, fishermen, Cartier/Iroquois, Champlain/French, Jesuits, Coureurs de bois, and relevant others). • Once the major players have been identified, students continue researching to determine what their role was in the settlement of Canada and add that to their mind map.	• Reading purpose: identifying major characters. • Add pictures to a mind map of major characters.	• Template of mind map for pictures • Scissors, glue
Transform	• Exit slip: Which story elements have we addressed today (who/what)? What information can we add to our rubric to help us with our final project?		

Lesson 4: The Why, the Where, and the How			
Phase	**Lesson Activity**	**Modifications**	**Materials needed**
Connect	• Read aloud: A picture book about settlement	• Second reading of adapted text, "Let's go to Canada"	• Adapted book • PCS symbols of major characters
Process	• Students chose which major player they will focus on for their summative assessment story. • Students continue researching using the various texts provided to answer the remaining essential questions on their mind map	• Reading purpose: identifying major characters and a detail about each one • Make a picture mind map of major characters and a detail	• PCS symbols of details • Picture mind map template • Scissors, glue
Transform	• Exit slip: In considering your strengths as a learner, what format (e.g., comic, picture book, pop up, other) do you want to choose to show your understanding? Why? • What additional elements/details should we add to our rubric to finalize it for our answer to the summative assessment question: What makes a powerful picture book?		

Figure 4.4 cont'd.

Lessons 5-6: Editing and Feedback			
Phase	**Lesson Activity**	**Modifications**	**Materials needed**
Workshop	• Students work on their stories through the format they have chosen • Students practise orally reading book to peers for feedback using the class generated rubric for reference	• Student continues to read adapted text, and practices reading aloud to build fluency for his final presentation • It is also videoed in case on the day of, Evan isn't comfortable sharing, he can chose to show just the video to his group • Continue to finalize picture mind map	• Adapted book • PCS symbols of major characters • PCS symbols of details • Picture mind map template • Scissors, glue • Video camera

Lesson 7: Showing what we know			
Phase	**Lesson Activity**	**Modifications**	**Materials needed**
Presentation day	• Break students up into groups to share their story in 2 rotations. • Students hand in their mind map for assessment.	• Student is included in a sharing group and reads his story aloud, identifying the characters and one detail about each. • Student hands in picture mind map for assessment.	• Adapted book • PCS symbols of major characters • PCS symbols of details • Picture mind map
Unit reflection	• Students reflect on the process of creating their book in a group reflection answering the questions: • What have you learned about yourself as a learner? • What steps did you take to be successful? • What did others say about your project? • What would you do differently next time?	• Select students are asked to provide some written peer feedback to Evan on his book on a post it note which are given to him during reflection time. • Evan is given a final picture quiz answering his essential question: "Who are the major players in Canadian settlement?"	• Picture quiz • Sticky notes • IEP checklist

© Portage & Main Press, 2014, *It's All About Thinking: Creating Pathways for All Learnings in the Middle Years*, BLM, ISBN 978-1-55379-509-4

Using Diverse Texts and Big Ideas to Enhance Student Engagement

Six educators from Dunsmuir Middle School, located outside of Victoria, BC, came together with the purpose of creating an engaging cross-curricular unit they called "Rock Stories." Hailing from different backgrounds and with varied teaching experience, these educators created a unit that engaged students in deeper thinking processes, and encouraged collaboration among both students and teachers. Using Information Circles and diverse texts as the catalyst, their Earth Sciences unit encouraged students to think about how rocks and minerals can "tell stories" about the past, the present, and the future.

The team included Lenore Clarke, grade 7 teacher and the curriculum support leader for the school; May Crompton, teacher-librarian and technology teacher; Justine Durrant, Aboriginal Education teacher; Barb Kersch, grade 7 teacher and Literacy Teacher; Jen Nixon, grade 7 Core Teacher; and Regan Rasmussen, Visual Arts teacher and a sessional instructor in Faculty of Education, University of Victoria. Working together as a professional inquiry learning team, these educators set out to create a collaborative cross-curricular grade 7 unit incorporating elements of visual arts, Aboriginal Education, science, and technology.

Earth Science unit "Rock Stories"

These six educators used diverse texts and Information Circles to engage all learners in accessing background knowledge, in seeking answers to questions that required deeper thinking, and in encouraging greater collaboration between students. They created an Earth Science unit for grade 7 that incorporated cross-curricular elements and perspectives centred on an open-ended, essential inquiry question. To scaffold student learning, the classroom teachers provided graphic organizers and strategy sheets, and they facilitated small-group discussions of the big ideas. "Rock Stories" is both process-oriented and product-oriented. The planners put great emphasis on student conversations during Information Circles and on thinking and instructional strategies. As a final performance task, their students had to create a mind map on which they were able to illustrate their varied understandings of the unit's big ideas and essential inquiry question.

When designing this unit, Lenore, May, Justine, Barb, Jen, and Regan used a backward design framework. The teachers collaboratively identified the overarching essential inquiry question, the big ideas that encompassed many learning outcomes, and the thinking strategies that they wanted their students to develop. Then they created the scope and sequence of the unit by planning individual lessons and various instructional strategies (Figure 4.5). As the classes progressed, the teachers adapted or changed the lessons when necessary to reflect the feedback they received from the students.

Figure 4.5 Unit plan for Earth Sciences "Rock Stories"

Essential Question: How can studying changes in the Earth reveal secrets from the past and impact our future?				
Big Ideas	• Rocks are made up of unique components. • Rocks can be recycled. • The Earth is made up of plates that move. • Movements of the plates cause both sudden and gradual change to the Earth's crust. • Rocks are important to humans in various ways (culturally, socially and economically).			
Thinking Strategies	Main ideas and details, Hypothesizing, Classifying, Synthesizing			
Lesson	**1**	**2**	**3**	**4**
Essential Question	What properties do geologists use to identify the minerals that make up rocks?	Can you identify unknown minerals by their properties?		
Lesson Topic	Properties of minerals	Identifying Minerals		
Thinking Strategy	Determining importance	Observing, classifying, interpreting, communicating	Observing, classifying, interpreting, communicating	Observing, classifying, interpreting, communicating
Teaching Strategy	Mini book	Lab: Indentifying Minerals 1st Block: Writing a lab report	Lab: Indentifying Minerals 2nd Block: Conducting lab	Lab: Indentifying Minerals 3rd Block: Analyze & Evaluate Results
Lesson	**5**	**6**	**7**	**8-9**
Essential Question	Are all rocks formed the same way?		How do rocks help us unlock the secrets of the past?	
Lesson Topic	Families of rocks		Formation of Fossils	Exploring Fossil Record
Thinking Strategy	Categorizing, Determining importance		Sequencing	
Teaching Strategy	Flow Chart with examples *Scaffold*	Create a Museum Box including pictures and descriptions	Flow Chart Graphic Organizer *Scaffold*	Fossil Trading Card

© Portage & Main Press, 2014, *It's All About Thinking: Creating Pathways for All Learnings in the Middle Years*, BLM, ISBN 978-1-55379-509-4

Figure 4.5 cont'd.

Lesson	10	11	12	13-15
Essential Question	How are rocks broken down and moved?	→	How can rock be recycled?	What would it be like to journey through the rock cycle?
Lesson Topic	Weathering	Erosion	Rock Cycle	Final Performance Task
Thinking Strategy	Sequencing, Determining importance	Sequencing, Determining importance	Sequencing, Determining Importance	Synthesizing, Communicating
Teaching Strategy	Magnet Notes *Scaffold* Compare and Contrast Chart	Magnet Notes *Independently*	Flow Chart Graphic Organizer *Independently*	Student choice for journey

Lesson	1	2	3	4
Essential Question	What is the structure of the Earth?	Does the surface of the Earth move?	→	
Lesson Topic	Layers of the Earth	Wegners's theory of continental drift		
Thinking Strategy	Main ideas & details	Main ideas & details	Interpreting	Synthesizing
Teaching Strategy	Place Mat in groups of 4	Graphic organizer for viewing DVD	Creating a model of Pangaea. 1st Block: Cut and layout	Creating a model of Pangaea. 2nd Block: Glue and label

Lesson	5	6-8	9-10	11
Essential Question	Does the surface of Earth move?	→		
Lesson Topic	Wegener's 1912 theory of continental drift	Theory of Plate Tectonics	Finding Patterns in Geological Data	→
Thinking Strategy	Synthesizing Evaluating	Main ideas and details, connections	Hypothesizing	Interpreting Synthesizing
Teaching Strategy	Creating a model of Pangaea 3rd Block: Complete questions	Model Information Circles and Mind Map *Scaffold*	Lab 8.5: Plotting earthquakes, volcanoes 1st and 2nd Block: Hypothesize and plot	Lab 8.5: 3rd Block: Analyze, write a conclusion, apply and extend

Lesson	12 Performance Task 2
Essential Question	Plates move, so what?
Lesson Topic	Reflecting on your learning
Thinking Strategy	What did you learn? How has learning about the theory of plate tectonics changed the way you think about i) the area in which you live; ii) Earth?
Teaching Strategy	Journal entry and "Somebody thought.... then.... so...... " chart
Resources	Activity sheet Journal on one side and chart on the other

Diversity and Unit Planning

The team designed the unit to accommodate the different needs, interests, and backgrounds of their students by incorporating many opportunities for student choice into the unit design, and encouraging student ownership, particularly through the Information Circle process and the final performance task. Students could choose from a diverse selection of titles to work through individually and with their group. In addition, after teacher scaffolding and guided student practice, the students chose the graphic organizer they would use not only to approach the Information Circles and performance tasks but also to build the necessary skills, confidence, and feelings of self-efficacy. At several points throughout the unit, teachers used the fishbowl strategy, that is, inviting one group of students to engage in discussion within an Information Circle while the rest of the students in the class observed and commented on the process, generating criteria for effective process. This was a powerful form of student-to-student modelling, and it highlighted the collaborative inquiry method of learning.

The teachers brought various backgrounds, skills, and teaching assignments to this unit, which required a high degree of risk-taking, flexibility, and collaboration. During the Information Circles, more than one teacher was in the room, promoting collaboration among the students, ongoing formative assessment, and increased descriptive feedback, along with modelling for their students.

Establishing the Information Circles

Prior to starting the Information Circles in her class, Jen facilitated a discussion with the class about the differences between Information Circles and the Literature Circles they had recently participated in. Using a book talk format, Jen introduced a collection of short diverse informational texts (9 titles with 5 or 6 copies of each) that she had gathered for the unit. The following process took three to five lessons to complete:

- During the book talk, students are invited to choose three titles they are interested in reading and to record them on a slip of paper.
- Jen then collates the requests, working toward giving each student one of their three text choices.
- Students are given one of their book choices and time to browse and record on sticky notes any areas of interest, noting, initial observations and queries.
- After several minutes, students move into groups based on their choice of text.
- These newly formed groups are then asked to collaboratively decide their plan for reading the text and the strategy sheet they will use during their reading.
- They then prepare for Information Circle conversation.

Preparing for Information Circle Conversations

- Students use a strategy sheet to help guide their learning. Although each strategy sheet is unique, they all follow the basic format—connecting, processing, transforming/personalizing.
- In their groups, students conduct a "think–pair–share" to brainstorm and record what they already know about the topic. This process of activating prior knowledge encourages students to record everything they know about the topic. They are then asked to share out within their group and add any new connections to their sheet.
- The process of reading the text is done independently using the strategy sheet to write down questions they may have, or points they need to clarify with the group.
- The strategy sheet becomes the "ticket in" to their Information Circle conversation the next day.

Information Circles Conversation

- During Information Circle conversations, students share their key ideas from the reading. Students work together to discuss main ideas, pose questions, clarify information, and share connections. Together, they build a shared schema of the text as they offer their opinions, questions, and inferences.
- Students discuss and record their deeper understandings of the topic, and connect what they learned to the unit's essential question and big ideas.
- Reflecting on what they have learned, students personalize their understandings and record their ideas on the strategy sheet.

Formative assessment

- Students reflect on the Information Circle conversation by discussing key questions: "What was the most important information we learned today?" "What worked in our Information Circle? What could we change or get better at?"
- Students choose another section of the same text or choose a new text and work with a new group.

Synthesis and Summative Assessment

Through the subsequent two to four lessons leading to the summative assessment, students create a mind map to show how their learning connects to the unit's big ideas and the essential question. The centre of the mind map holds the essential question, and each big idea forms a branch or strand of the mind map.

- Modelling and instruction are provided to facilitate the mind mapping process (images, words, use of colour, hierarchy). Samples of powerful mind maps are shared, and students also view the YouTube clip <www.videojug.com/film/how-to-mind-map-with-tony-buzan>.
- The criteria for their mind map is then developed, and the rubric is reviewed by the class (Figure 4.6). The teacher responds to questions and shows more samples.
- Students meet in groups to brainstorm how they want their mind map to showcase their learning related to the essential question. They pull pieces together, making connections between the essential question and big ideas, and create their own individual mind map.
- Completed mind maps are showcased in a "gallery walk" within the classroom.
- The mind maps are then assessed using the co-constructed rubric.

Figure 4.6 Final assessment rubric for students' Mind Map

Final Mind Map Criteria	
You must show how all the big Ideas are connected. Be sure to offer specific examples of the big Ideas. Remember your Mind Map must have the following parts:	
• A central image that relates to the unit	• At the bottom of your mind map write a reflective piece that responds to our unit question:
• Big ideas form branches that connect to the central image	• How can studying changes in the Earth reveal secrets from the past and impact our future?
• Key ideas form limbs off the branches – ideas move from most to least complex	• Be sure to include any questions or wonderings that have yet to be answered.
• Images and words show a clear understanding of the content	
• Clearly use text, colour, images and links to show connections between ideas	

Figure 4.6 cont'd.

	Beginning	Developing	Accomplished	Exemplary
Mind Mapping Process	• I can select a few important pieces of information that relate to the Mind Map • I'm not really thinking on my own yet; I need guidance from the teacher • I use one source to show all of my thinking; I generally copy text • I need evidence of using feedback	• I can select some specific pieces of information that relate to the Mind Map • I demonstrate straightforward thinking; I have yet to take some risks • I can think in concrete ways when I select/use pieces of information (paraphrasing the text) • I use some feedback from my peers and/or my teacher	• I can select and describe most important pieces of information that relate to the Mind Map • I demonstrate logical and predictable thinking and take few risks • I can think in some new and interesting ways when I select/ use specific pieces of information from multiple sources (use and apply information in a slightly different manner) • I use peer and/or teacher feedback to improve my work	• I clearly and accurately select and describe sophisticated and/ or unique pieces of information that relate to the Mind Map • I demonstrate flexibility, innovation and/or risk taking in my thinking • I can think in multiple ways when I select and use specific pieces of information from multiple sources (use and apply information in more than one manner) • I actively seek out peer and teacher feedback
Mind Mapping Product	• I demonstrate partial understanding of the concepts; I require teacher or peer assistance to do this • Some key ideas show extensions, 1 or 2 limbs off a branch; a few supporting details have been included • I need more evidence of using text, colour, images and links that help clarify and highlight connections in this Mind Map	• I demonstrate basic understanding of the concepts; I might require some teacher or peer assistance to do this • Most key ideas show extensions, 2 limbs off a branch; some supporting details have been included & most make sense • I demonstrate a basic use of text, colour, images & links that help clarify & highlight some connections in this Mind Map	• I demonstrate solid understanding and application of concepts; I can do this on my own with little or no assistance • All key ideas show clear extensions, 2-3 limbs off a branch; most relevant and supporting details have been included and make sense; attempts to connect to daily life are included • I demonstrate a good use of text, colour , images & links that help to clarify & highlight connections in most parts of this Mind Map	• I demonstrate complete and in depth understanding of concepts through analyzing and evaluating; I do this independently • Extensions of key ideas (limbs) show a deep understanding of the concepts; multiple and insightful details have been included; relevant connections to daily life are included (past and present) • I demonstrate innovation and flexibility with my use of text, colour, images and links that clarify and highlight connections in this Mind Map

Information Circles Using Text Sets

Building on the excitement she saw in Jen's class, Lenore aimed to employ the Information Circle strategy with a twist. Throughout her ecology unit, she had numerous resources stationed in the room, including a number of books on topics such as biomes, food webs, ecosystems, and endangered species, but not multiple copies of the same text as in Jen's class. Rather than having groups read and discuss the same text, she set up groups according to a book series or a specific topic. Each group member read a different text that was based on a common group theme.

The ecology unit was designed around the essential question "How do I fit into the living world?" Students had been working on activities that guided them to consider how plants, animals, and humans depend on one another and how they interact with their environment. The big ideas in the unit were:

1. How ecosystems support life.
2. Energy flow and matter cycles in ecosystems.
3. How human survival depends on sustainable ecosystems.

Lenore had modelled strategies like magnet notes (see chapter 3) and double-entry journals giving students practice in determining main ideas and details. Students were well-versed in the schema of connecting, processing, and transforming/personalizing.

The goal of the Information Circle part of this ecology unit was to have students use their newly developed knowledge base to synthesize information from different texts and explore connections, guided by the essential question and big ideas for the unit. Lenore built in choice by allowing students to select the text they would read and the thinking strategy they would use— magnet notes, double-entry journals, or a more personalized adaptation of either.

Setting the Stage

Lenore introduced the Information Circle process with a fishbowl activity, inviting a group from Jen's class to model the conversation process.

- Lenore's class observed the Information Circle meeting and jotted notes as to what worked.
- The class debriefed the model group, asking questions about the process.
- Lenore worked with her class to create a list of guidelines and strategies for a productive Information Circle. Ideas were recorded such as "be prepared" and "make connections" that promoted discussion and were posted at the front of the room.

Next, Lenore gave a book talk, highlighting the content and organization of the various books in the series or themed groupings. More than 30 different books were grouped as text sets under five or six topics.

- Using a document camera, Lenore introduced the books by projecting them for the students to see.
- Although there are five different books in the series (e.g., *Polar, Rainforest, Desert, Ocean*), she showed the table of contents of one to point out that all books had similar organization (e.g., climate, geography, flora, fauna). She explained how the table of contents could possibly become the focus for them in planning their reading and discussion.
- Next, she highlighted books that had been assembled by theme (e.g., endangered species, climate change), reading a short excerpt from a book or two in each set.
- At the end of the book talk, she gave students a chance to browse the collection and submit a list of three books that interested them.
- Lenore sorted through their lists to establish groups based upon the students' requests.

Group Meetings

Lenore planned two blocks of class time to work through the first round of Information Circles. She focussed the first block on reading and note-making, and the second on the sharing and discussion component.

- Students met with their group and browsed the books. They negotiated which text each of them would read and decided on a focus for reading (e.g., "climate" from the table of contents in a series, or "disappearing habitat" in the endangered species theme)
  - *Connecting*—Students chose a note-making strategy, either a double entry journal or magnet notes. They began by silently skimming their text, looking at pictures and headings.
  - *Processing*—Students read independently and used a graphic organizer to select main ideas and details relating to the group's focus; they also recorded questions and points requiring clarification.
  - *Personalizing (individual)*—Students continued to complete the independent note-making strategy and reflected on what they found most interesting and what they would share with the group related to the essential question. Each group member arrived at the next meeting ready to share both the process and the personalization pieces of their notes.
  - *Personalizing (group meeting)*—Students were reminded to refer to the discussion criteria for tips on holding a successful meeting. Each member shared their ideas and thoughts about their chosen text. The group worked together to discuss similarities, differences, and wonderings that arose from their group's focus and discussion; Lenore reminded groups to make connections to the essential question asked them to think of five to eight key ideas they identified.

- *Formative Assessment*—As the discussion concluded, each group completed a placemat (Bennett and Rolheiser-Bennett 2001).
- On their portion of the placemat, students independently recorded what they believed to be the most important ideas from the discussion related to the essential question/big idea for the unit. They then shared their portion of the placemat with the group. At the end of the sharing they negotiated one overarching statement for the centre of their placemat, synthesizing their understanding thus far. The placemat demonstrates their ability to synthesize the material. The placemat became an artifact of their thinking and discussion.
- *Gallery Walk*—Groups rotated around the class, viewing all the placemats and browsing the corresponding books to help them decide which text set they would like to use for their next Information Circle. Their ticket-out-the-door was a list of their next top 3 choices.

Art Component

As a visual arts teacher, Regan was able to build upon the learning in the grade 7 classrooms through art explorations. Depending on the time of year that students came to their art rotation, their exposure to the Earth Science units varied. Some had not yet started the rocks unit while others were in the middle of the process, or had completed it. Embarking upon this shared inquiry with grade 7 classroom teachers, students were afforded a richness and depth of learning by making connections across disciplines.

Establishing the Area of Inquiry

Students began by brainstorming the word *rock*, rotating in carousel fashion. They moved in groups of four from one chart paper to the next, elaborating upon what the previous groups had written. After sharing, students were asked to collectively brainstorm the word *inquiry*. When responses were posted, the class agreed that the phrase "To inquire is to wonder" reflected their consensus. Regan worked with the class to establish a shared inquiry question, extending from the essential question familiar to some from their Science classes. The essential art question became "What kinds of stories do rocks of the past and present reveal about our world and our place in it?"

Exploring "Rock Ideas" through Different Media

Students documented their process through writing and recording ideas and sketches in their Rock Journal. The following points summarize the journey they shared as they explored images, ideas, drawings, paintings, and clay media related to their inquiry:

- Viewing video clips about the ancient cave paintings of the world (e.g., Caves of Lascaux, Aboriginal paintings of Australia).
- Sketching some of the icons and patterns from the video clips.

- Writing stories about what the images might have been expressing (e.g., stories of creation, honouring Earth; images such as hunting animals, tools, and patterns that were important to early humans).
- Viewing contemporary rock paintings created by street artists on rock walls, buildings, subway stations, and similar. Students were particularly interested in the street artist, Banksy, known for his social commentary on international issues around the world.
- Writing stories about what contemporary street artists might be trying to tell us through their art.
- Looking at patterns and colours that occurred in rock faces over time from natural forces.
- Creating terra cotta clay tablets, using images from their Rock Journal sketches for the etchings.
- Writing art statements telling the stories, both historical and contemporary, associated with the images etched onto the clay.
- Learning about the chemical and physical changes of clay from plastic (wet state), to greenware (dry state); bisque-fired (initial kiln firing); and glaze-fired (final firing) processes.
- Brainstorming gemstones in carousel groups, during the final art rotation in the spring, many students asked to get their science binders to refer to vocabulary and processes they were studying during the Rocks unit. This was another ah-ha moment as students initiated making connections between their learning in Science class and their learning in the Art studio.
- Linking colour theory and exploratory studies to a favourite gemstone; students created large abstract paintings based on the chosen gemstone using only tints, shades, and complementary colour along with varied brush strokes and different amounts of water to alter the opacity of the hue.
- Writing a free verse poem to be placed either on or beside the painting, connecting something factual as well as something fanciful to their chosen gemstone.

Assessing the Learning

Teachers conducted formative assessments as their students explored, shared, and revised (through peer and teacher feedback), and expanded their understanding in discussions and written comments in their journals. The final assessment sheets summarized the steps in the process and allowed students time for reflective writing, including their thoughts on the art—the drawings, clay tablets, and gemstone paintings. Students also made connections to their Science class and notebooks, to the work of past and present artists, and to their own preferences and imaginative explorations. They shared their work by placing it on display for other classes to view, and they contributed to an electronic slide show documenting the process.

Working with a Teacher-Librarian

It was invaluable to have on the team the support of May, the school's teacher-librarian, who worked to develop a text set of Earth Science resources. Since this project was multidisciplinary, the focus had to be broad enough that everyone on the team could access several titles from the collection. May started by looking at the resources on hand in the school library, including diverse types of texts, hands-on materials, models, and nonfiction titles for Information Circle kits. She also supplied relevant website addresses and the school technologies available, which included animations and video, and age-appropriate materials that took student interest levels into account.

As the unit developed, May realized that they also needed First Nations texts and materials with an arts focus into their collection of materials. She also found additional online resources that were up-to-date and engaging, so that May's full set of resources included both print and digital titles and online websites.

Conclusion

We nurture deep learning in our students when we build from the Class Profile and the individual learning styles of our students. We can tap into their strengths, stretches, and interests as learners. By identifying the big ideas of a unit and the knowledge, strategies, and skills that we want our students to demonstrate in summative assessments, we embrace inquiry and choice as fundamental to our planning and teaching. Collaborating with colleagues is the secret ingredient in crafting learning opportunities that intrigue and inspire students to explore a discipline's big ideas and develop 21st-century skills. We can embrace and support our learners when we work together to design engaging big idea teaching and learning.

Chapter 5

Creating Pathways by Integrating the Arts

Educator Involved

Karen Deibert: Art Teacher, SD 5, Cranbrook, BC.

> Art involves molding of clay, chipping of marble, casting of bronze,
> layering on of pigments, construction of buildings, singing of songs,
> playing of instruments, enacting of roles on the stage, going through
> rhythmic movements in the dance. Every art does something with some
> physical material, the body or something outside the body, with or
> without the use of intervening tools, and with a view to production of
> something visible, audible, or tangible. (John Dewey)

Nicole Widdess thinks in terms of movement and, for her, movement through dance helps her express her thoughts and feelings. Linda Watson has to act out or dramatize through improvisation and performance, to sort out her thoughts and feelings. Leyton Schnellert translates thoughts and feelings into music, using rhythms to connect the ideas he wants to share. Karen Diebert makes meaning with her hands, shaping and creating her ideas in clay and other media. The arts have offered each of us varied pathways to learning, to creating our identities, and have helped us to be successful in the world.

When we think about our students' learning and how we can help them shape their own identity, we must work from the knowledge that people are diverse, that they learn in many different ways and at different times. The arts help us accept that we can never really be at the same place in our learning and social development at the same time as everyone else. The arts also guide us in how to tap into our potential and to recognize how each of us can make a unique contribution to a learning environment. The arts help us form natural connections to what we are learning. The arts should be integrated into our teaching and our students' learning—they offer us springboards for tackling the issues and ideas that matter. When students work with the arts to explore meaningful topics within new content, they have opportunities to access their prior learning, make connections, and pose questions that move them beyond the known to the unknown.

Each of the arts has its own forms of literacy. By integrating the creative and expressive arts into our units in core disciplines, we can offer our students varied entry points into challenging topics. Thereby, we help students strengthen their skill sets and build new ones. Learning through the arts requires alternative thinking. The creative process provides a way for students to relate to the content—they investigate their beliefs, they interact with concepts, and develop new ideas to create meaning. The arts create community. It is not by chance that societies and cultures are known by the arts they create and participate in.

Rationale for Integrating the Arts

It has been our experience that the arts provide more active learning experiences, which increases student involvement and engagement. They improve awareness of our senses, involve multiple forms of expression and feeling, including symbolic and non-verbal expression, and provide a basis for learning about the world from varied perspectives. We believe that instructional strategies and approaches that include one or more of the arts equals good teaching.

The concept of supporting and enhancing student learning through arts education is not new. The benefits and potential created through integrating fine arts with other content areas are many. These benefits include stronger achievement, engagement and understanding, skill development, confidence building, and ownership (Darby and Catterall 1994; Campbell, Campbell, and Dickinson 2004). When the curricula of the content areas are combined with the arts, students have the opportunity to delve into ideas more extensively, access different styles of learning, and present their understanding in a variety of ways.

Typical classrooms focus on only two of the multiple intelligences—the logical-mathematical and the verbal-linguistic. Just like their teachers, not all students work or learn effectively or completely in these two modalities. We do not need to be experts to integrate arts-based learning strategies that provide more diverse learning opportunities. We can, however, expand our repertoire as teachers so our students can explore other ways of knowing and learning. Trying new approaches can empower us and become contagious—by extending ourselves into the unknown, we encourage our students to also take risks. Doing so, however, requires that our assessments allow for students to demonstrate their learning by using the arts (Stiggins 2005).

When teachers integrate the arts into academic areas, students engage in learning more fully. Confucius wrote "I hear and I forget. I see and I remember. I do and I understand" (*The Analects* 551–479 BCE). Aristotle, Dewey, and many other educational thinkers have expressed their belief in "learning by doing"—and here we extend the concept to self-expression through the arts. Gardner (2006) points out that each of us has strength in one or two of the intelligences and that our strengths may overlap others. Bodily-kinesthetic intelligence, visual-spatial intelligence, and musical-rhythmic intelligence are the three most closely connected with the arts, but are not limited to them (Campbell, Campbell, and Dickinson 2004; Gardner 1999). Arts integration offers students an opportunity to actively engage in meaning making using several intelligences.

Some students can surprise and move us by expressing their perceptions of their learning through the arts: MacKenzie, a quiet and withdrawn grade 9 student, drew us into the eighteenth century—literally. What we could see from his visual art representations took us much deeper than the social studies text could ever do. In representing the emotional impact of slavery by creating a movement piece, many English-language learners in Nicole's class (who had not responded to the stories and artifacts they had explored or shared) showed in their dances their aching for the lives destroyed and their perspectives on restitution. We must revisit the shameful events of our country's past and present by tackling tough issues, and recognizing their impact on people other than ourselves.

The arts can enhance student confidence and engagement. When Hannah reflected on grade 9 Humanities, she wrote about her experience in Linda's arts-infused classroom:

> [It] made me start to accept myself for who I am. Last year I couldn't stand who I was. I didn't think I deserved to take up any space…you gave me many moments to shine…you gave me a new view on the world. You changed my life. The hugest change is that now I know that I can achieve whatever I set my mind to—be it writing a memoir, making connections, determining importance, chunking a reading, or taking a risk.

With success in the classroom comes engagement (Heink and Farnau 2008; Respress and Lutfi 2006). Many students who struggle academically have not had an opportunity to discover, understand, or use their particular strengths (Campbell et al. 2004; Respress and Lutfi 2006). Confidence in one's ability to learn and excel does not come easily when there is constant struggle and failure in the classroom (Campbell et al. 2004; Levine 2002). As middle years educators, we have a responsibility to nurture young people, help them develop belief in their abilities, and express their learning through their own strengths and talents. Exploring the arts provides students with another pathway to learning and increases their self-confidence, their sense of self-worth is enhanced, strengthened and supported.

Drama as a Pathway

Drama is about engaging in discussion, observing perspectives, navigating through numerous possibilities, making and supporting decisions, and taking personal risks to gain confidence. When we use drama as a tool, students learn how to:
- build relationships
- work in groups in a collaborative way
- accept and implement diverse ideas to create a shared experience
- become their authentic selves and learn to nurture their own and others' creative ideas
- make meaning through democratic processes
- share thinking and feelings in a safe environment
- suspend disbelief by becoming willing to let go of limited thinking and constraints
- learn through representation how powerful symbol and metaphor can be
- appreciate the impact of their actions, what it takes to make change, and how hard it is to make a difference
- value critical thinking, self reflection, and taking action
- appreciate and seek out non-dominant perspectives

Teacher Responsibilities

- Get to know your students' confidence level, and what they are willing to risk in front of their peers.
- Build trust with your students, helping them learn to trust each other so that they do not feel at risk of embarrassment or criticism.
- Ensure students understand why you are asking them to step outside their comfort zone.
- Know your students' strengths and limitations, how to get the best work from them, by building their skills and developing their confidence.
- Become familiar with various dramatic forms and how to use them effectively for purposes of integrating them into the unit and theme.
- Provide structure to lessons when integrating drama into projects.
- Build time into lessons for student reflection on the activity.
- Provide students with choice within the dramatic activity.
- Provide varied opportunities for student leadership.

Forms of Drama

The Greek word *drama* was incorporated directly into English—it means *act, acting, business,* and "*an action represented on stage.*" Many people have the impulse to re-enact life, to retell their stories and the stories of others—which might come from our natural need to give meaning and structure to our experiences. When we as teachers can connect our students to the experiences of figures past and present through dramatic activities, we can help them empathize with issues, and conflicts and understand their complexities, thereby making their learning personally relevant.

We have successfully integrated into content teaching many forms of drama:

- tableau
- physical theatre (mime)
- games
- choral speaking/reading
- readers' theatre
- puppetry (sock, stick, shadow)
- sketch/scene
- role play

Among the numerous resources we have used in planning activities are *Improvisation: Learning through Drama* (Booth and Lundy 1985); *A Drama Approach to Reading Comprehension: Strategies and Activities for Classroom Teachers* (Kelner and Flynn 2006); *Asking Better Questions* (Morgan and Saxton 2006); *Drama Worlds: A Framework for Process Drama* (O'Neill 1995); *Action Strategies for Deepening Comprehension* (Wilhelm 2002); *Building Plays:*

Simple Playbuilding Techniques at Work (Tarlington and Michaels, 1995). Teachers should feel free to adapt them to create their own learning sequences when planning lessons.

Linda and Leyton use dramatic techniques and action strategies including *tableaux vivants* to help students delve deeply into the lived experience of historical characters and events (Wilhelm 2002). Working in tableaux, students create both a visual and a visceral understanding of a pivotal moment in history—another pathway to learning and exploring. This technique takes the class beyond activities into deeper thinking and rich, personalized, and meaningful responses to the content. Tableaux are inductive and exploratory and require students to consider multiple perspectives and interpretations.

> Tableaux vivants *are "living pictures" of people motionless and silent in a scene evocative of a momentous situation.*

Tableaux

Tableaux can be a rehearsal technique used by theatre directors to engage actors in deconstructing physical action beyond what is already understood or assumed about a moment in time. Within a tableau, the director and actors play with that moment to emphasize particular emotions, relationships between self, others, and artifacts within the overarching theme. We have found that words alone cannot explain the meaning of a moment the same way that acting it out can. When Linda teaches a unit on the French Revolution she uses tableaux to engage students in the emotions of the time (e.g., various depictions of Marie Antoinette, Louis XVI, and Robespierre).

Tableaux can also be collaboratively created by a group as a form of cooperative learning used to communicate ideas and provoke critical thinking. The "actors" engage in a process of exploring, illuminating, and selecting from the content the compelling aspects to highlight. It could be teacher-guided to support aspects of the curriculum. Leyton and Linda have found great success with getting students to create tableaux and then record, journal, reflect, and draw on the experience. As they mentor the students in the technique, they help them develop skills for examining the situation from multiple perspectives. Using the gradual release of responsibility we engage our students in drama-related learning modalities and away from instruction and learning dominated by reading and writing. Students who are familiar with succeeding in school using only those modalities have to think differently. Those who learn hands-on, or through interpersonal and emotional means, or who are reflective and intuitive have a chance to shine. All students get an opportunity to access and develop these ways of knowing.

In essence, working on tableaux involves heightening aspects of a text and creating, inferring, and re-creating events in "pictures." We don't always know the layers of meaning within a moment until we stop that moment to explore possible relationships between the people and artifacts, and the possible emotions, motivations, and outcomes. We ask questions like "*What would you do in this moment?*" "*What would you say in this moment?*" "*What might you be feeling in this moment?*" "*What do you think should happen next?*"

Once students experience a physical connection to the content, we find their learning is more meaningful and deep.

The first building block for using tableau as an integrated teaching strategy is to build student confidence starting with parallel action. This entails having all students in class perform particular actions individually at the same time and as a whole class. Then move them into partner work, and finally small groups of four. Some students need support when working together, so we scaffold lessons as we go. Having an open space to work is also helpful, but we have done this work in regular, desk-filled classrooms. Give some thought to a control device: Linda uses her voice, but Leyton likes to use a drum—it's an individual choice.

Warm-up
1. *Freeze Tag*
Students move around an open space, and you appoint one student as "It." It tags students. When tagged, the students must "freeze" and remain in control until It has tagged all players. Appoint a new It, and continue the game. Linda usually debriefs the game by asking students to reflect on the nature of cooperation versus competition. (You might allow variations by suggesting how a tagged player can be "thawed." One caution: this could add a competitive feel to the game and counter act the purpose of building cooperation.)

2. *Freeze /Act*
The entire class moves around the space in a random manner (walking by changing direction and pace). The idea is for students to catch themselves in a very random and unique pose when Linda calls out the word "FREEZE." A different signal can be used as well (e.g., a drum, tambourine, classroom lights flashing). On the command, students freeze their position and then, on the next command "ACT," bring their position to life and act out what their position suggests to them, for example, an animal, object, or action the person is posed for.

This strategy develops the skill of reacting spontaneously to a stimulus and develops some confidence with each other. The activity can be varied, depending on the group, to allow for groups of student to "FREEZE" and then "ACT" in a scene or by the teacher being more exact in the commands.

Control
At first, students find it challenging to control their movement and their emotions, but by focusing on control, they develop skill and confidence and their tableau work is of a higher quality. Have the entire class move randomly around the space, and call out the following command sequence:

- *"Move around the room. Avoid eye contact and physical contact."* Be patient and coach them to remain in control: hands to themselves, no bumping into each other, avoiding collisions, remain neutral by not laughing, smiling, or talking.

- *"Move around the room. You can make eye contact"* (coach control and cooperation) *"Do not break focus and control"* Challenge them to control their emotions and their physical selves.
- *"Move around the room. You can nod and make eye contact and add a handshake. Still no words, control your laughter."*
- *"Repeat and add a verbal greeting to your handshakes and eye contact. Try greetings like 'Hello', 'Good day', 'Cheers', "What's up?"* Encourage them to be brief and pleasant.
- A final challenge is to add compliments (fun gushy words which push them to break concentration) to the verbal exchanges, or to add other verbal and non-verbal exchanges.

In our experience, students struggle to remain in control and positive toward each other, which provides opportunity for discussion or for reflection in journal writing. They need time to debrief the experience, to understand the physical and emotional skills involved, and to realize that by playing these games, they have been building relationships, skills and confidence in taking risks.

Sculptures in pairs

The premise of this activity is that students will "sculpt" their partner into a statue, first following teacher suggestions. One partner plays the role of the "sculptor"; the other is the "clay" taking shape by cooperating and following instructions. Partner work raises the level of difficulty for students and requires a greater level of trust between partners. It is important not to start pair work until students begin to experience success in performing the freeze/act sequences. Because pair work involves some physical contact, students need to feel safe, so it's best to allow them to adapt the sculpture activity to their own level of comfort. Linda suggests they could just use voice commands instead of touching. Leyton has students use imaginary puppet strings, that is, students don't touch each other but pull on the imaginary puppet strings demonstrating the desired actions. Linda always starts with what feels most safe for her students, then gradually adds more challenge. Teacher modelling is the key here — introduce gesturing, pointing, and modelling what you want as helpful techniques.

While students are working in pairs, instruct them to stay focused on controlling their emotions and remaining "in character."

- The sculptor manipulates clay into a statue position suggested by the teacher (e.g., a sports-related activity, an occupation, an emotional moment).
- Reverse the roles of clay and sculptor.
- Allow partners to create their own topic using concepts from the content units of study (e.g., mitosis, melting, landforms, king, lord, ratio, a poetic device). You might have pairs do so in parallel action, then share in small groups or for the entire class. Next, move from

pairs to small groups for selecting and preparing the tableaux scenes they will represent—from suggestions from the "sculptor," the teacher, or from the unit content. Linda uses all of these stimuli depending on the situation and confidence level of the class. This is the beginning of tableau work.
- Move to slightly more complex concepts from the curriculum that require more layers and students (e.g., revolution, feudal system, double replacement reactions, succession, solving for x in a polynomial)

Statue Museum

The next step in the sequence activity brings students back to working on their own, then in pairs, and finally in groups of four, as they begin to add creative interpretations to their work.

Guided imagery

- Linda uses creative imagery as she leads a closed-eye activity, having her students imagine their journey through a museum from the entrance doors, sensing the floors, the lighting, the temperature, sounds, and smells to heighten attention to the senses.
- As they return to reality, show pictures of statues from actual museums (content-related or theme-related). Then ask students to write or draw their reflections and images in their journal.

Creating museum statues

- Ask the students to imagine that the classroom has become a room in a museum, a room full of statues that are all variations on a theme, themes that start out concrete and move to abstract. They are to become the statues, and to use creative thinking as they assume a pose representing the characters or concepts you call out:

    the traveller, the opera singer, the scientist, the pop star fan or groupie, the artist, studying, shopping, eating, hunger, pain

- During the entire sequence, students engage silently in their pose, exhibiting the self-control they have been developing from previous activities. Linda counts down from 5 as students find the pose that best expresses the title. The countdown builds in student self-control.
- When they are ready to share their work, we split the class in half so that one half can demonstrate their poses while the other half watches and interprets. We have found that when students see others' statues, the level of their subsequent work deepens. Seeing a group all together provides perspective, but also reduces the students' sense of risk and exposure.
- Eventually, we work toward solo sharing and performances.

Increasing complexity

- Repeat the sequence, this time in pairs with different titles, but still asking for silence. This helps students to react spontaneously and decreases self- and peer-censorship.
- We give more time during the count down (count back from 10) to assume a pose and freeze, and we encourage partners to lead and follow each other. They have to figure out how to fit in to, or relate to, each other's ideas without talking about or planning an image completely. For example, if one partner poses as a baseball player up to bat, their partner completes the picture. Some titles to consider are:

    at the dentist, the driving lesson, the first date, the proposal, the secret, the interview, the accident, the argument.

- Linda sometimes uses book, story, or poem titles, depending on the purpose of the lesson or the skill level of the class. Introducing a content-specific concept can focus students' thinking on key ideas in the unit.
- The next step is to form groups of four or more, depending again on the class. We challenge the students to work from silence. With these tableaux the goal is to refine the skills of control, cooperation, trust, and risk-taking. The titles are more suited to a group picture as opposed to pairs and the concept of interrelationship and dependence is emphasized to a greater degree. Some titles to consider:

    lunch in the cafeteria, visit to Grandma's, feeding the animals, math exam, the fishing trip.

- At this point, students will find it challenging to capture all their ideas in one tableau, so introduce the idea of multiple tableaux that "tell the story." This works well in science and math because concepts are progressive (cell reproduction, factoring, growth cycles, neutralization, changes in eco systems, algebraic patterns).

Pulling it together

- The final step in this sequence comes when students are ready to create multiple tableaux to tell a simple story based on a title.
- Planning out the story requires discussion and time for trial and error (rehearsal). Linda introduces basic story elements or simple stories, picture books, or fairy tales to support students in creating original stories. Leyton shows four successive images of a transformation process like the water cycle. Some classes need these samples first before they feel confident enough to create their own.
- We start by asking students to create a series of three tableaux. We use the formula "beginning, middle, end" or "before, during,

after" to help students pick dramatic moments from the unit's content. Possible titles:

the scene of an accident, the wedding, the trial, the bus ride, graduation, the market, the operation, the robbery.

Invite students to think carefully about how many tableaux they will need to effectively demonstrate their concept. The tableau sequence prepares students for tableau work as a pathway for learning. You can then use tableaux to connect curriculum in many areas.

Dance and Music as Pathways

Nicole began dancing at the age of 3, and her world was consumed with dance for many years. Nicole still experiences great joy to see how people of all ages enjoy dance and find ways to communicate thoughts and feelings in movement. Nicole believes that dance offers something for everyone as a way to express feelings and explore the creative process through shape, sound, texture, and rhythm.

Dance is a language in which the body does the talking; "the concepts that dancers translate into movement may be extremely complex, possibly beyond their capacity to express in spoken or written forms" (Newbald and Goodwin 2004, p. 105). Nicole knows how dance makes her feel, whether through performance or choreography for self and others, but it wasn't until doing professional reading that she felt that she could bring non-dancers into the experience.

What is dance? Physical and Health Education Canada (2013, <www.phecanada.ca/programs/dance-education>) suggests "dance is a forum for collaboration…it is a site for deep learning for everyone." In the arts, we sometimes forget the social and communicative importance of the process and focus only on the performance. As a dancer, Nicole knows that dance requires teamwork and a common understanding of the message to be shared. Reflecting on dance as a teacher and learner, she now realizes that dance was always about feeling—her personal feelings and the feelings evoked in others. Yet dance is something that is rarely done alone. A collaborative piece involves making meaning together. We get ideas from inspirations, events, other dancers, and we share and we question with audience members who watch us. In dance, deeper learning comes from within. Our personal feelings and interpretations deepen further through discussion with other dancers or audience members that help us to make connections and ask self-reflective questions.

Ann Dils writes that "dance underscores the importance of bodily experience as an integrative agent in all learning" (2007, p. 107). Bodily experience requires us to pay attention in new ways to honour and teach to kinesthetic students.

Integrating dance into content area learning requires music and
language (non-verbal and verbal). We work between these forms to enrich
student learning. Newbald and Goodwin (2004) explain that "children
need a foundation from which to develop their work…when setting out to
respond or create through dance, teachers should aim to use other art forms
to engage all the senses to assist children's understanding and guide their
responses" (p. 107). We see dance as a natural way to provide learners
with a new pathway to showing and sharing their understanding of a
concept or issue.

Dance as a tool provides students with opportunities to:

- appreciate the aesthetic inherent in dance
- develop critical-thinking skills through the creative process of dance
- communicate information, ideas, understanding, and emotions
- develop self-motivation and enhance self-esteem through participation
- appreciate the role of dance in society
- strive for physical well-being by developing our bodies
- develop qualities of cooperation and respect for diversity through a
  knowledge and understanding of dance in various cultures and time periods

British Columbia Ministry of Education, 2010. *Dance Curriculum K–7.*

Reading Tina Hong's *Developing Dance Literacy in the Postmodern: An
Approach to Curriculum* (2000) excited Nicole as a passionate literacy teacher.
She took Hong's ideas about dance literacy and compared and connected
them to learning in English language arts (Figure 5.1).

Pink Day flash mob to Lady Gaga's "Born This Way"

On February 29, 2012, one hundred and sixty grades 6 and 7 students from
Ferris Elementary School in Richmond, BC, performed to Lady Gaga's "Born
This Way" to recognize and build awareness around the International Day of
Pink. Students met together in the gym to rehearse and learn choreography
for six 45-minute blocks. Nicole choreographed the piece so that a flash-mob
surprised the rest of the students and staff at a school assembly. Performers
used the lyrics and movement to portray their understanding of how to
appreciate our differences.

It was an engaging way to help students make meaning, but it was also
an example of how dance can be used to send important messages. Students
were fully engaged and excited about portraying to the entire school their
thoughts on acceptance through dance. Students could be seen at recess or
lunch practising the steps and working on incorporating their own dance
style. The emotional and kinesthetic aspects of dance will help students
remember this event later in life—perhaps even more than if they were
to explore the topic in more traditional ways and settings. The audience
members took away a powerful message from the dance, moving beyond the

Figure 5.1 The relationships between Dance and English Language Arts

Speaking	Listening
• Discussion, collaboration, negotiation • Working as a member of a group (contributing to the discussion, hearing voices and opinions) • Recognizing and celebrating success through think-pair-share	• Listening and responding to others' ideas respectfully • Working as a member of a group by piggybacking off of others' ideas
Reading **(Viewing & responding to the dance)** **(The performance)**	**Writing** **(Choreographing the dance)** **(The creation)**
• Building background knowledge prior to the dance • Making connections from the dance to self, texts, and the world • Determining the importance of the movement piece • Asking questions about the dance • Inferring what the movement might mean • Synthesizing the performance	• Recognizing and celebrating success through exit slips or quick writes • **Meaning:** the dance is enhanced through communication and expression that is personally or socially important • **Style:** contributes a sense of images, ideas, and feelings that are personally and socially significant • **Form:** representing patterns and sequences in the dance and considering transitions between each • **Mechanics:** the technique of the dance steps as they are executed

language barriers of the school's culturally and linguistically diverse students. Nicole's work with 160 students in grade 5 to create the anti-bullying flash mob helped students understand what Pink Day was all about.

Slavery mini-musical (Classroom approach)
In 2004, Nicole taught a grade 5/6 class at Cook Elementary School in Richmond, BC. Many of the students had recently immigrated to Canada and needed support with language acquisition and building background knowledge. Nicole began to integrate the arts with language arts and social studies in her units and lessons. As a summative assessment for the unit of study on slavery, her students developed a mini-musical that showed how they could make connections and more deeply understand the injustices of slavery. Figure 5.2 shows the weekly lesson sequence of how the class collaborated to develop the musical with teacher support. Part 1 outlines the music taught. Part 2 describes how dance was incorporated. Part 3 describes the synthesis of the whole unit. Lessons from music and dance are described week by week.

Figure 5.2 Three-part music and dance lesson sequence

© Portage & Main Press, 2014, It's All About Thinking: Creating Pathways for All Learning in the Middle Years, BLM, ISBN 978-1-55379-509-4

PART 1 – Music	
Week 1	**Building Background Knowledge through Sensory Images**
Listening and Responding to "Kumbaya"	**Lesson:** • Listen to the song "Kumbaya." • Ask students to fill in their four quadrants (see Figure 5.3) while listening to the song more than once. Students should pay particular attention to the images, words, questions and feelings the song evokes.
Materials: • Four quadrants template • Song on CD, "Kumbaya"	• Ask students to share their four quadrants in small groups and decide on one image, word, and feeling that describes the song for their group. • Share small group ideas in large group while teacher records thoughts on to chart paper.
Week 2	**Building an Understanding of Schema**
Listening and Responding to "Jump Down Turn Around"	**Lesson:** • Review the last lesson of "Kumbaya." Listen to the song again and ask students to quickly suggest images, words, questions, and feelings that the song evokes.
Materials: • Four quadrants template • Song on CD, "Jump Down Turn Around" • Copies of lyrics to all songs	• Listen to the song "Jump Down Turn Around." • Ask students to fill in their four quadrants while listening to the song more than once. Students should pay particular attention to the images, words, questions, and feelings the song evokes. • Ask students to share their four quadrants in small groups and decide on one image, word, and feeling that describes the song for their group. • Share small group ideas in large group share while the teacher records thoughts on to chart paper. • Begin learning the lyrics to "Kumbaya" and "Jump Down Turn Around"
Week 3	**Building an Understanding of Schema/Imagery**
Learning to Sing New Songs	**Lesson:** • During this lesson, the students and teacher sing in various ways with both pieces of music to get used to the song. Practise the songs in a variety of ways:
Materials: • Lyrics to "Kumbaya" • Lyrics to "Jump Down Turn Around"	• In rounds • With one person singing the first line then all join in at the second line • Solos/Duos • Learning the songs early on is important for the final mini musical.

Figure 5.2 cont'd

Week 4	**Building Questioning Skills**
Questioning the lyrics of a song **Materials:** • Music books with current lyrics to the songs practiced in class	**Lesson:** • Ask the students to sing "Kumbaya" and then "Jump Down Turn Around." While they are singing, ask them to listen for words and feelings that make the song capture the lives of the slaves. • Some students may choose to record their thinking during singing while others may wish to record their thoughts after singing. • Have a whole class discussion to capture what students think makes a powerful song about the life of a slave. Record student thinking. **Note:** If there is time, allow students to create their own songs depicting what they think life for a slave would have been like. Remind them of the chart the class made together to guide them – think of it as class generated criteria.
Week 5 & 6	**Building Questioning to Determine Importance**

During these two weeks, students practise the lyrics to "Swing Low, Sweet Chariot," "Nobody Knows the Trouble I've Seen," and "Plantation Boy."

Students needed this much time to become comfortable with the lyrics, but they also needed the time to learn how to move with the rhythm of the music and show emotions to the lyrics of the song.

PART 2 – Dance	
Week 1	**Building Background Knowledge through Movement**
Listening and Responding to "Kumbaya" through movement **Materials:** • Four quadrants template completed from Music, Week 1: Lesson 1 • Song on CD, "Kumbaya"	**Lesson:** • Listen to the song "Kumbaya." • Ask students to review their four quadrants in small groups and decide on one image, word, or feeling that describes the song for their group. • Teacher models what image, word or feeling describes the song for her. For instance, for "someone's crying Lord," show students how you can move and cry by moving the body slowly across the floor with shoulders and head contracted over the chest; show that it's okay to move your body at different heights, speeds, and patterns (i.e., include turns). • Students work in pairs to show one another their movement interpretations of the lyrics. • Pairs come together to share with one another.
Week 2	**Building an Understanding of Schema through Movement**
Listening and Responding to "Jump Down Turn Around" **Materials:** • Four quadrants template completed from Music, Week 2: Lesson 1 • Song on CD, "Jump Down Turn Around"	**Lesson:** • Review the last lesson of "Kumbaya." Listen to the song again and ask students to quickly show images, words, or feelings that the song evoked through movement. • Listen to the song "Jump Down Turn Around" again and review four quadrants from last class. • Teacher models what image, word or feeling describes the song for her. For instance, for "jump down turn around pick a bale of cotton," model the action of jumping down to the ground, touch the floor, turn around while coming up to a half standing position to lean over and reach forward with the right hand as if ready to "pick a weed." • Students work in pairs to show one another their movement interpretations of the lyrics. • Pairs come together to share with one another.

© Portage & Main Press, 2014, *It's All About Thinking: Creating Pathways for All Learnings in the Middle Years*, BLM, ISBN 978-1-55379-509-4

Figure 5.2 cont'd

Week 3 & 4	Building an Understanding of Schema, Imagery through Movement, and Building Questioning Skills
Learning to freely move while showing emotion by questioning the lyrics of the songs	**Lesson:** Return to the criteria for words and feelings that make a good song to capture the lives of the slaves. This comes from Music, Week 3: Lesson 1. Begin to model emotions to the class through facial expressions combined with body movement (sad, tired, angry, hurt, lost, worried, ashamed, surprised…) using instrumental music that evokes the particular emotions. You may model one emotion at a time, so that students have a chance to explore and discover what that might look like for them.
Materials: • Lyrics to "Kumbaya" • Lyrics to "Jump Down Turn Around"	Continue exploring this idea of showing emotions in pairs and allow time for pairs to share with other groups to get feedback or to "borrow" movement ideas.
Week 5	**Building Questioning to Determine Importance**

During this week, practise movement to "Swing Low, Sweet Chariot," "Nobody Knows the Trouble I've Seen," and "Plantation Boy."

Students needed this time to become comfortable with the meaning behind the lyrics as well as to become familiar with the speed of the music. Allow time to learn how to move with the rhythm of the music and continue to show emotions to the lyrics of the song.

PART 3	
Week 6 & 7	**Synthesis to Tying It All Together**

Plan the format of the mini production together. Nicole began by asking students to brainstorm scenes that they thought should be included in the musical.

• On chart paper, Nicole wrote all of the ideas down

• Together, categorize the ideas into big ideas to help create scenes.

• In the end, the plan looked like this (with consideration of the songs we already knew):

  ◦ Scene 1: Opening, "Nobody Knows the Trouble I've Seen" (solo)

  ◦ Scene 2: Cotton fields "Jump Down Turn Around" (all; scenery & props)

  ◦ Scene 3: Slave quarters "Kumbaya" (solo and all; scenery)

  ◦ Scene 4: Escape to Canada (no music just drama; forest scenery)

  ◦ Scene 5: Freedom "Plantation Boy" (all; props)

Note: Props and scenery were done during Art class. Small groups worked together to create the scenery. Groups signed up for what they were interesting in pursuing.

Rehearsal: Nicole's class rehearsed everything without costumes about 5 times. Students used their emotions and body to move to the music, embracing the thoughts and feelings of slaves and the injustices they felt.

Nicole videotaped the performance. The class celebrated by watching the video together.

Sometimes movement and feeling precede words and it is important for students to have a chance to work together in other forms and languages. The musical was a chance for students to use music and movement—exploring and representing the big ideas and their response to what they learned in their unit of study.

Figure 5.3 Four Quadrant template to describe response to "Kumbaya"

Name:_____	Date:_____
Title: _____	
What I See...	What I hear...
What I wonder...	What I feel...

Within both examples, music also offered a rich collection of practices and modalities to make meaning, to explore and challenge their own and others' perspectives, and to represent their new understandings. Just like drama and dance, music can deepen students' perceptions of themselves, the world around them, and the knowledge they are acquiring. Participating in and creating music, drama, dance, and art together enhances their sense of belonging in their classroom community.

Visual Arts as a Pathway

As a child, Karen Deibert played with clay dug from her garden. In elementary school, she struggled a great deal with most of her academic classes. In secondary school, her art teacher allowed her the freedom to pursue art in a variety of media, and she began to experience feelings of success. As Karen became more confident, the many positive results of her art spilled over into her other areas of learning. Opportunities to become involved in different forms of art provide some students with alternative means to succeed. The following quote from Einstein illustrates one of Karen's firm beliefs:

> "Not everything that counts can be counted, and not everything that can be counted counts."

Karen believes that integrating the arts provides opportunities for students to strengthen their confidence, engagement, and achievement—traits, attitudes, and emotions that cannot be easily measured but are essential in the pursuit of a meaningful and relevant education. Currently, Karen is teaching at Parkland Middle School in Cranbrook, BC, where she has an opportunity to work with students from different grades and to collaborate with teachers outside of middle school.

Cross-Curricular Unit: Using clay to enhance the study of Japan

The lessons in this unit address different cultures and their beliefs and values about integrating the arts into student learning. The key focus here is cross-content learning with clay.

Topic: Sushi dishes and traditional ceremonial tea-bowls

Objective: Students will study the lifestyles of the Japanese people. Students will become familiar with the customs associated with the tea ceremony, and with the history of Japanese culture. Students should have an opportunity to celebrate by making sushi and having a traditional tea ceremony in their classroom.

Teacher responsibilities
Be prepared. The opportunities and experiences for the students will be intensified, strengthened and much more positive when all the materials are easily available and there is a clear lesson objective and direction. Let the students know what the project is, and what the desired outcomes are and invite students to ask questions related to the new project early on and throughout.

Teacher collaboration
When team-teaching, set aside time for a meeting to clarify goals of the project. Address each teacher's responsibilities and which responsibilities the teachers will share. Tentatively schedule the start and end dates, however, do consider and allow for shifting of the scheduled dates to take place.

Materials
- paint brushes, sponges, wooden knives, plastic knives and forks, pin tools, pencil crayons, pens, scissors, small containers
- paper for designing the work (photocopy discards; recycle when you can)
- plastic bags (from grocery shopping, dry cleaners)
- card stock for templates (e.g., old file folders)
- 1 box of clay (e.g., 20 kg to 25 kg per box; keep extra box available, just in case)
- several sheets of 3-in. foam (approximately 16 in. x 20 in.). The foam makes a great surface to work on and allows the dishes to be shaped easily. Have several "foam stations" set up although students use the foam sheet for about 5 min.
- glaze (4 to 8 colours)

- boards cut to approximately 9 in. x 12 in. (22 cm x 28 cm) Note: Pieces of cardboard or mat board (picture framing) might save cost or time. Check with galleries or framers for leftover pieces.

Make the sushi dishes on a bed of plastic so that the work can be slid (with care) onto the board. This will lessen the chances of the dish warping.

Suggestion: This lesson outline is suited for the study of Japan in connection with Social Studies at the grade 6, 7, and 8 level, but not limited to this grade range or subject area. This lesson idea can be modified to include various other grades and/or subject areas such as a food science class or a study on culture, race, or heritage.

Summary: Students have an enhanced learning opportunity to explore and "experience" both the ancient and modern culture of Japan through the medium of clay. Student planning, reflecting, and evaluating are all important steps in art-integrated activities (Figure 5.4).

The Lessons

Lesson 1: Japanese customs
These lessons occurred on alternate days from lessons focused on social studies that helped students build their background knowledge. Through discussion, address the study of the Japanese culture. Introduce the project to the students. Let them know they will have an opportunity to create a sushi dish and a ceremonial tea bowl from clay.

Students are already in engaged in research related to both ancient and modern Japanese culture, including a mini report.

Lesson 2: Research continues
Ask students to brainstorm with a partner, using the following question, "What are some examples of food or drink that are connected to ceremonies or rituals?" Ask students for their responses. Show images of a tea room, a tea ceremony, a Japanese garden and ask the students to infer how they connect together. Show them a summer tea bowl and a winter tea bowl. Ask students to discuss the similarities and differences. This is a great opportunity to send students off to do more research about tea ceremonies and tea bowls which will help them decide the type of pinch-pot tea-bowl they would like to make by making a mini sketch, using the text sets.

Lesson 3: Introduce examples and demonstrations of the work
If student exemplars are not available, search the Internet for images of tea-bowls and sushi dishes. Share the criteria of the project with the students and have them discuss the "Pretty successful" results column. Ask partners to share ideas that come to mind for their own dishes (Figure 5.5). Use the remaining class time to research design ideas or a Japanese symbol to use later as part of the design on the sushi dish.

Figure 5.4 Student planning sheet for a cultural study of Japan

Name: _____ Date: _____

1. Something I learned from the student exemplars and teacher demonstration.

   _____

   _____

2. What were some ideas that interested you? Complete three mini-sketches.
   This is just a starting point!

3. The idea I am most interested in doing for the sushi dish set is sketched below!

   Include dish, wasabi dish, chop stick rest, tea-bowl – OTHER?

4. Three or more steps I will need to follow to achieve my goal:

   _____

   _____

   _____

5. Things I may need to remember:

   _____

   _____

   _____

6. Things I will need to bring from home:

   _____

   _____

   _____

Lesson 4: Planning and making templates

Review the steps necessary for a successful project (Figure 5.4). Have students complete a plan and pattern for their sushi dish set, including a sketch of their planned tea-bowl. However, the tea-bowl might change as the clay is molded and formed with the fingers and thumb. Organize the items the students will need for the projects. Have students review their planning sheet. They may need to bring items from home to complete their plans.

Lesson 5: Creating the tableware

Karen recommends several classes, back-to-back, for this stage. Have the students make the tea-bowls using their plan during the first class, then make the sushi dish during the second class.

To make the ceremonial tea bowls, use a ball of clay slightly larger than a golf ball, but not as large as a tennis ball. The ball of clay should fit comfortably in the palm of the hand. The clay can be gently pinched and turned until the tea-bowl is formed. The shape of the tea-bowls may vary. If a student plans a square tea-bowl, follow the process for making a round pinch-pot and then use a wooden paddle to alter the shape.

With all items and clay ready, approximately 50 minutes to one hour (including setting up and clean-up) should be adequate for students to build beautiful tea-bowls. Remind the students to be gentle and gradual with the shaping of the clay for the tea-bowl. Gradual and gentle pinching and turning of the clay will produce better results. If students work the clay too harshly, it may crack. If the clay shows any sign of cracking, have the student blend in one drop of water at a time. Too much water in the clay can cause a problem; but so can not enough water.

Note: When students' hands become hot, have them cool their hands under cold running water. Hot hands tend to draw the moisture from the clay too quickly, which can cause cracking. Before students set their tea-bowls aside to dry, ensure they mark their work with initials or another identifying mark.

Time-saver: Have the slabs of clay rolled out ahead, perhaps inviting parent helpers. The average size of sushi dishes may range between 5-in. x 5-in or 6-in. x 6-in. for a square set and 5-in x 6-in. or 5 in. x 7 in. or 4 in. x 8 in. for a rectangular dish set. Dishes shaped as a leaf, fish, flower or other organic item should also fall into these size ranges. Of course, a smaller dish for the wasabi (a condiment made from a root plant) can be made much smaller and from scraps of the clay.

Lesson 6: Making the tableware

Once the tea-bowls are made, have the students proceed with their sushi dish set. Remind them that they may want to include a chopstick rest or a separate wasabi dish. The time for making the sushi dish may be between one and a half and two hours. Some students who are particular about detail will likely require a little longer to follow up.

Figure 5.5 Student Reflection and Evaluation Sheet

Name: _____ Date: _____

Sushi Dish Ticket

Please complete the following to the best of your ability.

1. What did you find important about making the sushi dishes?

   _____

   _____

2. How did this opportunity enhance your learning with respect to understanding more about the Japanese culture? Explain.

   _____

   _____

3. What did you enjoy about making the tea-bowls and sushi dish sets?

   _____

   _____

4. What difficulties did you encounter when you were working with the clay? Explain.

   _____

   _____

5. Did you understand the explanations and class demonstrations?

   _____

   _____

6. What else could have been done to have helped you be more successful or to have helped you learn better? Explain.

   _____

   _____

7. Please include any other relevant comments, questions (concerns) about the project. Such as: What worked for you? What DID NOT WORK, Why?

   _____

   _____

Figure 5.5 cont'd

8. Finally, use this rubric to assess your project.

	4 **You did better than your PLANS! Powerful use of techniques**	**3** **Pretty special results! You can be proud of your work.**	**2.5** **Solid effort, with room to grow.**	**2** **On your way. You have some room to improve.**	**1** **Good start More planning, and effort will help.**
DETAIL on all pieces included in the set!	Details are easily viewed. PLANNING and care evident.	Project details work together well. Pieces are attractive and functional.	Most details are successful. Some areas need improvement.	Results of details not strong or not effective. More effort overall required.	Results not complete, strong or effective. Room to improve.
ATTRACTIVE and positive results on all pieces. Glazing results too!	The project shows the student was focused and concerned with details The work is NEAT (pride). Construction is strong effective!	The dish set shows the creator took pride in the project. The design & construction look planned and executed well.	Designing and assembling the dish set was completed, yet flaws are evident (bumps, uneven work, poor joins). More care was required.	The dish set looks rushed and/or thrown together. Little thought, planning or care evident. Much more effort over all was required.	The project looks rushed and/or is incomplete. Messy or careless work is apparent. More work and effort over all was required.
CREATIVITY of the tea-bowl and dish set.	Very original thought was used to create the project.	Some original ideas & some borrowed ideas were used.	Creative aspects noted.	Little individuality or creativity shines through in the final results.	Lacks creativity. None of the pieces stand out as being creative.
Classroom Growth Work ethic and contribution to the classroom community	Class time used wisely. Effort & strong focus evident. Helpful and cooperative! "Classroom community minded."	Time was used wisely and carefully. Clean-up help was also good Willingness to wait, share, and help was very evident.	Some time was used wisely; some was wasted. Clean-up effort was minimal. More effort overall.	More focus and effort overall in use of time, effort, and cooperative working required.	Much more focus and effort required overall in use of time, effort, and contribution to a "community". More focus on cooperative work required.

9. My OVERALL RATING for my SUSHI DISH SET is _____

    because _____

© Portage & Main Press, 2014, *It's All About Thinking: Creating Pathways for All Learnings in the Middle Years*, BLM, ISBN 978-1-55379-509-4

Lesson 7: Glazing the tableware

Unlike the shaping of the pieces (which should be completed in a day or two at the most), the glazing stage can take place over two or more periods. However, allow between one and a half to two hours to glaze the pottery. If applying glaze by brush, ensure complete coverage by having the students use 3 or 4 coats. If you plan to dip the items in the glaze, have the students wax the bottoms of each piece first.

Lesson 8: Presentation and celebration

Students present their findings about the Japanese culture. The class could hold a traditional tea ceremony, prepare or purchase sushi to serve on the newly created sushi dish sets.

Pulling It All Together

Self-reflection and assessment involves students judging their individual work and progress. Their judgment (reflection) and evaluation (self-assessment) are based on the specific set of criteria set out at the beginning of the assignment. Self-evaluation leads to improved student learning in assignments and project work in subsequent units of study and future grades. Self-assessment helps students understand the main purposes of their learning and thereby grasp what they need to do to achieve (Black and Wiliam 1998). This stage of student reflection and evaluation helps them connect to the important concept of "becoming better learners." (Figure 5.5)

Service learning connection

This project can also be completed with a connection to the health and career education curriculum. One class of Karen's students made a number of sushi dish sets, which were then sold through the school and through a local (and very popular) sushi bar. They raised approximately $500 which they donated to two local charitable agencies in the community. Teachers can vary the connection to education and the curriculum to learn about and address a social issue in the community.

Conclusion

Learning through the arts engages our students. We learn to tap into our senses; we think with our bodies. Integrating the arts into our teaching fosters student creativity, helps students to take risks, and deepens their understanding of important concepts. As well, the arts reinforce and extend community. We begin to see and understand how many ways there are to explore, contribute, and learn when we work in new expressive and creative ways.

Chapter 6

Creating Pathways Using Inquiry and Project-Based Learning

Educators Involved

Matt Rosati: Classroom Teacher, SD 42, Maple Ridge, BC

Marna Macmillan: Classroom Teacher/ Learning Support Coordinator, SD 43, Coquitlam, BC

Jacquie Moniot: Teacher-Librarian SD 43, Coquitlam, BC

Brenton Close: Classroom Teacher, SD 74, Ashcroft, BC

Darcy McNee: Classroom Teacher, SD 63, Saanich, BC

Nadine Stofer: Classroom Teacher, SD 63, Saanich, BC

Sandi Johnson: Classroom Teacher, SD 63, Saanich, BC

It may be hard to believe, but even today, we can walk into a classroom and see students sitting in desks in rows, listening to teacher presentations, answering the same questions, in the same way, at the same time. Where is the engagement, the critical thinking, the creativity? How can we break through this out-of-date approach to teaching and learning? One answer is—through inquiry and active project-based learning (PBL). We want our students to be actively posing questions, planning projects, and drawing upon prior and new knowledge to explore concepts and issues. We want our students to be generating new and personalized perspectives and plans of action. Ultimately, we want them to take action and to make a difference in the world around them. It can all start from a wondering mind. Inquiry can spark curiosity, deep learning, and advocacy. Through inquiry, we can help students learn to think critically and creatively.

Project-Based Learning

We asked Matt Rosati, a teacher from Maple Ridge who has been thinking about and exploring project-based learning for years, to share his wisdom and experience. He co-authored the opening section of this chapter.

Learning through projects is certainly not new—teachers have always used projects to engage learners and create more authentic learning experiences. However, we now have more research on PBL, and that research recognizes it as a very powerful method for teaching and learning. Matt's initial foray into PBL was prompted by his concern about the power dynamics in his classroom. Simply put, he no longer wanted to coerce students into engaging with the curriculum; he felt there had to be a better way, something that was more natural and authentic.

He knew that his learning and understanding are products of his experience, and believed that the same must be true for his students. Matt initially struggled to find strategies that he could implement in his teaching to allow his students to demonstrate their learning in their own way—their "constructs of knowing." He now points out that the most important contribution project-based learning has, as a teaching and learning approach, is that it invites and encourages students to demonstrate their learning in ways that they understand and are comfortable with but that also requires them to go outside their comfort zone.

Project-Based Learning and Inquiry Learning

Although project-based learning isn't an all-or-nothing approach, teachers can use it with their students in any content area. The key is to provide appropriate instruction in the skills of inquiry and guide students in personal development of those skills through inquiry projects. For example, the teacher must teach the skill of time management before expecting students to learn and do it on their own. Teaching using PBL can take longer than traditional methods, but the learning for students is deeper and long-lasting.

- The power dynamics in classroom communities can be crucially important to student success. We want students to take control of their own learning gradually, and PBL allows students to acquire some power over what and how they learn.
- Learners engage in solving meaningful questions about real-world problems led by their natural curiosity. The projects also offer choices so that students can follow their own passions and interests to greater or lesser degree.
- In a group, students exercise and further develop their abilities in collaborative problem solving and critical thinking skills—making decisions about what they will learn, how they will learn it, and how they will demonstrate their learning in the assessment. Doing their research, students have to make critical decisions about the merit and relative value of the ideas and content in the texts and other resources they use—which makes PBL the perfect framework for 21st-century teaching.

Implementation of PBL and Inquiry Learning

Many teachers worry about how the day-to-day activities will play out, and about how it will all come together. It is important to allow the projects to progress naturally, to be led by the wonderings and connections that students bring to the collaboration. The role of the teacher is in no way reduced; rather, within this framework, the teacher must adopt a more responsive approach. Teachers can plan major topics, how to bridge between them, what skills might have to be strengthened in order to deal with the next challenge, but how and when such teachable moments present themselves comes from the students.

In Matt's experience, mapping out the skills and content that he wants the students to encounter and use is very important. Matt peruses curriculum outcomes, mapping out the topics that relate to the enduring understandings or essential questions for particular units of study. From that map, he focuses on what content should be covered, how much has to be presented by direct instruction—the things that students may not know they need to know; what skills the students need to use or strengthen; what activities will engage the class in using their skills to investigate and understand the content; and what kind of assessment, both formative and summative, will best reveal what the students have learned.

His planning template (Figure 6.1) is anchored in curriculum outcomes, but also offers the flexibility needed when introducing PBL. Some students might ask for more structure because they are not used to following their own path, but over time they become comfortable directing their own learning. PBL's open-ended structure allows for a great many possibilities and for the students to make their own meaning.

The projects start with one or more questions that are essential for exploring the curriculum topics. Developing essential questions is a skill that

Figure 6.1 Template for curriculum mapping

Curriculum Mapping

	Subject/Course/Unit
Essential Questions and Enduring Understandings (What content is worthy of understanding? What *enduring* understandings are desired?)	
Content (What facts, concepts, principles are most important to know and understand?)	
Skills (What processes, procedures, strategies should we implement?)	
Activities (What activities will equip students with the needed knowledge and skills?)	
Explicit Teaching (What will need to be taught and coached? How should it best be taught, in light of performance goals?)	
Assessment (How will we know if students have achieved the desired results? What will we accept as evidence of student understanding and proficiency?)	
Resources (What materials and resources are best suited to accomplish these goals?)	

becomes easier the more you do it. Essential questions should relate to the human condition, be open-ended, and be subject to debate and research; for example: *How do our prejudices affect us? What happens when ideas are more important than people? How do our environments shape us? How are statistics used to influence society?*

Teachers can conduct PBL in many different ways—there is no *one* way. The key to PBL is not the exact process but the recognition that students are making their own meaning and constructing their own learning out of the curriculum content—and they have choice in what to learn, how to learn it, and how to demonstrate their learning.

Matt devises a focus question to present to his students as the inquiry that will shape the project they will work on with his help. As a class, the students discuss what the question means and how it can be interpreted, sharing some examples. He then asks the students to develop their own focus question from the overall theme. For example, if his focus question is "How do our environments shape us?" he encourages his students to develop their own question about "environment." Students need lots of help with this process, especially in the beginning. It's advisable to have some general questions available to adapt, modify, or use. Students who are new to this very different way of teaching and learning will need some time and support to become comfortable and trust that these methods will be beneficial to them. In this situation, it's best to introduce PBL first as a class project (co-inquiry), then follow up with individual student inquiry projects on related topics.

Teachers should direct and model aspects of the class project, demonstrating (and teaching, as needed) the skills, abilities, and content mastery that they expect students to use in their individual projects. Ensure that the students are also learning and applying all the elements set out in the curriculum map for the unit of study. This method also has an effect on creating genuine, student-based content that merges with the teacher's required content. When the students are engaged in their own projects, everyone generates content and examples. The teacher is no longer the sole supplier of topics; everyone's work has the potential to influence everyone else's work and ideas. It's very powerful and very exciting to see in action.

As PBL starts to take shape in your learning community, there are a few things to keep in mind.

- Find out initially through assessment for learning what the students already know about the topic, skills, or content. In PBL everyone, teacher included, is both a learner and a teacher—there may be experts about particular topics sitting in your class.
- Make the first few assignments or activities easily accessible and always open-ended. Plans should have entry points that allow all students in the class to participate and have some connection to the topic. Suggest that students take a picture or draw or write about their current understanding of the topic.

- Do formative assessment in the moment. Use the abilities in the room to give students examples of your expectations. If Matt's students are writing an inquiry question or statement of topic to be researched, he circulates and reads as they are writing. When he sees a model example, he stops the class, shares that student's work, and asks the class to reflect on what makes this example a strong one.
- Keep student reflection a part of every class. PBL works best when metacognition is embedded within it. Have the students reflect often about what they're doing, why they are doing it, how they could do it better, what they want to know next, and the steps of the process in which they are engaged.
- Teachers should constantly be modelling the skills and abilities being used and developed during the class project, so that the students will know how to apply them to their individual projects.
- Ask students often who their audience is and how they might demonstrate what they are learning.

Lessons in Decoding Texts and Constructing Meaning

The following is a sequence of lessons Matt uses with his students to support them in their inquiry learning.

Lesson 1 — Introduce the Focus Question

In this example, the focus question is an essential question for the unit. The focus question is the most important piece for both the class project and individual projects. It provides an important guide as the projects become complex and, possibly, chaotic. Introduce the focus question to the class: "How do our prejudices affect us?"

Facilitate a class discussion (whole group or small group with reporting out) about possible answers and examples based on their experience and understanding of the question. As part of respectful teaching, every serious attempt to address the question must be accepted as a legitimate example of what a student knows or understands.

Scaffold for support

Teachers may also choose, depending on their students, to structure more of a discussion. A possible prompt could be:

> *Tell about a time that you decided something about a person or situation you just encountered. As you got to know the person or the situation better, was your initial decision right or wrong?*

This is also a great opportunity to introduce skills and content from your curriculum map.

Practise skills, focusing on outcomes

To include descriptive writing in this unit, ask the students to write a descriptive paragraph about the situation in the above prompt, which also provides practice in critical thinking and metacognition.

Lesson 2—Decoding Text

Set the stage for a shared learning experience in which all students feel their contributions are meaningful and that they matter. This activity introduces the activities cycle of "teacher introduces and demonstrates; students practise skills."

Choose a text to read together

As a class, read your first text together. Matt recommends children's literature regardless of the age group. It can be read in a relatively short amount of time and the text features are easily identifiable. Some examples are *The Sneetches* (Seuss), *The Island* (Greder), *Sister Anne's Hands* (Loribecki), or *Voices in the Park* (Brown).

Invite students to summarize understanding

From the text, as a class, choose the most powerful image. Then, ask students, in small groups, to address the focus question in relation to the image. As in this example, curriculum content is offered and used as opportunities to apply or practise the learning skills

Read the book pausing every few pages to ask what students are learning that is related to the focus question.

After the book is read, ask students how the whole book related to the focus question, and what other books, experiences, and current or past events also relate to the book and the focus question.

Lesson 3—Set Targets for Reading Comprehension

The class project is a model or a standard toward which each student should strive. Teacher feedback and student self-assessment and reflection are crucial because they let students know where their efforts stand and how they can improve. Still using the story image that the class agreed upon, introduce the reading handout (Figure 6.2). Introduce and discuss the terms "Retrieve information" (remember), "Recognize meaning "(understand), "Interpret texts," and "Analyze texts." With the class, apply these four skills to the image. With students in pairs or trios, have them pick one of the skills and use it with the picture. Have students share out their responses.

Have some additional images ready on which students can use these skills. The more diversity in the images the better. Give each pair or trio their image, a transparency (overhead) sheet, and a fine-tipped erasable pen. Have them choose one of the reading skills to write their responses on the transparency. Students can put the transparency sheet over top of the image.

After 5 or so minutes, have them trade pens with another group to get another colour pen. Then have students choose another of the reading skills and use the new coloured pen to write, diagram, or jot down their responses.

Figure 6.2 Categories of reading skills

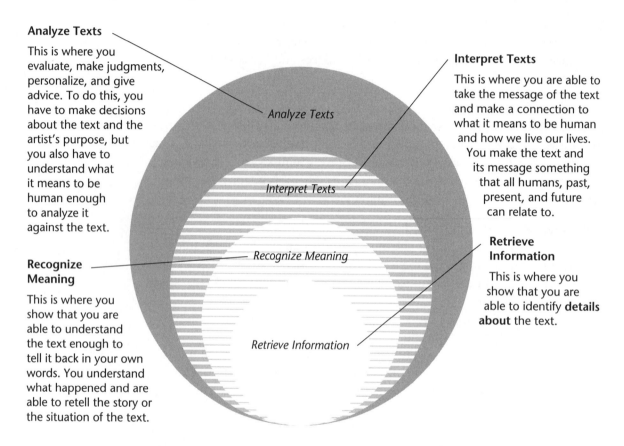

Analyze Texts

This is where you evaluate, make judgments, personalize, and give advice. To do this, you have to make decisions about the text and the artist's purpose, but you also have to understand what it means to be human enough to analyze it against the text.

Recognize Meaning

This is where you show that you are able to understand the text enough to tell it back in your own words. You understand what happened and are able to retell the story or the situation of the text.

Interpret Texts

This is where you are able to take the message of the text and make a connection to what it means to be human and how we live our lives. You make the text and its message something that all humans, past, present, and future can relate to.

Retrieve Information

This is where you show that you are able to identify **details about** the text.

Analyze Texts

Interpret Texts

Recognize Meaning

Retrieve Information

Practise formative assessment
Find examples from pairs or trios whose responses demonstrate the skill they were using and share those examples with the rest of the class, using an overhead projector or document camera. Using a metacognitive approach, ask the students what is good about the exemplar, how it compares to their attempt, what is needed to improve. Allow the students time to reflect on their work and set goals.

Use authentic and meaningful exemplars to set goals
Initially, what the class produces might not be the very best examples, but by choosing exemplars from within the learning community and sharing them in the moment of doing, a teacher gives students more immediate and authentic feedback that makes the goal of being a model become approachable for all.

Lesson 4—Transfer Skills to Personal Projects

Students are developing the skills necessary to engage in a project based on their own question.

This lesson leads students to expand and incorporate ideas and skills into their own projects while still learning important expectations from the class project. Ask students to locate and bring an image of prejudice, as they understand and interpret it, to class. Be prepared for lots of different ideas and explanations.

Gradual release of responsibility

Students will be able to speak as an authority on their own ideas and understandings. Teachers may also notice, and can certainly point out or expand upon, some powerful cross-curricular connections from what the students have chosen. Lesson 4 can be about practising the reading skills developed in the previous lesson and gradually releasing more responsibility to the students. Organize students in small groups of three. One student is the interviewer, one is the interviewee, and one is the recorder. The students will rotate roles.

To start the lesson ask the students to generate examples of effective questions to ask their peers in an interview about their image. Once there is a sufficient diversity of sample questions recorded on the board at the front of the class, it's time for the interviews to begin. Sample questions may include *"Why did you select this image?" "How does it relate to the focus questions?" "What does it remind you of?" "What do you wonder about the image?"*

The interviewer interviews the interviewee for approximately four minutes about their image. The recorder takes notes. The interviewer has to keep the interview flowing by asking follow-up questions.

After all three interviews have been completed, ask students to look for commonalities in all three interviews. This is an excellent opportunity to reinforce how to work with information to find confirming evidence of an idea or theme. Trios then meet with another trio to share and compare what they have learned. Ask groups of six to share out their common themes and two of the groups' images that they believe communicate these ideas.

At the end of the class, have students reflect on (1) what makes for an effective interview, (2) what their personal strengths and stretches were as interviewer, recorder, and interviewee, and (3) a burning question they have about prejudice and how it affects us.

Future Lessons: Self-Assessment of Applied Knowledge and Skill

The next steps in this PBL process involve allowing students the time, space, and freedom to develop their own understandings within the context of the classroom models and exemplars. More model texts can be introduced or sets of texts related to the focus question. Students use these texts collaboratively to develop their knowledge and understandings related to the topic. These are the skills that students will apply to their own projects. The teacher makes it clear that the expectations established in the group project should be applied to each student's project.

Next steps

- In a co-inquiry or individual inquiry, as work on projects continues, the methodology should remain consistent:
  1. The teacher introduces new skills or content (from the curriculum map) to apply to the project as a modelling activity.
  2. The students respond and practise, then demonstrate their skill with the content in their own project.

  Remember that teaching and lessons now occur in the context of student learning and teachable moments and opportunities, so teachers need the flexibility of a strong curriculum map that provides choice from a variety of lessons and topics that fit overall unit goals.

- Community is a crucial component of PBL. Start building community early and keep building it throughout the year. It can take the form of ice-breaker activities, or even just working with and supporting each other. This method of PBL relies a lot on shared understandings and meanings. If all the projects share a theme, every student's project and every student's understanding have the potential to fuel every other student's project and understandings. Students must trust and feel a sense of belonging to achieve the ideal cooperative environment.

At the end of the unit, consider having the students present their projects as a culminating activity. Because the projects have been constructed together, presentations should be considered a celebration of the new learnings and understandings that each student has made. For this summative assessment, teacher and students can work together to develop a rubric with clear, student-friendly, descriptive language that helps the teacher give helpful feedback about what each student has achieved (Figure 6.3).

Inquiry-Based Research

Marna Macmillan, a Humanities 8 teacher, and Jacquie Moniot, teacher librarian, who teach in a grades 6 to 8 middle school in Coquitlam, collaborated on many student research projects for over twelve years. Grade 8 students are at a perfect age, developmentally, to question the world around them, take on contentious issues, and argue for what they believe to be right. Marna was struck by the curiosity and engagement her students had when discussing current news events, issues from a global perspective, or issues connected to their personal lives. She wanted to create a classroom culture that invited that kind of energy and discussion on a daily basis, providing an opportunity for students to explore important issues and events through personal investigation and connection.

Figure 6.3 Sample rubric for summative assessment of student projects

Aspect	Not Yet Within Expectations 1	Approaching Expectations 2	Fully Meets Expectations 3	Exceeds Expectations 4
Focus Question	Did not fulfill the project's proposal; unclear thesis; information included does not seem to support the thesis; sources not credited.	Minimally fulfilled the project's proposal; some information is not clearly connected to the thesis; credit for sources not complete.	Adequately fulfilled the project's proposal; sufficient information that relates to the thesis; many good points made; credited sources.	Completely fulfilled the project's proposal; an abundance of material clearly related to the thesis; points are clearly made and all evidence supports thesis; varied use of materials; credited sources.
Research Skills and Time Management	Time not used well; used few or no resources; little evidence or examples; spent little time preparing.	Time could have been used more efficiently; used minimal resources; used little evidence and examples; minimal preparation time.	Managed time well; used several reliable primary sources; used several reliable secondary sources; used appropriate evidence and examples; used preparation time well.	Managed time very well; appropriate primary sources; used many reliable appropriate secondary sources; used appropriate evidence and examples; used preparation time to go beyond basic research.
Creativity	Repetitive with little or no variety; insufficient use of multimedia; few connections; no personal interests	Little or no variation; material presented with little originality or interpretation; few connections; few personal interests	Originality apparent; good variety and blending of materials and media; makes connections; taps into personal interests/passions	Very original presentation of material; uses the unexpected to full advantage; captures audience's attention; makes connections; taps into personal interests/passions
Visual Elements of the Project	Produced a product that is disorganized, and difficult to see and understand; produced a product not related to the purpose of the project; exhibited little effort; little or imbalance of multimedia	Produced a product that is somewhat interesting but difficult to see; somewhat supported the purpose of the product; minimally supported the main idea; exhibited a fair effort; multimedia not clearly connected	Produced a product that is interesting and easy to see and understand; supported the purpose of the project; communicated main ideas; exhibited excellent effort; some use of multimedia	Produced a product that is creative, interesting, and easy to see and understand; supported the purpose of the project; fully communicated main ideas; exhibited outstanding effort; balanced use of multimedia materials
Coherence and Organization	Presentation is choppy and disjointed; does not flow; development of thesis is vague; no apparent logical order of presentation	Concepts and ideas are loosely connected; lacks clear transitions; flow and organization are choppy	Most information presented in a logical sequence; generally very well organized but better transitions from idea to idea and medium to medium are needed	Thesis is clearly stated and developed; specific examples are appropriate and clearly develop thesis; conclusion is clear; shows control; flows together well; good transitions; succinct but not choppy; well organized

© Portage & Main Press, 2014, *It's All About Thinking: Creating Pathways for All Learning in the Middle Years*, BLM, ISBN 978-1-55379-509-4

Marna's collaborations with Jacquie on the research process made it clear how important "questions that matter" are in motivating students to search for answers. Many of the articles, novels, and books that most engaged this age group of students were those that dealt with complex moral and ethical issues (i.e., bullying, child labour, human rights, slavery, war and genocide, and women's equality). Therefore, Marna and Jacquie provided their students with a chance to explore a wider, more global perspective of "persecution and compassion" by having them develop and pursue their own questions and their own topic areas that connected back to an overarching, essential question.

It was also important for the students to acquire the specialized literacy skills of "reading for information." They needed help to navigate the digital world where information is so easily accessible, ever-changing, and expanding into multiple formats. Students need to locate and select appropriate information from a variety of sources, to read for key ideas, and to ensure that the information they use is reliable. From their new learning, they make connections to their own lives, begin to recognize dehumanizing language and understand its impact, or understand how to nurture compassion and empathy by seeking to understand others.

Investigating Persecution and Compassion

Essential question

- What are the factors that lead people to acts of persecution or acts of compassion?

Enduring understandings

- Effective readers make meaning using a variety of reading strategies to connect new information to background knowledge (process).
- Effective research starts with engaging the curiosity of the researcher, who then asks their own questions in order to search for deeper understanding. This includes determining importance of information, synthesizing information to build knowledge, and reflecting on new understanding (process).
- Good researchers check sources and determine reliability of their sources (process).
- Dehumanization can lead to acts of persecution, both large and small (idea).
- Listening to and understanding other perspectives nurtures compassion (idea).

The following lessons are organized under "The Points of Inquiry" from a BCTLA document (Ekdahl, Farquarson, Robinson, and Turner 2010) that includes outcomes for grades 4 to7 inquiry skills <bctf.ca/bctla/pub/index.html>. Marna and Jacquie chose the outcomes most relevant to their lessons, and included them in checklists, like that below, or rubrics when assessing students for each section of their project.

Connect and Wonder

· Ask focus questions related to aspects of the topic or issue.

· Ask a question that will generate meaningful inquiry and that is interesting and worth answering (inquiry-based learning).

· Recognize that differences in interpretation of stories are important aspects for discussion and consideration (inquiry based reading).

Working with questions

It is important to nurture a classroom where asking questions becomes the norm. Students need to trust that they will not be ridiculed for asking questions, no matter how simple or complex. It is helpful to empower them with a better understanding of types of questions and the purpose each serves. For example, reading a novel aloud to provoke, scaffold, and practise the asking of questions is a wonderful, quick way to encourage students to have discussions about categories of questions, and to raise students' awareness about how a question can signal confusion or ask for inference, or lead to more discussion.

Many read-aloud books embed the themes of persecution and compassion, but Marna's favourite is *Iqbal*, by Francesco D'Adamo (2003). Initially, Marna facilitated some simple activities to define "thick and thin" questions and to categorize questions so that students begin to think about effective questions (Harvey and Goudvis 2007).

Marna read aloud for 10 to15 minutes each morning, and asked her students to write three questions that came to mind as they listened. They could write on sticky notes or on an organizer that has room for questions before, during, and after the reading.

See pp. 131–134 for Nicole's set of lessons on how to develop more powerful questions.

- Compile the students' questions (no names attached) into a list in no particular order. Present the list to class the following day, and have students work in partners to categorize them.
- Debrief the class as a whole, and have students discuss their reasons for their choice of category.
- After the class has followed this process a few days and students have become comfortable with question categories, challenge them to develop one discussion question or research question out of the three questions they wrote down during each read-aloud session.
- At the front of the classroom, keep a running record of the student-generated discussion and research questions as a reminder of what they look and sound like. Marna used those questions to model to the class how one might begin to find information that might contribute to the answers. For example, if the question were "Why would a family give away their child to a carpet factory?" Marna might bring in a short

article explaining the effects of poverty, modelling a think-aloud, and show a section of text while describing how to determine importance of information and discover possible answers to this question (Harvey and Goudvis 2007).

Provocations

Use a text set to further develop student questions and possible topics for research. In order to expose students to a variety of topics or issues quickly without dense text, Marna and Jacquie used a text set, a collection of texts (books and/or articles) with a common genre, theme, author, topic, or purpose. This text set had mostly sophisticated picture books, articles, and nonfiction text pieces about a variety of events, people, and issues—both current and historical (Figure 6.4). Photos, artifacts, quotes, films, music, or stories are all effective ways to provoke students' curiosity and inspire questions.

- Students sit in an Information Circle with the text set books spread out in the middle.
- Students choose a book of interest to them to start with. They have a few minutes to examine it, then pass it to the right. The process gives them a sense of the range of events, issues, and stories included.

Figure 6.4 Inquiry text set on theme "Persecution and Compassion"

Inquiry Text Set
"Persecution and Compassion"
One Hen by Katie, Smith Milway
Planting the Trees of Kenya: The Story of Wangari Maathai, Claire A. Nivola
Brothers in Hope: The Story of the Lost Boys of Sudan, Mary Williams
The Carpet Boy's Gift, Pegi Deitz Shea
Shi-shi etko, Nicola Campbell
Shin-chi's Canoe, Nicola Campbell
Fatty Legs: A True Story, Christy Jordan-Fenton
This Child, Every Child: A Book About the World's Children, David Smith
Anne Frank, Josephine Poole
The Story of Ruby Bridges, Robert Coles
Rosa, Nikki Giovanni
Martin's Big Words: The Life of Dr. Martin Luther King, Jr., Doreen Rappaport
Confessions of a Former Bully, Trudy Ludwig
The Bracelet, Yoshiko Uchida
My Freedom Trip: A Child's Escape from North Korea, Frances Park and Ginger Park
(We added many more articles and non-fiction books, and often added to the text set according to the students in our classroom and the areas they expressed an interest in.)

- Debrief the students about the themes and issues they notice as they skim the books. Generate a list of themes and issues with the class (e.g., racism, bullying, segregation, courage, poverty, displacement, kindness, slavery, freedom). Discuss what they might learn when they actually read one or more of these books. The big ideas/concepts of "persecution" and "compassion" may surface through this discussion.
- The Frayer model (Figure 6.5) helps a class begin exploring big ideas or concepts. Give students time—individually or with a partner—to come up with examples and non-examples of one of the themes or issues they identified. The essential question can be introduced after students have completed and shared their Frayer models. (You may want to limit the focus to persecution and compassion.). This is a key step in setting up safe processes for student sharing in order to begin an ongoing, open dialogue about personal connections and new learning.

Frayer Model: <www.worksheetworks.com/ miscellanea/graphic-organizers/frayer.html>.

Using the text set, students choose a book or article that interests them in order to read and respond in more depth. This allows students to practise and apply thinking skills while reading, and further develop skill in shaping effective questions. It also gives students time to explore topics they might be interested in pursuing further. Marna provided time in class to read and respond, using a response organizer with categories as in Figure 6.6. She asked them to complete a response for a minimum of three pieces they had read; many students read more books and articles than that, but weren't asked to complete a response for every book. It's important to model how to use a Reading Response Organizer and allow students to practise each reading response skill. Then students use the back of their Organizer page (Figure 6.6) to note the examples of persecution and compassion they find in the articles and books they read.

Figure 6.5 The Frayer model for analyzing big ideas

Define in your own words.	Describe characteristics (What does it look, feel, sound like?)

(persecution/compassion)

Examples from your experience and/or background knowledge	Non-examples (When it doesn't happen and possible reasons why)

Figure 6.6 Layout for a Reading Response Organizer (front and back) for student notebooks

Activating prior knowledge: What do I already know about this topic?	
My questions (I wonder):	**My connections:**
Images that stay with me:	My response / reaction / opinion:

On the back of this organizer, have students start to collect evidence of the concepts, noting the examples they find in the articles and books they are reading.

Examples of Compassion (quote and page #)	**Examples of Persecution** (quote and page #)
p. ___	p. ___
p. ___	p. ___

Building criteria

- Build a set of criteria with your students for their responses. Don't make it onerous, but be clear about what you want them to demonstrate.
- Choose examples of good responses (or aspects of those responses) to share with the students on a regular basis. Discuss why each response "fully meets" the criteria, or ask them to tell you why they think it demonstrates the criteria. Give students an opportunity to improve on their own responses after these sessions. The class spent two weeks with the text set and, at the end of each week, Marna asked each student to choose their best response to hand in for assessment.
- It is important to give students regular feedback on the response skills they demonstrate and have regular conversations or individual conferences with them about what they are learning. A class Information Circle helps build class community, and lets you hear from everyone to get a sense of what students might be interested in pursuing.
- During a conference or in a circle, students bring their favourite book (or response) from the week, and share highlights of their learning (e.g., *What is the book about? What was the most interesting thing you learned? What sticks with you and why? What questions do you still have?*). It is during these conversations that students begin to get a sense of what their peers are interested in, hear about books they might want to read next, and talk about questions that they might want to develop.
- After four or more responses, have students list the topics and questions they feel most passionate about.

It is important to listen and encourage students to find such a topic. Sometimes, the text set is only a jumping off point for other topics that weren't included in the text set. Often, students will discover issues of persecution that have happened in their own family (e.g., Japanese internment camps or residential school experiences), or want to find out more about an organization that helps people (e.g., Doctors without Borders, Free the Children). In an authentic inquiry experience, students have to be allowed to investigate questions that they care about and are motivated to research and answer.

Locating, Selecting, and Evaluating Sources

Students best develop the following skills from The Points of Inquiry (Ekdahl, Farquharson, Robinson, and Turner 2010) in the context of their inquiry with the teacher-librarian and teacher:

- Evaluate resources and information critically for perspective, purpose, currency, authority, relevance, coverage, and quality.
- Check for reliability and credibility of a source.
- Understand the differences between the various tools and resources for searching, and use each appropriately.

- Prioritize resources by usefulness.
- Use different kinds of resources to expand and verify information.
- Use a graphic organizer to keep track of sources of information.
- Interpret information from graphic representations, statistics, and media sources.
- Use information responsibly.
- Report sources cited in appropriate format.

Before any research took place, Jacquie explicitly taught some of these skills—such as how to check for reliability and credibility, searching for and keeping track of many useful sources, and understanding various tools and resources for searching. However, students learned these skills best in the context of their own search for information, when both Jacquie and Marna could support their decisions around prioritizing, evaluating, and interpreting the sources and the information found. Sometimes, as a result of their observations, Jacquie and Marna would plan a follow-up mini-lesson or reminder lesson on key inquiry skills. Their collaboration was important in responding effectively to their students' needs, and for ensuring that they had the tools needed to find reliable information.

Finalizing individual topic questions

To support students in narrowing down their topics and their final questions, remind them that their question should reflect their real interests. Brainstorming sub-questions supports them in the process of developing the bigger research question. Again, Marna and Jacquie found it easiest to set up conference times with each student, and meet with them during a time while others finished their responses, developed and finalized their questions and began to locate and select relevant information that might contribute to their research. They had students use an organizer with headings:

Final Questions: Narrowing the Focus	
Question #1: Type	**Question #2:** Type
Sub-questions	Sub-questions

Student examples of inquiry questions

- What was a residential school? Why did these schools exist? What was their impact on First Nations communities?
- What is bonded child labour? Where does it occur? How can it be stopped?
- Why were Japanese Canadians taken to internment camps during World War II? What impact did the internment have on them?
- Who is the Dalai Lama? Why was he exiled to India?
- Who are Craig and Marc Kielburger? What have they accomplished and why is it important?
- Who was Martin Luther King? What did he accomplish and what was his impact as a leader?

Determining importance and citing sources

Students worked in the library for double blocks of time (two 45-minute blocks) twice a week. By this point, teachers should have signed off on students' main questions. Students should also have a list of at least 4 or more sources of information. They used a two-column fact/response sheet to record important ideas, samples of evidence, and the sources they were using.

Source Title: _____ Author: _____ Date: _____	_____ _____ _____
Facts/Important quotes p. ___	My connections, questions, reactions, thoughts

Marna used the class time between library blocks for mini-lessons on how to determine the importance of information, modelling strategies such as Marking Text. This strategy involves students marking their thinking on the text using sticky notes or an overhead transparency sheet. They could use a code such as: K for key idea, I for inference, Q for question, S for surprise, T:T for a text-to-text for connection, T:S for a text-to-self connection, and T:W for a text-to-world connection. Students' notes became the focus of their research for their next library time, and connected the information they were learning to their main questions (Figure 6.9). They wrote a summary of their findings to help them reflect on what they had learned, and to consider what they still needed to know.

Synthesize understanding

Students were expected to demonstrate their ability to mark their text as a strategy for determining its importance, to write a detailed response, and to provide evidence of their learning. Both half way through and at the end of the research for their project, students were also expected to:

- choose the best information article read so far, and provide a photocopy of the article that showed their marked text
- cite the source properly
- write one paragraph summarizing the article
- write four paragraphs working through reflective questions like *What did I learn? Why is this information important? How does it connect back to my questions? What do I still wonder about? What are my opinions about this information?*

- This process helped them ensure that they met all the criteria, and provided evidence to support their efforts. They included this self-evaluation along with their article and response.

Self-evaluation

- How did "marking text" help you better understand the article for this response? Explain.
- Select your two best sentences from your summary, and explain why you think they are the best.
- Give an example of new learning that helped answer your questions.
- Give an example of a thoughtful part of your response. Explain why you consider it "thoughtful."

Finally, Marna used the following criteria to give feedback on each student's response:

Organization

· Typed

· Photocopied article

· Rough draft

· Good copy with all parts of response included

Knowledge and Thought

· Marked text of article

· Summary captures gist of article

· Response is detailed and thoughtful

· Uses evidence from article to support ideas and opinions

· Response clearly connects important learning back to your questions

Writing Skills

· Response has been proofread (by a peer) and edited (by you!)

· Ideas are organized into paragraphs

Marna prepared feedback and a number of mini-lessons for the whole class after she marked the first set of responses — areas she felt they were strong in, and areas they needed to work on — so that they had an opportunity to improve their second response.

Sharing what we know now

Marna and Jacquie wanted students to be able to share their learning and exchange ideas and connections to the essential question with their peers. They asked students to prepare a five-minute talk with visuals for a small group of their classmates, with reference to the following:

Reporting out: My sharing outline

· Introduction: What are my major questions? Why did I become interested in them?

· First question and the answers/information I found out

· Second main questions and the answers/information I found out

· My response to what I learned: My thoughts, opinions, reactions to my learning and why

· Conclusion: What do I understand now about why people persecute others? What leads people to compassionate acts? How did my research help lead me to these conclusions?

As an optional part of the final presentation, Marna and Jacquie gave students an open-ended challenge to prepare a creative project that synthesized their learning and their conclusions about the essential question. The class brainstormed questions that would help them consider what to create: *Why do humans hurt each other? Why do they help each other? How does it feel to be persecuted? What is the impact? What does an act of kindness feel like? Why is it important?*

Encouraged to tap into their passions to represent their learning, students produced paintings, sculptures, poems, songs, short stories, structures, skits, and even movies that helped explore the essential question. When they presented their final product, they were asked to explain what they were trying to capture, and their peers shared positive feedback. This part ultimately takes more time, but asking students to tap in to other ways of showing what they know evokes powerful responses, honours different strengths and talents in each student, and demonstrates the many other ways that they can represent their learning.

Inquiry in a Differentiated Math Class

Something had to change for Brenton Close. Brent's classes were always diverse but as a group his class had a shorter collective attention span and greater disparity of pace and expertise than he had previously encountered in his rural school. Brent has been working to build open-ended teaching into his classroom, but this year several students struggled even with simple computation and the meaning of basic symbols; others showed signs of boredom almost every day; and in one lesson a grade 8 girl held a model of a cylinder, described the process for finding its surface area, and derived the surface area formula — all before he had set up the task! Two other students really benefited from repeatedly assembling and disassembling an actual model of the figure to determine how a cylinder is represented by a net drawing.

He realized that he needed an approach that allowed all students to work inductively with the big math ideas, to work at their own pace, but also to work in small groups of students to reinforce key concepts. Brent had heard about "flipped classrooms" (that is, providing students with electronic access to lessons and working with teachers only when they have questions), so he did some investigating. He saw promise in aspects of this approach, but wanted to ensure that he met the learning needs of all his students by using a variety of instructional techniques.

To do so, he created a website and started to record short lesson segments, then asked his students to work through the lessons at their own pace and do the assigned practice questions. Brent encompassed this within the framework of units of study designed to keep the class together as a cohesive social group. His intentions were to:

- help students focus during times of direct instruction to facilitate greater concentration.
- allow students to engage in and practice their learning at their own pace.
- encourage students to aim for mastery rather than bare-minimum passing grades.
- make better use of adults' time by providing more individual and small-group assistance for students.
- encourage inquiry study for students able to work through curricular material quickly and independently.

To implement this new approach, Brent designed a basic weekly structure (Figure 6.7) that allowed individual self-paced study through the middle of the week, with Mondays and Fridays focused on whole-class activities. Within the first week, he found that some adaptations were necessary. Many students embraced the idea of more accessibility to individual help, but others took the implicit freedom as an opportunity to escape mathematics, especially when they could find individual spaces to access Facebook or digital games.

Figure 6.7 Brent's weekly structure for grade 8 Math class

Monday (Whole-class or small-group activity)	• Problem solving: challenging, realistic problems • Vocabulary: word wall, personal math dictionary, modelling on mini-whiteboards
Tuesday	1. Introductory exercise: multiplication drill, 1-question or 2-question quiz, question of the day on mini-whiteboards
Wednesday	2. Independent study: students work on curricular assignments at their own pace, either viewing lesson recordings or completing practice questions as quiet seatwork
Thursday	
Friday (Reserved for 5-day weeks, so that if we miss a day at any time, the activities are shuffled accordingly)	• Games Day – logic games, strategy games, problem solving games, First Nations traditional games … all played either in small groups or as a whole class *None* of the games we played were technology based *All* of them involved students moving in the classroom, interacting with each other.

Brent divided the students who either struggled to work on their own or avoided any assigned work among himself, the classroom assistant, and the First Nations support worker so that each student had one adult monitoring their progress quite closely. He asked a small group of students to abandon the recorded lessons altogether, and to work through lessons and assignments with direct assistance from Brent himself.

During the independent study part of the week, Brent expected students working at all levels to be engaged in mathematics on a continual basis—watching recorded lessons, completing practice questions, working with a teacher or classroom assistant, or working independently. He spot-checked completed practice assignments for accuracy, and worked with students to have them correct errors in methodology before they considered each assignment finished. At the end of each unit of study, the class wrote the unit test together at the same time.

Brent invited the students who had worked quickly and accurately through curricular assignments to use their class time on an inquiry project of personal interest that involved mathematics (Figure 6.8). He wanted to expose students to some applications of mathematics in real life.

Figure 6.8 Inquiry project for Mr. Close's Math classes

Inquiry in Mathematics

Your project is intended to extend your mathematical thinking into one or more areas of personal interest, and to help you learn something beautiful about mathematics. Your choice of topic can be personal and individual to you, but your teacher must approve its relevance to the study of mathematics. The following ideas might help you select a topic for inquiring into the use of mathematics:

Number systems (e.g., binary, hexadecimal, dozenal)	Cryptography	Art (e.g., painting, sculpture, origami)
Architecture	Music (music notation or a musical instrument)	Nature (e.g., patterns in nature, plants, landforms, water)
Fractals	Space (e.g., natural order of celestial bodies)	Space travel and technology
Microbiology	Computer programming	Business and accounting
Finance	Investment	Stock markets
Publishing	2-D or 3-D Animation	Trades (e.g., carpentry, electrical system, instrumentation, fabricating, machining)
Flight (e.g., kites, airplanes, helicopters)	City planning	Demographic study
War (e.g., logistics, movement of troops and equipment)	Water treatment (e.g., personal, municipal, or systems in developing countries)	Economics
Farming	Genetic engineering	Tessellations
Nanotechnology	Robotics	

Writing an Inquiry Question

The question you phrase as the topic of your research is the most important part of your project because it states your purpose and provides the focus for your final presentation. Your question must be thoughtful and challenging to answer. In some cases, you might not end up with an "answer," but the process of trying and learning about the topic can still make a great project. Your inquiry question must be approved by your teacher. The following might help guide you to a great question:

• What is it that most interests you about the topic you have selected?

• What do you most wonder about when you think about that topic?

• Does the question you are wondering about have a simple answer or will it likely lead you on a path of discovery?

© Portage & Main Press, 2014, *It's All About Thinking: Creating Pathways for All Learnings in the Middle Years*, BLM, ISBN 978-1-55379-509-4

Figure 6.8 cont'd

Final Product Options

Your final product is your chance to present the results of your research and what you learned along the way, and to share your learning with your teacher, support workers, and classmates. Your final product should respond to the following:

- What is the topic, and how does it relate to mathematics? (Describe it and define it for people who might not know anything about it.)
- What made you choose this topic? What aspects of the topic are of personal interest to you?
- What did you learn about your inquiry question?

Here are a few options. You are welcome to use an idea of your own, as long as your idea is approved by your teacher before you put hours of work into it.

- Poster
- PowerPoint slide show
- Illustrated essay
- Construction project with oral or written explanation
- Product of choice, with teacher approval

Self-Assessment

Your self-assessment should include a brief written reflection on each of these questions:

- What aspect of the project do you believe you have done well?
- What you would like to change or do differently next time?

Assessment

In the final assessment of your project, I will consider both the time and the effort that you put into your work, and the quality of your final self-assessment reflections. Here is a breakdown of how your inquiry project will be assessed.

Area of Assessment	Scale				Weighting	Mark
Preliminary research (3 topics)	1	2	3	4	x 1	
Inquiry question	1	2	3	4	x 1	
Connection to mathematics	1	2	3	4	x 1	
Final product: Creative and attractive presentation	1	2	3	4	x 2	
Final product: Amount and accuracy of content information	1	2	3	4	x 3	
Sources: Number and quality (Sources must be cited)	1	2	3	4	x 2	
Self-assessment reflection	1	2	3	4	x 3	

Developing Powerful Questions in Humanities

When Nicole began to introduce her grade 6/7 class to the inquiry process for the first time, she felt that it was important for the whole class to work on a common theme, so that her modelling and their learning would occur in a community of learners.

When the class was working in social studies on the theme of persecution, Nicole had them begin reading the novel *Iqbal*, by Francesco D'Adamo (2003), during their Reader's Workshop block of time. *Iqbal* is a powerful, true story that often hooks readers right away. It tells the heroic story of a young boy from Pakistan who stood up for his rights as a bonded child labourer in a carpet-making factory. Often, students are shocked to hear that this kind of treatment happens in our world today. They become passionate and want to know more. Their wonderings are genuine and caring.

To help develop the students' questioning around this idea, Nicole created lessons to identify different kinds of questions and determine which are more powerful. She began her own research on questioning by looking closely at Jeffrey Wilhelm's *Improving Comprehension with Think-Aloud Strategies* (2001). Wilhelm provides a lovely visual of question types for the inquiry approach. Nicole began to think about the following four kinds of questions:

"In the Text" Questions	"In Your Head" Questions
• Right There	• Author and Me
• Think and Search	• On My Own

The question for Nicole, then, was how to represent these in her lessons so that students could use the information in a thoughtful way. She began by providing the students with an essential question to consider for the entire unit:

What experiences does Iqbal have and what choices does he make that shape who he is?

Nicole decided that the final performance-based assessment would be a questiongram and, with that end in mind, she developed lessons that supported her students in two ways:

1. in their understanding of different kinds of questions
2. in understanding how research/responses lead to success with the final assessment.

To do this, she modelled the skills that students would need to build in order to be successful, and outlined steps that would lead to just that.

- Each week, students work in small Literature Circles.
- At the beginning of the week, they read together and develop a two-column note-taking organizer with headings "My Thinking" (on left) and "Evidence" (on right).

- Students return the following day and use the organizer as an aid in their Literature Circle discussion. In addition, students use the "Say Something" strategy (Brownlie 2005) in which students take turns sharing one quote from the book and describing their thoughts about it. After everyone takes their turn sharing, the conversation opens up and becomes more fluid.
- During the third class of a weekly cycle, students continue working in their Literature Circle groups to compose a "response-write."

This routine continued for 3 to 4 weeks to allow lots of practice, both collaboratively and independently, and of modelling (gradual release) before Nicole began the questiongram performance-based assessment. This gave students the time to develop the skills required for the questiongram (Figure 6.10). Nicole returned to the essential question and reminded students that this activity would help them connect what they read, different kinds of questions, and the various texts they had read.

My Thinking/Evidence

Before digging into the novel, Nicole built background knowledge with her students by using the picture book *The Carpet Boy's Gift*, by Pegi Deitz Shea (2006). She provided chart paper to each desk grouping of four students and asked them to write, as she read the book aloud, their thoughts and questions, creating a "graffiti wall." She had previously noted that there were no right or wrong thoughts or questions, and it was okay to scribble them all down. After the end of the story, she asked the groups to pick out their most important ideas on the graffiti wall. As the groups shared, Nicole recorded their thinking. During the next class, she returned to this list as she modelled how to insert their thinking into a graphic organizer like a T-chart:

Book Title	
My Thinking/Questions	Evidence

Students recorded their list of thoughts and questions from the story in the left column. Then they looked for specific evidence that supported their thinking to record in the right column. Nicole's modelling of how to use the organizer gave students the chance to explore this process both in small groups and as an entire class. The picture book, with its small amount of text at an entry reading level and its pictures, was suitable for all learners. When students asked her "How many do I have to do?," Nicole suggested they find 3 to 5 points, allowing students to make their own decisions based on what they felt they could thoughtfully contribute. This lesson purposely prepared students for the questiongram performance-based assessment.

Understanding Question Types for Inquiry Approach

Nicole also wanted her class to explore different types of questions and help them learn to apply this knowledge across curricula. She developed a table (Figure 6.9) to help them organize the names of question types (in the left column) and brief descriptions and examples (in the right column). Together the class modelled what they thought each question type might sound like and added it to the chart. Wanting to take student thinking further, Nicole modified Figure 6.9 by covering the examples provided on the right side and copying the page again for her students to try coming up with their own examples, either together with a partner or the class or alone. By allowing her students time to talk, she further benefitted their learning. It reinforced the skill and gave her an opportunity to assess student understanding.

Response-Write

The response-write activity (Figure 6.9) pulled together the idea of shaping powerful responses and of stretching student thinking to provide evidence that supports that response—the skills needed for the summative (performance-based) assessment. Nicole modelled the following example in front of the class; later, she provided a copy to the students who found the exercise difficult and needed a sample to support them. Most students started off by relying on the sentence starters modelled, but by the end, most grasped the concept and were able to write without the structures put in place.

Figure 6.9A Kinds of Questions/Now You Try

Question	What you need to know...
Right-There Questions	• Factual questions • Answer is found in the text • Yes or no answer **For example:** What is the Master's name?
Think-and-Search Questions	• You need to infer, that is, think about it, then try to piece together the details from the book (search) to come to an answer (*inference*). • Try to fill in important gaps in the text by searching to find evidence for a hunch you may have. **For example:** Why do the child slaves think life will be better with Iqbal's arrival?
Author-and-Me Questions	• Connect your own life experiences and beliefs with the text **For example:** How would you react to Iqbal when he says, "Have you ever seen anyone pay off their debt?" (p. 20) What does the author want me to think about Salman's response to Iqbal when Iqbal tries to tell them that Hussain Khan is not a nice man?
On-Your-Own Questions	• Questions usually stirred by the events, topics, or theme of the text. However, the answers to these questions are not found in the text. • Think about the book's issues in a much wider context (the world) and raise questions about those issues. **For example:** What are the causes of and solutions to child labour? How would it feel to be a child slave? What can I/we do to help end child labour?

Figure 6.9B Response-write activity

> **I think I will use the question:** *"Does the kite represent the idea of freedom to Fatima?"* (p. 57)
>
> I will try to use specific evidence from the novel as I write. "On page 57, the quote I found connects my thinking to the idea of a kite being a possible symbol of freedom:
>
>> "You run and the kite rises higher and higher in the sky; sometimes it even touches the clouds, and it soars and veers with the wind. You have to be very careful, though. If you let go of the string, you lose the kite and after a while it floats away."
>
> Now that I have some evidence, I think that I can interpret it.
>
> Some suggested sentence starters might include:
>
>> *I think … because …*
>> *This connects with … because …*
>> *This is important because …*
>
> I think the kite is important because Fatima thinks of it as her key to freedom. I know this because she explains how the kite "rises higher and higher…and veers with the wind." This makes me think that Fatima may compare herself to the kite.
>
> *End with a connection, a thought, a feeling.*
>
> I feel hopeful for Fatima because freedom is what every child deserves instead of being required to work long, hard hours for a master.

Figure 6.10 Process for questiongram activity

Literature Circle Questiongram

"Thinking about Our Essential Question"

Process:

1. In thinking about the Literature Circle books you have read, record the following essential question in the middle of your paper:

   What experiences does Iqbal have and what choices does he make that shape who he is?

2. On the inside ring, attach quotes from the novels you read that provide evidence relevant to the essential question. Choose a character from one or more of the novels you read when thinking about how to respond to the essential question. You have read at least 3 novels, so try to include a character from each of them.

3. On the middle ring, include images that reflect your thinking. The images can be drawn, taken from the computer, cut from a magazine, and so on.

4. On the outside ring (the perimeter of your paper), include connections (T-S, T-T, T-W) or the wonderings you still have about to your essential question.

Example:

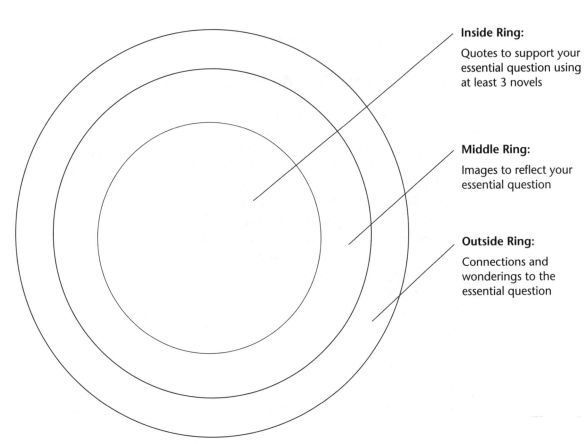

Inside Ring:

Quotes to support your essential question using at least 3 novels

Middle Ring:

Images to reflect your essential question

Outside Ring:

Connections and wonderings to the essential question

Figure 6.11 Literature Circle questiongram criteria

Criteria for Literature Circle Questiongram

What choices does Iqbal make and what experiences does he have that shape who he is?

Mark	Criteria
4	5 or 6 quotes support your essential question
	4 or 5 powerful images that reflect the essential question
	Strong connections and/or wonderings relate to your essential question
3	3 or 4 quotes support your essential question
	3 or 4 powerful images that reflect the essential question
	Some connections and/or wonderings
2	Few quotes
	Few images
	Few connections and/or wonderings
1	Limited response; few quotes included
	Few to no images
	Few to no connections and/or wonderings

(Adapted from *Student Diversity*, Brownlie and Feniak, 1998)

Deep Inquiry Learning: An Integrative Unit

Open-ended learning through inquiry invites more than one question, more than one answer, and more than one way of thinking. Instead of arriving at the same place at the same time, we want to generate multiple approaches and ideas within an activity or a task. Darcy McNee, Nadine Stofer, and Sandi Johnson, all classroom teachers, have worked together at North Saanich Middle School for several years. Sandi and Nadine have team-taught in an open classroom model for eight years, while Darcy has had her own classroom. For the past four years, these three teachers have collaboratively planned their units across all core subjects, often integrating the disciplines to facilitate deeper and broader learning and to meet students' diverse needs. Their collaboration has allowed all three teachers to deliver the same curriculum and assessments, and allows each to bring her own strengths to the planning and instruction, creating a rich foundation for their students.

Forensic Science

North Saanich recently moved to a model of ten combined grades 7/8 classes. In order to accommodate them and ensure students were not repeating curriculum, the teachers created a Forensic Science unit, integrating the grade 7 and grade 8 Prescribed Learning Outcomes (PLOs) in Chemistry and Optics. In a highly engaging unit with numerous hands-on activities, their backward design plan provided an opportunity for students to choose how to best demonstrate their learning, and to meet the widely diverse needs of students within these classrooms.

They decided which big ideas were needed to solidify student learning (Figure 6.12), and decided that the final product would be a Crime Scene Investigation.

Figure 6.12 Crime Scene Investigation (CSI) Unit Map

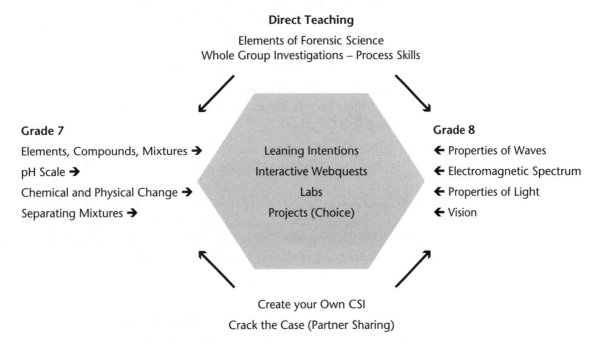

Big Ideas Phrased as Questions

- What is forensic science?
- How can we use forensic science to understand and solve problems and issues?
- How do we use forensic science to develop understanding in the curricular areas of chemistry and optics?
- How can we use forensic science to reinforce the science process skills?
- How can we examine forensic science to understand how science is used in the real world?

Direct Teaching of Elements of Forensic Science

They began the unit with direct teaching of forensic science skills—processing a crime scene, interviewing witnesses, handling evidence, and documenting the crime scene. Students used labs for hands-on explorations of topics such as fingerprinting, hair analysis, bite marks, and tire track impressions to practise and solidify these process skills.

Grade 7—Separating mixtures

To demonstrate prerequisite skills for separating mixtures, teachers gave groups of students baby-food jars filled with two or three different items (from *BC Science Probe 7*, Carmichael et al. 2006, p.150). Students followed the inquiry method by brainstorming methods they could use to separate the items. For one jar that held marbles and nails, one student group used a magnet to extract the nails, another used a pair of tweezers to pick apart the mixture. Students further explored the concept using interactive sites online.

Hands-on application of skill and knowledge

Students then used their knowledge and skills to complete a hands-on, concept-based crime lab (Figure 6.13).

> **Note to Teacher:** Prepare your evidence jars ahead of time. Wide-mouth Mason jars work best. They should contain water, mud, iron fillings, tar, grass, blond hair, sand, wood chips, salt, and oil in differing combinations and quantities Each group should receive a jar with a different label. Only one of these jars should have all of the substances—this is the guilty party. You also need ice cream buckets, magnets, paper filters, mesh filters, tweezers, evidence bags, labels, magnifying glasses, and petri dishes.

Planning for project

Students chose how to demonstrate the knowledge they acquired while researching the essential question. The teachers allowed them to complete a project, either independently or in small groups, and gave them a copy of the Forensic Science: Project Planning Guide and Rubric with evaluation terms for self-assessment (Figure 6.14). They discussed with their students the different ways they could demonstrate their learning —including Glogster, Prezi, PowerPoint, mind maps, models, written stories, songs, taped interviews, and YouTube. As well, they provided time and support during class, as needed, and encouraged the students to work toward their strengths. When projects were completed, students shared their projects during a presentation process for the whole class, and received feedback from both their peers and their teachers. From beginning to end, the process inspired and motivated students to try new ways to represent their learning, take risks, and take their learning deeper.

Figure 6.13 Project: Crime Scene Investigation

Project: Crime Scene Investigation
of death in Gowland Todd Provincial Park

Part One

Your challenge

To think like a CSI Scientist while examining evidence collected, plan a method of separating your mixture, and come to a conclusion (based on your evidence) to prove the innocence or guilt of the suspect.

Your team will be provided with a water sample from inside the suspect's boot that you are to investigate. Prior to extracting and separating the substances from your mixture sample, devise a plan for separation so that you do not destroy any evidence. Once you extract each substance, you need to preserve it in a labelled evidence bag because it is needed as evidence when the case goes to court. Then, examine your evidence to conclude whether the suspect could have committed this crime.

Preliminary collection of evidence

Saturday, April 18, an assault occurred on the edge of a salty marsh in Gowland Todd Provincial Park. The victim, a 5' 4" blonde, Caucasian female, had been struck by a hard object, presumably a metal bar. When the police arrived, they found a suspect in the area. Gowland Todd is a popular trail used by hikers and, therefore, many sets of footprints were found, but with no distinctive footwear. However, the police did find that the suspect's boots had water in them.

Secondary evidence

The salt marsh where the assault occurred is accessible on foot by a public hiking trail through a golf course. The hiking trail's surface is woodchips while the ground where the assault occurred is fine white sand. The only access to the hiking trail is through the parking lot at the nearby golf course. The golf course parking lot has recently been resurfaced with asphalt. While walking through the parking lot, police notice an oil stain, perhaps a leak from a car's engine. There is a small blacksmith's shack on the perimeter of the golf course close to where the victim was found.

© Portage & Main Press, 2014, *It's All About Thinking: Creating Pathways for All Learnings in the Middle Years*, BLM, ISBN 978-1-55379-509-4

Figure 6.13 cont'd

Part Two: Plan

Observation: What do you see in your sample?

_____

_____

_____

_____

Identify the PH (acidity or alkalinity) of your sample

_____

Separation techniques

Substance	Method

Conclusion

Could this suspect be the guilty party? Why or Why not?

How do you explain all the materials present in the sample?

_____

_____

_____

_____

Figure 6.14 Forensic Science: Project Planning Guide and self-assessment rubric

Forensic Science: Project Planning Guide

Learning Intentions

I can explain how forensic science is used in the real world.

I can explain how _____

_____

_____

_____

Ways to Show What You Know	My Plan: Sketch, list or describe the end result of your project.
• Create 2D art (i.e., cartoon, painting, drawing or diagram). • Perform a dramatic piece. • Create something with technology (movie, prezi, glogster, PowerPoint). • Write a newspaper article. • Create 3D art (i.e., pottery, papier-mâché, sculpture) • Write a song. • Negotiate another project with the teachers.	

Project Due Date: _____

Reality Check:

☐ Do I feel confident in my overall plan? Is it realistic?

☐ Do I know what materials I need? Do I know where to find them?

☐ Can I manage my time so that so I can work at a comfortable pace without cramming it all in at the last minute?

© Portage & Main Press, 2014, It's All About Thinking: Creating Pathways for All Learnings in the Middle Years, BLM, ISBN 978-1-55379-509-4

Figure 6.14 cont'd

Forensic Science: Project Rubric

	Good Start!	On Your Way!	You Are There!	Wow!
Demonstration of Knowledge and Learning Outcomes	Demonstration of knowledge is under developed. May contain vague or inaccurate information.	Demonstration of knowledge is generally straight forward and clear. Unevenly developed.	Demonstration of knowledge is fully developed and shows depth.	Demonstration of knowledge is fully developed and shows depth and originality.
	Product demonstrates a minimal understanding of learning intentions.	Product demonstrates a basic understanding of learning intentions.	Product demonstrates a thorough understanding of learning intentions.	Product demonstrates an insightful understanding of learning intentions.

Grade 8—Inquiry Using Online Interactive Websites

Optical illusions
Students went to computer stations to explore and discuss different illusions like Blind Spot and Size of the Moon from <www.indiana.edu/~ensiweb/lessons/unt.illu.html> and others from <www.opticalillusions.com>.

Eyeball dissection
This webquest (Figure 6.15) allowed all students to engage independently with the concepts, while enabling easy adaptations such as closed captioning, text reader, and others.

Hands-on Application of Skills and Knowledge

Students then use their knowledge and skills to complete a hands-on, process-based lab in which they follow a procedure to dissect a cow's or sheep's eye. The point is to gain an understanding of the eye, of dissection skills, and of forensic pathology (Figure 6.16).

Figure 6.15 Webquest Activity 8

C.S.I. Investigator Training

The Eye and Dissection Skills

Go to this website: <studyjams.scholastic.com/studyjams/jams/science/human-body/seeing.htm>. Observe and listen, filling in the blanks in the following statements.

1. The parts of the eye work together to _____ light and send _____ about it to our brain.

2. Pupils are the _____ , _____ part of our eye that lets light travel _____ it. They control the _____ of light that _____ the eye. In the dark, our pupils are _____ and in bright light they _____.

3. The coloured part of the eye is called the _____. These are usually _____ , _____ or _____.

4. _____ in the iris control the _____ of the pupil.

5. We need our eyes, _____ and _____ in order to see.

6. The light passes through the _____ , the transparent outer layer of the eyeball that covers the iris and pupil.

7. The _____ is under the cornea and together they _____ the light rays that pass through them, like a _____ in a movie theatre.

8. It projects an _____ image on the retina.

9. The _____ is the lining at the back of the eyeball. It is _____ to light. When light hits the retina, it _____ off the things you see to the brain through the _____.

10. The optic nerve is a _____ of nerves that sends _____ between the retina and the _____.

Click on "Close" and then "Test Yourself"
Go to page two.

© Portage & Main Press, 2014, *It's All About Thinking: Creating Pathways for All Learnings in the Middle Years*, BLM, ISBN 978-1-55379-509-4

Figure 6.15 cont'd

Page Two

Go to the following web site: <www.brainpop.com/>.

Click "Log in" then username: northsaanich password: vikings

Click Health > Body Systems > Eyes

How is your eye like a film camera?

1. The lens _____ it _____ , depending on

   what you are trying to focus, just like a camera _____ .

2. The retina acts like the _____ in the camera.

3. When a camera lens focuses an image on film, it ends up

   _____ . When the lens of your eye focuses an image on

   your retina, it also ends up _____ .

Draw it:

Pick an object in the room. Daw the object the way you see it in one square.
Draw it in another square the way you think it might appear on your retina.

Take the Graded Quiz. Record your answers here:

1. _____   6. _____

2. _____   7. _____

3. _____   8. _____

4. _____   9. _____

5. _____   10. _____

Figure 6.15 cont'd

Page Three

Go to the following website: <www.eschoolonline.com/company/examples/eye/eyedissect.html>.

Click on the Eye Anatomy to help you identify the following parts of the eye.

You can click on the view of sliced eye to help you as well.

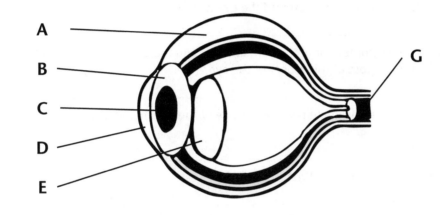

A: _____   B: _____   C: _____

D: _____   E: _____   F: _____

G: _____

Close the window and try the virtual eye dissection. Go to the following website: <www.exploratorium.edu/learning_studio/cow_eye/index.html>. Click "Watch Online," then click "Watch Step One Video." After each step, click on "Next Video."

© Portage & Main Press, 2014, *It's All About Thinking: Creating Pathways for All Learnings in the Middle Years*, BLM, ISBN 978-1-55379-509-4

Figure 6.15 cont'd

Page Four

Video 1: Why do they do cow eye dissections at the Exploratorium?

_____

Video 2: How are the muscles in cow eyes and human eyes different? How does this affect the movement of the eyes?

_____

Video 3: What does the fat around the eye do?

_____

Video 4: What comes out of the cornea when you make your first incision? What is the purpose of this aspect of the eye?

_____

Video 5: What is the white part on the side of the eye that you cut in order to cut off the cornea?

_____

Video 6: What is the iris? What shape is it?

_____

Video 7: What does the vitreous humor look like, what is it made of, and what does it do?

_____

Video 8: How is the lens like an onion?

_____

Video 9: What does the lens act like?

_____

Video 10: What does the retina do?

_____

Video 11: What is the spot that the retina is attached called?

_____

Video 12: What does your retina become?

_____

Video 13: How is the back of human eyes different from the back of a cow's or a cat's eyes?

_____

Investigator Training: Dissection Skills

A forensic pathologist is a specialized CSI investigator who performs dissections in order to solve crimes. In this lab, you will dissect a cow's eye in order to gain an understanding of dissection skills and of the eye.

Safety first!

You will use a scalpel or a razor to cut the cow's eye. Be careful. These tools can cut you just as easily. Whenever you handle raw meat, you must wash your hands thoroughly afterward to wash away any bacteria you picked up from the meat.

Materials

- One cow's eye for every two participants
- One single-edged razor blade or scalpel for every two participants
- Scissors and tweezers
- Wax paper and paper towels
- Dissection tray
- A sheet of newspaper
- Gloves
- Eye protection

Diagram of eye before dissection

1. Examine the outside of the cow's eye. See how many parts of the eye you can identify. Draw a diagram and label it.

2. Use the scissors to cut away the fat and muscle.

3. Use a scalpel to make an incision in the cornea. (Careful! Don't cut yourself!) Cut until the clear liquid, the aqueous humor, under the cornea is released.

4. Use the scalpel to make an incision through the sclera in the middle of the eye. Then use your scissors to cut around the middle of the eye, cutting the eye in half, so you have two halves, with the front half having the cornea. Draw a diagram with these labels: Front half with Cornea; Back half of Eye

5. Remove the cornea and place it on the tray; then cut it with your scalpel. Your scalpel will crunch through layers of clear tissue.

6. The next step is to pull out the iris. The iris is between the cornea and the lens. It may be stuck to the cornea or it may have stayed with the back of the eye. Find it and pull it out. It should come out in one piece. Draw a diagram of the dissected iris.

© Portage & Main Press, 2014, *It's All About Thinking: Creating Pathways for All Learnings in the Middle Years*, BLM, ISBN 978-1-55379-509-4

Figure 6.16 cont'd

7. Remove the lens. It's a clear lump about the size and shape of a squashed marble. Hold the lens up and look through it. Put the lens down on a newspaper and look through it at the words on the page. Draw what you see, using these titles: Looking through Lens; Lens on Newspaper

8. If the vitreous humor is still in the eyeball, empty it out. On the inside of the back half of the eyeball, you will see some blood vessels that are part of a thin fleshy film. That film is the retina.

9. Use your finger to push the retina around. The retina is attached to the back of the eye at just one spot. Can you find that spot? That's the place where nerves from all the cells in the retina come together. All these nerves go out the back of the eye, forming the optic nerve, this bundle of nerves carries messages from the eye to the brain. Draw a diagram of the retina

10. Under the retina, the back of the eye is covered with shiny, blue-green film. This is the tapetum. It reflects light from the back of the eye.

11. Look at the other side of the back of the eye. Can you find the optic nerve? To see the separate fibers that make up the optic nerve, pinch the nerve with a pair of tweezers or your fingers. Diagram of Retina

Clean-up

Follow your teacher's directions for disposal and clean-up procedures.

Conclusion

Reflect and respond to the following questions:

1. How did this dissection add to your understanding of the parts and functions of the eye?

2. Why is it very important to document (draw labeled diagrams) as you complete the dissection.

Project Based on Learning Outcomes

The Project Planning Guide and Rubric (Figure 6.14) for the grade 7s can also be used for the grade 8 project. At this point in the unit, the grade 7s and the grade 8s had been working concurrently to solve crimes (based on the learning outcomes for their grade) via the online interactive webquests, labs, and student projects. These outcomes were framed as focus questions for students to answer.

Grade 7 Learning outcomes as focus questions

- How can we use our understanding of elements, compounds, and mixtures to explain the behaviour of matter?
- How can we use our understanding of the pH scale to explain the properties of acids and bases?
- How can we use our understanding of chemical and physical changes to explain the reactions of matter?
- How does our knowledge of the behaviour of matter allow us to separate mixtures?

Grade 8 Learning outcomes as focus questions

- How can we use our understanding of the properties of waves to explain the behaviour of waves?
- How can we use our understanding of waves to explain the electromagnetic spectrum?
- How can we use our understanding of the properties of visible light to explain the behaviour of visible light?
- How can we use our understanding from dissecting an eyeball to explain how the eye functions?

Interactive webquests were created using a number of web-based materials such as Brain Pop, Study Jam, and BBC Bitesize Learning, among others. These sites gave students opportunities to interact with the concepts independently—watch videos, play games, and take self-marking quizzes. Teachers could easily adapt these webquests to meet diverse learning needs. Students solidified the concepts they learned through the webquests in the hands-on labs, then took this learning further in their projects.

The CSI labs

Sandi, Darcy, and Nadine ran labs concurrently for students to explore further the grade-specific PLOs in non-violent crimes. The students had to use the forensic process skills previously learned and combine them with what they learned from the webquests to solve the crime. These labs offered students a chance to see real-world applications of the skills they were developing.

Cumulative Project

Throughout the unit, students were reminded of the summative assessment for which they would have to create their own Final Scene, independently or in partners. The assignment:

> *"Choose a CSI topic (impressions, fibres, fingerprinting, chromatography) to explore.*
>
> *Create a CSI crime scene and present it to a partner and together use CSI skills to solve the crime."*

In order to prepare the students for this final project, the teachers created mini crime scenes for them to solve (Figure 6.17). This highly engaging activity demonstrated how to combine the process skills with the learning objectives. It also gave our students choices in how to frame their own crime scene.

Assessment of Project

The structure of the unit allowed for assessment *of* learning through completed webquests, lab reports, and the culminating project, and for assessment *for* learning through the projects, in which students could self-assess and receive peer and teacher feedback. As students worked their way through these assessments, they showed tremendous growth in both their learning and the ways in which they represented their understanding. Their repeated exposure to the curriculum brought deeper understanding of each concept studied.

This Forensic Science unit proved to be very engaging for the students, and they gained a deeper appreciation for the application of science in our world.

Conclusion

Learning through inquiry can be messy, but it helps us rethink what is taught, how it is taught, and how learning is assessed. Learners learn from posing questions, investigating those questions, and working with multiple resources offering different perspectives. Project-based learning requires us to know our students and help them develop their passions, their skills, and their capacity for research and representation. All forms of inquiry are best served by students being in the driver's seat for their own learning—by having *choice* in what they inquire into, in the resources they access, and in their methods of documentation and representation. Students work toward creating their own understanding instead of guessing the responses their teachers might want or of replicating what has been handed to them.

Yet, in all the examples of inquiry in this chapter, there is a role for teacher-led instruction. Matt guides learners in developing their inquiry skills

Figure 6.17 CSI Scenes to examine and determine applicability to suspect

Examining Evidence

Station #1

A torn T-shirt was found in the back seat of a suspect's car. Two pieces of torn cloth were found at the scene of the crime.

Are the two pieces a match to the t-shirt found in the suspect's car? Explain your thinking.

Station #2

A note was found at a crime scene at a bank. A notepad with a similar type of paper was found in the desk drawer of the prime suspect.

Can the note be traced to the pad? Explain.

Can fingerprints on the note be traced to a person? Explain.

Station #3

A shoe print was found at the scene of a hit-and-run automobile accident.

How can a suspect's shoe be matched to a print? Explain.

Station #4

Some powder was found in a plastic bag in the suspect's pocket. A similar powder was found on the victim.

How could you determine whether the two powders are the same? Explore and explain.

Station #5

A piece of duct tape was taken from a victim of a Break and Enter. This piece of duct tape had hair fibres stuck to it. A roll of the same brand of duct tape was found at the suspect's home.

How can you determine if the piece of tape came off the roll found at the suspect's home? Explain.

Station #6

A glass with a lovely lipstick pattern was left at the crime scene. There were several women who had entered the victim's apartment over the last week. They have all willingly given a lip print.

Does the lip print on the glass match any of the suspects?

To process the evidence at each station, read the evidence card and determine whether the evidence collected by the investigators can be matched to the suspect in custody.

© Portage & Main Press, 2014, *It's All About Thinking: Creating Pathways for All Learnings in the Middle Years*, BLM, ISBN 978-1-55379-509-4

and helps his students create a schema of what inquiry is. Marna and Jacquie use think-alouds and model learning strategies. Nicole teaches students about different kinds of questions, and supports them in developing this key skill. Brent uses inquiry as an extension in mathematics. Students choose topics of interest to them, and Brent conferences with them to support them in developing their questions and inquiry plan. Darcy, Nadine, and Sandi take science back to its roots—they teach their students content-specific inquiry through inquiry.

Chapter 7

Creating Pathways through Social-Emotional Learning

Educators Involved

Marna Macmillan: Classroom Teacher/Learning Support Coordinator, SD 43, Coquitlam, BC

Sabre Cherkowski: Assistant Professor, Faculty of Education, UBC Okanagan, Kelowna, BC

Kim Ondrik: Classroom Teacher, SD 22, Vernon, BC

Murray Sasges: Classroom Teacher, SD 22, Vernon, BC

Julie Hearn: Classroom Teacher, SD 42, Maple Ridge, BC

When teaching middle years students, it's crucial that we attend to their social-emotional learning (SEL). By building students' understanding of personal and social responsibility, we help them construct their identity, their character, and their connections to others. When talking with parents about their hopes for their children, we are amazed by how often a strengths-based list emerges that does not include many, if any, traditional academic skills. Instead, the list includes words like caring, empathetic, happy, adaptive, compassionate, cooperative, along with phrases like good relationship skills, responsible decision maker, active citizen, makes healthy choices, and emotionally, mentally, and physically healthy.

Creating a safe, caring learning environment where healthy, trusting relationships are important used to be considered "the invisible curriculum." In the last decade, however, research into social-emotional learning has exploded, and we now have a deeper understanding of the importance of such a learning environment. We educators should—with explicit intention—promote and nurture these attributes in our classrooms and our school communities.

Social-emotional learning is an integral aspect of middle years philosophy. We asked Marna Macmillan from School District 43 and Sabre Cherkowski from UBC Okanagan, who have been thinking about and exploring social and emotional learning for years, to share their wisdom and experience. Marna and Sabre co-authored the opening sections of this chapter.

Developing a Learning Community

According to the Collaborative for Academic, Social, and Emotional Learning (CASEL), social-emotional learning "involves the processes of developing social and emotional competencies in children." It is reflected in five core capacities:

- self-awareness
- self-management
- social awareness
- relationship skills
- responsible decision making

The research supports a direct link to academic success when these capacities are nurtured and promoted in a supportive, engaging learning environment (Achor 2011).

Social and emotional learning is based on the understanding that the best learning happens in the context of supportive relationships that make learning challenging, engaging, and meaningful. Social and emotional skills are critical to being a good student, citizen, and worker. Many risky behaviours (e.g., drug use, violence, bullying, dropping out) can be prevented or reduced when integrated efforts are made year over year to develop students' social and emotional skills. This is best done through effective classroom instruction, student engagement in positive activities in and out of the classroom, and parent and community involvement in program planning, implementation, and evaluation (Bond and Carmola-Hauf 2004; Hawkins, Smith, and Catalano 2004; Nation et al. 2003; Weare and Nind 2011).

Social and emotional competencies are developed within the classroom community—a community that is built intentionally with the following features:

- instruction that is inclusive, active, and engaging, that consistently includes student voice and choice and that emphasizes formative assessment (e.g., problem-based, project-based, or inquiry-based learning)
- opportunities for cooperative learning in authentic learning experiences that help students see the benefit of collaboration and mutual support
- guidelines co-constructed by students and teachers about how they want a successful, safe, engaged learning environment to look, sound, and feel
- positive discipline approaches (restorative practices, restitution) assisting students to solve problems and designed to strengthen students after mistakes are made
- consistent practice (by all adults in the building) of effective social and emotional competencies, particularly in moments of conflict and agitation
- opportunities for students to dialogue, to share their stories, and to listen and find value in each other within, for example, the structure of talking or listening circles

Using Circles to Build Community

Understanding the power of Circles will not happen by reading about them. The power of Circles happens when one is *in a circle*. What is a Circle and how does it work? Nancy Riestenberg, author of *Circle in the Square: Building Community and Repairing Harm in School* (2012), describes Circles in schools. Rooted in the wisdom of indigenous peoples, the talking or peacemaking Circle is an intentional communication process guided by a community's values. The Circle can be used to acquaint, direct, teach, support, or hold someone accountable for harm. Within the shape of the circle is equality—there is no head-of-the-line or back-of-the-room. All participants can see one another, and everyone can hear. It is critical, however, to take the time to first create a set of guidelines that everyone agrees to follow in the Circle.

Although Circles can be combined with other processes, they have several unique characteristics that distinguish them from other dialogue or conflict-resolution processes. Commitment of participants in the Circle to building relationships before discussing core issues is a very intentional and important strategy of the Circle process. Circles deliberately delay the dialogue about sensitive issues until the group has done some work on building relationships. An introductory round of responses to a question invites people to share something about themselves. The follow-up rounds identify the values that participants want to bring to the dialogue—and the guidelines needed for participants in the space to feel safe. A storytelling round on a topic tangentially related to the key issue may also precede discussion of the difficult issue that is the focus of the Circle.

In their book *Restorative Circles in Schools: Building Community and Enhancing Learning* (2013 e-book), Bob Costello and Joshua and Ted Wachtel talk about the effectiveness of starting with check-in and check-out circles in the classroom. Check-in Circles may have different purposes: to find out how students are feeling, to review a project's high points and challenges, to set or review goals for the day or week, or to provide an opportunity to reflect on learning that has happened in previous classes. Check-out Circles may also be used for either academic or interpersonal purposes: synthesizing important or significant learning from the day, acknowledging contributions of fellow participants, reflecting on academic goals and setting new ones, or assessing the successes or challenges of a project.

In *Reading, Writing and Rising Up*, Linda Christensen (2000) describes how she uses a Read-Around Circle to develop a community of writers who become more willing to share their writing and their writing process, and who respond and provide encouragement and supportive feedback to each other. She builds trust slowly, facilitating the sharing and feedback sessions. She is also a participant and shares her own writing along with the challenges or successes she has experienced, which promotes an atmosphere of respect and trust that is essential for student engagement.

Many of the teachers who work with Marna start using Circles with the intention of building relationships among their students, giving voice to the diverse experiences in the room and giving time and space to build understanding and empathy for each other. After consistently using the Circle process with her students, one teacher in Marna's district reflected:

> *During Circle, my students are thoroughly engaged, attentive listeners and thoughtful, empathetic participants. In the peacemaking Circle format, we have explored topics such as inclusion, kindness, moderation and self-care, friendships, acceptance and diversity, perspective taking, and problem solving. It has become a special time for sharing and learning—a time to discover our own voice and truly hear the voices of others.*

Getting started with Circles

To get started with Circles in a classroom setting, try one of the following:

- Discuss with your class the range of feelings and needs in the two lists on their copy of Figure 7.1. When ready, ask them to think about and mark their five most important ones—My Hi-5.

Figure 7.1 Graphic organizer for students to self-describe

Name: _____

My Hi-5

Think about what you need to feel or what you need others to do for you so that you can do your best learning.

Do you need to feel respected? Do you need to be able to laugh?

Do you need to feel accepted for who you are?

Look at the list of **feelings** below, and check off the 5 (Hi-5) most important to you.

Add other feelings that are important to you, but are not listed.

I need to feel...

☐ respect   ☐ love

☐ compasion   ☐ appreciation

☐ kindness   ☐ support

☐ belonging   ☐ _____

☐ _____   ☐ _____

Look at the list of **needs** below, and check off the 5 (Hi-5) most important to you.

Add other needs that are important to you, but are not listed.

I need to...

☐ be happy   ☐ share my work

☐ be quiet   ☐ move

☐ think by myself   ☐ laugh

☐ think with a group   ☐ cry

☐ _____   ☐ _____

_____

_____

- Create an interesting way to present your Circle Guidelines (i.e., in a poem, rhyme, or meaningful statement).
- Invite students to bring a talking piece. One teacher uses this as a way to incorporate student "show and tell" into the week.
- Use art lessons to have students create talking pieces that symbolize different or unique aspects of themselves.
- Start with questions that invite safe and positive sharing, such as *"What is the best thing that happened to you this week?"* or *"How do you feel coming to Circle today?"*
- End the Circle with positive affirmations for each other, including the adults in the room (*"I'd like to compliment _____ today for …"*; *"I really appreciated …"*; *"I liked it when …"*)
- Start small. Be patient.

How Positive Psychology Informs Our Teaching

"What we pay attention to will grow." Put another way, we get more from what we give attention to. We know that attending to strengths and positive outlooks can increase resilience, vitality, and happiness, and that doing so can decrease stress, anxiety, and depression (Lyubomirsky, King, and Diener 2005). How can we use what we are learning from the science of positive psychology to cultivate a learning community in which our students flourish?

Social-emotional learning is recognized as an important element for student development and success in school and in life (Zins, Weissberg, Wang, and Walberg 2004), and it is linked to increased academic achievement (Cohen 2001; Elias and Arnold 2006). Learning is also a social process, and schools are social contexts. Students learn in collaboration with their peers, their teachers, and others in their learning community. Positive community-building practices can be designed to build and encourage the development of positive outlooks, habits, and mental models among our students. The research findings (Seligman 2011; Lyubomirsky, Tkach, and DiMatteo 2006) suggest that our perceptions and expectations can influence our reality. We must look for ways to awaken our students' sense of personal and communal agency, to see that they can influence the community in a positive way.

Integrating Social-Emotional Learning and Project-Based Learning

The previous chapter introduced inquiry and project-based learning (PBL). This example offers a glimpse into Kim Ondrik's grade 6/7 classroom in Vernon, BC, where project-based learning and social and emotional learning are integrated.

"Are you giving us a new challenge today, Mrs. O? You said you would. Remember?" Josh teases as he enters at the morning bell. *"Oh, what*

is it about? I can't wait to see," follows Beccs. *"I hope I can use the photograph of the Pygmy Owl I took last week in the Wetlands. I've been writing poetry about it in my head ever since."*

The energy and smiles are contagious as the students hang up their backpacks, slide off their coats, and greet their friends on this chilly Monday morning as they move to the Circle. Each day in "The Ozone" dawns in an eclectic oval of short benches, wooden boxes, old military chests, and thrift-store cushions. They connect before any plans for the day are discussed. Listening deeply is their discipline and practice.

Learning in Relational Trust

The Ozone is a grade 6/7 learning community of sociocultural and economic diversity. It seeks to be inclusive of all preferences, perspectives, and experiences grounded in community. In the Ozone, the teachers and teaching assistants have a shared philosophy that, if a child does not wish to learn, they respect that wish, while at the same time designing exciting and invitational learning opportunities that bring forth the child's passion and questions and, in doing so, develop trusting attachments to others.

The Ozone accepts human frailty and assumes daily conflict. Their Talking Circles, rooted in restorative justice practices, provide opportunities for each member of the community to voice their point of view. Relationships are repaired through owning mistakes (intentional or accidental) and giving and receiving forgiveness. The Ozone believes that punishment does not strengthen people, it shames them and weakens their resolve to do the right thing. In all things, the focus of the Ozone is on growth and learning.

The Ozone is an environment that stimulates exploration and discovery. It is a place that sees belonging, honesty, and compassion as the rich soil in which each unique "plant" can comfortably be the person he or she is, one who can safely begin to express his or her unique gifts and differing needs. The Ozone encourages "root" growth with deep learning:

- to understand material for oneself;
- to interact critically with others when discussing content or processes;
- to determine most decisions democratically;
- to relate ideas to prior knowledge and experience; and
- to examine issues with care.

When the learners challenge themselves, they learn to tolerate confusion as they push branches out of their comfort zones in every way—expressing their ideas, presenting their projects, self-identifying which Math group they should join, mentoring younger students, or serving at the Upper Room Mission, a local soup kitchen.

The Challenge

"As you know, we received an Aboriginal grant to publish our Okanagan Coyote Stories *from last year. Since then, I've been doing a lot of thinking about the best way to do this. Or, should I say, the most engaging way to do this,"* Kim smiles. *"So, I have a proposal for you to consider."*

All eyes are riveted on her. Even after a weekend's unstructured adventures, the attention directed toward anticipating the new project is astonishing. This is one of the reasons Kim has fallen in love with projects.

"I propose that we research and create books. It's your choice to work alone or with a partner."

Kim listens to the response by attending to the words and mood that come from the children. She usually crafts the challenges herself (Figure 7.2) and, mindful that she may not always be in tune with the passions and perspectives of all students, she comes each day to The Ozone with an attitude of willingness to shift and change.

"I have given some boundaries to challenge your problem-solving skills. You'll notice that you need to choose your book's title from a list." John and Sam groan. For these highly creative minds, any perceived restrictions engage their "counter-will" (the will to oppose). She continues with enthusiasm hoping to woo them and draw them back into community:

"As a natural conclusion to our recent "family life" learning, I suggest The Power of Hormones *or* The Mystery of Human Reproduction.*"*

Marin, the future midwife, is delighted. She and Hannah immediately begin to whisper their ideas.

Colton and Kim have had many conversations about stress hormones, so she thought this would give him an opportunity to understand more about himself. He smiles.

"Or if you would like to more fully reflect on those projects we did in downtown Vernon before Christmas, The Impact of Joy *may interest you."*

Jessica gestures to Faith, the classroom education assistant, with a fist pump. Faith nods her head and chuckles.

"Those of you who enjoyed last week's Survival Challenges may like to pursue The Wonder of the Wetlands.*"*

Kim knows this one will capture John's imagination: *"Can I do a comic strip, Mrs. O?"*

"Finally, there is the title The Challenge of Adolescence. *I know that many of you are experiencing challenges outside of school, so I thought you might like to process those thoughts and feelings through writing, drawing, and research. It works for me sometimes."*

Georgia's hand lifts her chin as her eyes stare off into the distance. Soon, she is moving from the only home she has ever known—so many memories to pack away.

Figure 7.2 The Ozone Challenge

OZONE CHALLENGE
research & create a book

ONE MUST ALWAYS be careful of BOOKS, & WHAT IS inside them, FOR WORDS HAVE THE Power TO CHANGE us.
—TESSA GRAY
CLOCKWORK ANGEL BY CASSANDRA CLARE

for a richer, fuller life
READ

Be courageous and try to write in a way that scares you a little.
—Holley Gerth

BOOKS aren't just made of words, you know...they're also filled with places to visit & people to meet.

Before creating the book:

1. Choose <u>one</u> of these titles for your book:

   i. The Wonder of the Wetlands

   ii. The Power of Hormones

   iii. The Impact of Joy

   iv. The Mystery of Human Reproduction

   v. The Challenge of Adolescence

2. Choose to <u>work alone</u> or <u>with a partner.</u> *As you make a wise decision, consider these questions:*

   i. What are my strengths ? What are my weaknesses ?

   ii. Is there someone else with *complementary* abilities ?

3. Research your topic by collecting information:

   i. <u>autobiographically</u>: YOUR experience & perspective

   ii. <u>interviews</u>: OTHER'S experiences & perspectives

   iii. <u>published information</u>: online, magazines, books

4. Decide upon <u>"10 nuggets of gold"</u> that you would like to highlight or feature in your book. *As you make a wise decision, consider these questions:*

   i. Who is my *audience* ?

   ii. What information would be the most *interesting & engaging* for that audience ?

   iii. What nuggets can I most effectively *illustrate* ?

kim ondrik

© Portage & Main Press, 2014, *It's All About Thinking: Creating Pathways for All Learnings in the Middle Years*, BLM, ISBN 978-1-55379-509-4

Formative Assessment

Over the past six years, Kim's understanding of project-based learning has deepened significantly in regard to students' energy, enthusiasm, and engagement. Now she has posted on the white board (Figure 7.3) a chart of stages and questions to guide students through the creative process with their projects. Students refer to the chart throughout their project work—sometimes independently, sometimes with reminders. Kim refers to it when learners are anxious, stuck, or distracted, or when they are tempted to walk away rather than persist. She respects the uniqueness of each learning journey—the speed, the route, the destination. In conferencing with individual students, Kim refers to one part of the process that can serve to stimulate that student to take a chance, to try something new, or to remember something lost. This interaction might occur many times before there is any observable growth. Repetition and reminders without judgment meant that Kim must be constantly attuned to herself.

For some learners, risk-taking is tightly bound to relational trust. Without attachment, learning does not happen. Each time that Kim is gentle and attentive, trust is nurtured. Each time she is willing to take the time to stop and listen deeply, trust is nurtured. Each time she speaks hopefully and reminds the child of past triumphs, trust is nurtured. Confidence replaces insecurity through tiny, incremental growth, not according to Kim's timeline, but to each child's unique schedule.

Supporting Students to Negotiate Their Own Learning

The students scatter throughout the school, finding private nooks and crannies, journals in hand, chatting, laughing, debating, brainstorming. As the room empties, Kim spots Sam seated at a table with his head down.

"Hey Sam. What's up?" "I really wanted to write a book about Agent Orange. I've been doing a lot of reading about it lately." "Hmm. If it interests you that much, go for it." Sam lifts his head. *"Really, Mrs. O?" "Of course. It's all about growing and learning for me. I'm flexible. Did you forget that?"* Sam smiles, thinks for a moment and states with confidence *"The Corruption of Agent Orange. How's that for a title?" "If researching and creating a book about Agent Orange will stimulate your growth, go for it, Sam!"*

When the recess bell rings, only Ben jumps to go outside. He has been wandering since the Circle gathering. Everyone else is actively engaged, unwilling to stop, pausing only to grab a snack. *"Do you have some ideas, Ben?" "Not really." "Would you like some help?" "Not really." "Enjoy your body break. Maybe you'll feel more inspired afterwards."*

Ben has found the transition from a teacher-directed, individual-first, model of education to the community-first, democratic, hands-on structure of The Ozone very difficult. He has to generate his own learning energy, explore

Figure 7.3 The Ozone Process for creating powerful projects

PBL Flowchart for Students

Beginning	Research	Organize	Project Design	Polish	Present	Celebrate
How can I best be successful? • work alone? • with a partner? • in a group, with roles assigned, based upon strengths? **Begin with the end in mind.** • learning outcome demonstrated • deep question answered • a challenge met **Study the rubric levels of expectation criteria.**	**What are the possible sources?** • books, newspapers, magazines • libraries: class, school, community • Internet • films • interviews • conversations with experts **Have I explored at least 3 points of view?** • importance of triangulation **How is the research shared among group members?**	**What are the most effective methods?** • cut and paste • in a binder? Journal? • lists • webs/clusters • word documents • save on the server? • flash drive? **Guiding Questions** • 3 points of view • 3 sources for each • on track with criteria in rubric? **How can the group stay organized and share the work?**	**What kinds of projects could I use?** **Should I use something new?** **What has been effective for me or others in the past?** **Who will the audience be?** **What will most engage the audience?**	Review, edit, proofread. **Feedback** • from at least 3 peers • from one adult **Respond to the feedback; revise?** • Does it make sense? • What part should I/we use? • What part should I/we ignore? Compare project to the rubric criteria. Prepare for presentation. Share "air time" equally among group members.	**Day before** • Do we have everything we need? **Night before** • Get a good night's sleep. **Day of** • Get presentation ready. • Talk to partners. • Briefly rehearse. **Who is invited to view presentation?** **Who will assess the presentation?** **After the presentation**	Cake??

© Portage & Main Press, 2014, *It's All About Thinking: Creating Pathways for All Learnings in the Middle Years*, BLM, ISBN 978-1-55379-509-4

his own thinking, and reflect on his own learning. Working with others, considering others' perspectives and presenting his learning publicly is also far outside Ben's comfort zone. Still, with gentle nudging, deep listening, and the provision of many daily opportunities to share his voice with the community, Ben is growing. He returns from recess and nervously asks John if they could work together. John explains that he already has plans for a comic strip, but Ben could work beside him, if he'd like. Ben begins.

Classroom management is less of a focus when children are engaged. Inquiry learning in a learning community offers many opportunities for problem-solving. This provides the teacher with freedom to observe and document their learning as she moves from group to group posing questions, offering descriptive feedback and, if asked, voicing concerns. Kim journals what she sees, as well as taking photographs and capturing video clips. She selects observations and powerful images to include in the anecdotal part of The Ozone report cards each term. The students can't wait to view which photos she chooses to best capture their journey each term.

Assessment that Deepens the Learning

After ten days of production, the class gathers in their morning Circle and begins a conversation about the value of a rubric at this stage in the process. *"What are the important aspects of this project?"* Kim asks, *"What do you think should be assessed?"*

The intent behind her questions is not to focus on grades, but to stimulate the learning process and to deepen the students' understanding of the critical features of a powerful project. In particular, she has been noticing how many students have not considered checking and revising their work before they prepare their good copy. Others have created illustrations all around their writing so they believe that correcting their spelling will ruin their drawings.

> In The Ozone, the class frequently explores the role of editors and the power of feedback in polishing their work. Developing a spelling conscience is a vital lifelong skill, so Kim asks what a "4" (Exceeding expectations) would look like in terms of spelling when the books are assessed on presentation day. The students agree that a "4" would have perfect spelling, no mistakes. *"I'm okay with a 2, Mrs. O.,"* states Joel. *"It would take way too long to re-draw everything and I really like what I've done."*

Kim encourages the students once again to consider that one does not have to be a strong speller to produce excellent writing, but one does have to be wise and brave to ask others for feedback, and then to be willing to persevere and make corrections.

Continuing with the rubric, Chris suggests that they also need to consider how appropriate the books are for their intended audiences. Hannah reminds the group that reader engagement is probably the most important feature. *"How interesting is the story? How detailed are the illustrations?"* she queries. Kim creates a rubric chart of their ideas and encourages The Ozone to use it as a guide as they work toward next week's presentations. *"Remember, while you will be assessing yourself and your peers using these criteria; I will be assessing you, too"* she reminds the class (Figure 7.4).

Kim tries to conduct assessment conferences in a relaxed, democratic manner, focusing on individual development and growth, rather than making an A the goal for all. Many students, even the most developed ones, say that getting feedback can be difficult *"because people don't always know how to be gentle with people's hearts."* Assessment should inspire and stimulate growth in the middle years instead of being connected with anxiety, stress, and judgment. Creating a culture of care in all things is essential to Kim.

Rarely in The Ozone do students ask what letter grade they achieved on their projects (although Kim uses the rubrics to determine report card achievement). The focus is on revising their final product and learning from one or two pieces of peer feedback after their presentations. Kim has the learners reflect on their growth at the end of each term, and they share what they are good at and what they need to work on as opposed to increasing their marks. Frequently, in fact, students say that they need to get better at accepting feedback and learning from it—a lifelong skill to be sure.

> For most learners, the stage of polishing a project is where they have to exercise their "perseverance muscles." Although the class has a clearly laid-out process, it's difficult and sometimes unsettling for some, because they have to stop creating and for others, because they have to take feedback and respond to it. According to Dalton, *"The worst part is not being able to think of anything because you're so overwhelmed by the feedback."*

During the inquiry process, the revising, and the polishing, Kim tries to draw in many other adults in the school for support. The learners can select those that they feel the safest with to receive feedback from; sometimes it's the principal, sometimes it's a high-school peer tutor. Requesting and accepting feedback at the publishing phase is a life skill. *"I'm not a big fan of the polishing part, but I think it helps me grow,"* Marin reports.

Presenting and Celebrating the Learning

The time for student presentations of their projects may require up to three days. Kim has found that for every hour of attentive listening and descriptive, non-judgmental feedback per presentation, middle years students need a 20-minute break (physical, intellectual, sometimes nutritional). The usually confident volunteers cannot wait to do their presentation first; she has to draw names for the more reluctant. When students offer their projects in varied "texts" (slideshows, puppet shows, storytelling, posters, keynote presentations, models, or other format), the students can review several in one day.

Figure 7.4 Rubric for summative assessment of Book Project

Aspect of the challenge	Not yet meeting expectations	Minimally meeting expectations	Fully meeting expectations	Exceeding expectations
What is the quality of the story or text?	• No elaboration • "Tip of the iceberg" understanding • 6 or less nuggets	• Some elaboration • Slightly "under the water" understanding • 7 to 8 nuggets	• Most information elaborated • Quite deeply understood • 9 nuggets of gold	• All information elaborated • Very deep understanding • 10+ nuggets of gold
What is the quality of the illustrations?	• No illustrations are detailed, colourful, thoughtful, or creative	• Some illustrations are detailed, colourful, thoughtful, and creative	• Most illustrations are detailed, colourful, thoughtful, and creative	• All illustrations are detailed, colourful, thoughtful, and creative
How connected is the book to the intended audience?	• Very little text and few illustrations are appropriate for the intended audience • Intended audience is not clear, even with the explanation	• Some text and some illustrations are appropriate for the intended audience • Intended audience is clear only with explanation	• Most text and most illustrations are appropriate for the intended audience • Intended audience is clear with some explanation	• All text and all illustrations are appropriate for the intended audience • Intended audience is very clear without explanation
How engaging is the book?	• Text is not connected to the title • Few illustrations are hand-drawn (<5) • Illustrations are not used to enhance the text	• Text is somewhat connected to the title • Some illustrations are hand-drawn (6 to 7) • Illustrations are partly used to enhance the text	• Text is connected to the title • Most illustrations are hand-drawn (8 to 9) • Illustrations are used to enhance the text	• Text is well-connected to the title • All illustrations are hand-drawn (10+) • Illustrations are used to powerfully enhance the text
How is the spelling?	• 6 or more mistakes	• 3 to 5 mistakes	• 1 or 2 mistakes	• No mistakes
Presentation	• No Pow! • Not engaging	• Little bit of Pow! • Engaging at times	• Mostly "Pow-ish" • Engaging	• Huge Pow!! • Very engaging
Creativity	• Inside the box • No risk-taking	• Little bit outside the box • Wee bit of risk-taking	• Lots is outside the box • Evidence of risk-taking	• Completely outside the box • Lots of evidence of risk-taking

The final aspect of an Ozone Project is the celebration of learning. The class decide together what would honour their hard work and they collaborate to plan the event. *"There has to be food!"* laughs Dalton. *"Can we share our projects in the wetlands? That's my favourite place in the world!"* cries Lila. *"Let's try something different this time,"* laments Chris, *"Can't we mix it up a bit?"* Kim explains that books are often launched with a party, and perhaps this time they could try a celebration at the same time as the presentations.

Kim ensures that her units and lessons are project-based and that they focus on inquiry learning within their community. She plans projects in a cycle (Figure 7.5) so that her assessments *of* learning become assessments *for* learning, as new projects are based on students' questions and their emerging areas of strength and needs for growth. She then creates a stimulus, an event that provokes and makes the students curious, a challenge that requires them to form groups to research and explore. Although she offers them criteria for designing their projects in a way that supports self-regulation of their learning, she leaves room for negotiation. Integrating these aspects of pedagogy can be powerful and feel authentic for middle years learners.

> *"Project learning is so engaging because it's a choice. I'm not being forced to do something I don't really want to do. Bossing us around just brings out counter-will. I like projects because I learn/think a lot more than I would if a teacher slapped a piece of paper with words in front of me. I liked the book project because I love to write, and I liked to use my ideas to create a book."*—Marin, age 12

Service Learning

Inclusion, openness, vulnerability, and diversity are principles that help to create a rich and meaningful community. Deep levels of personal engagement in the community and in the process are also critical. Volunteerism can be a powerful way to ensure a deep commitment. Service learning is one approach that supports students in building personal and social responsibility. The Association for Middle Level Education (AMLE 2010) notes that "in today's society, genuine community involvement is a fundamental component of successful middle schools." Intentionally building students' understandings of personal and social responsibility helps to deepen their identity, character, and connections to others. It is an important piece of the middle years learning puzzle. Teachers should capitalize on integrating provincial curriculum with real-world experiences by providing adolescents with opportunities to follow their special interests and aptitudes, and by engaging them in exploratory activities through community involvement, both locally and globally. Service learning reframes the role of teacher and learner—developing practices of deep listening, civic participation, and ultimately engaging with others in

Figure 7.5 Flow chart of Project-Based Learning

STIMULUS
poem, lyric, newspaper clipping, novel, photograph, hands-on object or collection, oral story, YouTube video, documentary, film, experiment, field trip, guest speaker, serving others in the community

Determined by:
- observing, listening, bringing issues into the classroom that affect individuals, schools, families, neighbourhoods, city, province, country, world
- accessing prior experience
- accessing prior knowledge
- accessing prior skills

Within the classroom community; teacher as initiator; as facilitator

- questions
- concerns
- connections
- conversations
- dialogue
- activities
- challenges
- responses

Within the teacher's brain/metacognitive processing

ASSESSMENT OF LEARNING
- opportunity to individually show what you **now** know
- documentation of student learning
- designed by the teacher and connected to the big ideas presented by the projects

PRESENTATIONS
- questions
- concerns
- connections
- conversations
- dialogue
- activities
- challenges
- responses

The students' work

Within the teacher's brain/metacognitive processing

PROJECT DESIGN
The students' work
How do I best...
- guide students into appropriate roles for each group
- guide students in organizing information: what they already know and what they are finding out
- provide examples of organizational structures throughout the process to stimulate thinking
- encourage students to experiment with different ways to "show what you know"

PROJECT LEARNING Flow Chart

PROBLEM SOLVING AND PERSEVERANCE reflection; critical thinking; understanding and expressing point of view; debate and negotiation

- point out examples of presentation formats and demonstrate possibilities
- encourage students to refer to the rubric to guide research and exploration
- create an emotionally safe place so students can present to their peers
- record the learning outcomes that the projects cover (in all subject areas); note those outcomes that remain unexplored for future learning opportunities

CREATING A CHALLENGE
Embedded with the opportunity for learners to:
- find their own will, interests, affinities, voice
- find their own reasons, explanations, understandings
- initiate, take chances, push out of their comfort zone, be creative
- share their gifts, talents, vulnerabilities
- self-regulate

Within the classroom community; initiated by students, teacher, parent, ed. assistant

FORMING A GROUP
- Know self: strengths, weaknesses
- Find complementary skills/abilities
- Create the "most effective" team
- Can I problem-solve with you?

RESEARCH AND EXPLORATION
- Questions
- Research and exploration
- New understandings
- Questions

respectful, reciprocal ways. Moreover, placing others' interests ahead of our own is at the heart of service learning.

Leyton's teacher education students explored the wetlands that Kim Ondrik and her grade 6/7 class care for as part of their service learning. Together, university and middle years students learned how community-based approaches "involve the application of academic skills to address or solve issues and problems in the world" (Henkin, Harmon, Pate, and Moorman 2009). UBC-Okanagan middle school teacher candidate Steve Fisher noted that Kim Ondrik

> "discussed the attributes that are critical to successful service learning. She made an analogy of a tree and its roots; the tree is the actual project and the roots are the attributes that are 'rooted' in successful service learning. The two roots are perseverance and attention; in order to be successful, the people doing the service learning must pay attention to detail so that the project runs smoothly and they, as well as the other participants, must persevere through any challenges that may arise. By addressing this before they went out on their day of service learning, the students were grounded in conversation about why and what service learning is good for, and what they need to be thinking about as they go out to complete the project."

Learning in and through Community

Kim is co-teaching 56 students in a multi-grade program in Vernon Community School (VCS) with Murray Sasges. A significant proportion of Murray's and Kim's time with these grades 7 to 9 students is spent outside of the school building. Traditional teacher-directed whole-class lessons, textbook readings, and assigned paperwork are rare. Students participate in a range of hands-on activities aimed at making a positive contribution to a variety of communities.

Their desire as educators is to consider each student as rare and precious, honouring his experience, her feelings, his opinions, her development, and then stimulating deep root growth—so that fruit will be produced in its right time. Shifting family and economic structures as well as personal technological attachments like iPods have contributed to many children arriving in our middle years classrooms without a sense of identity, purpose, or relational capacities.

> "Simply by keeping us away from one another, isolated in our homes, television has made us less trusting. And the content of many programs has made this worse." (Perry 2010, p. 229)

School is something that children have to do. It's not a choice. They are disinterested and numbed by "those boundaries that would confine each pupil to a rote, assembly-line approach to learning." (hooks 1994, p. 13)

As educators, Kim and Murray engage in layered and complex work. They ask themselves questions such as: How do we create spaces where both children and adults have the opportunity to become vigorous, self-directed learners, rooting themselves in community life and yet growing into their unique and diverse potentials? How do we transform the classroom into an incubator of the magnificent and astonishing? These are daunting and exciting questions, stimulated even further by BC's 21st Century Learning initiatives.

The work of VCS is inspired by the story and principles of Reggio Emilia, a city in northern Italy. This story also offers a unique body of theory and practice about working with children and their families, produced from a very particular historical, cultural, and political context. The schools in Reggio Emilia do not dismiss technical practices, nor do they ignore matters of organization and structure. They do, however, put them in their place — as a means to support an educational project that understands "the school" as first and foremost a public space, a place of encounter and connection, interaction and dialogue among citizens, younger and older, living together in a community. Reggio Emilia has been a pedagogical experiment for more than 40 years; it is unique, to the best knowledge of Murray and Kim.

Principles for planning service learning

Service learning should be rooted in the local community, based on needs identified by the community. Murray and Kim are passionately seeking to root this kind of process in their town, Vernon, BC, which has a distinct historical, cultural, and political context. They live on lands inhabited by the Okanagan people for thousands of years. Later settlers to the valley brought agriculture. Many artists, drawn to the ecological diversity and beauty, call Vernon home. However, Vernon faces many challenges, both economic and environmental. The current local government is facing the challenge of how to "grow" Vernon for a sustainable and vibrant population. As educators deeply grounded in the community, Murray and Kim work from several essential questions:

How do we honour these dynamics in the daily work of our children?

How do we find solutions to problems that are particular to Vernon?

How do we inspire lifelong learning in students as citizens who understand and care deeply about this place?

The image of service learning for Murray and Kim flows from these kinds of questions and concerns. Social and emotional learning need to be attended to within the classroom community to effectively go out and work with the community in a respectful and collaborative manner. The first principle in VCS is respect. The teacher serves the students by asking each child "What is it that you need?"

Murray and Kim feel the need to reflect upon and clear any inner debris that impedes the flow of other-orientedness within their hearts and minds. This challenging work is rooted in family-of-origin experiences, personal stress, or perhaps institutional presuppositions of what proper schooling should look like. They listen first. Deep listening, the capacity to consider critically what is being communicated by others, happens best in different learning circles—so there are no desks in their rooms. Reflection and feedback are ongoing. Their purpose goes beyond formative assessment as a tool to encourage the diversity of viewpoints without judgment—an initially scary process for students who have never encountered such personal and vulnerable teaching and learning.

The second principle in VCS is reflection on experience—as expressed over a hundred years ago by John Dewey:

> **"We do not learn from experience. We learn from reflecting on experience."**

Believing, along with others, that people think most clearly when confronting a challenge, Murray and Kim ask their students to consider problems (questions, projects, and issues) that originate from the students' own questions and concerns. These well-considered provocations ruffle feathers, reveal strengths and areas of weakness, and stimulate rich conversations. Trust and respect are deepened and relationships form—self to self, self to others, self to abstract ideas, self to ideas in action. From this perspective, absolutely every circumstance becomes an opportunity for learning as long as time and opportunity are provided for processing—frustrations at home, intolerance of differences, new insights, sharing of successes, current events, interesting facts. Cross-curricular threads are then teased out as they engage in the service or project-based learning. Within the emotional safety of this community, the students begin to reveal assumptions, opinions, concerns, or motivations.

> "The exciting aspect of creating a classroom community where there is respect for individual voices is that there is infinitely more feedback because students do feel free to talk—and talk back" (hooks 2003, p. 42).

Murray and Kim have discovered that as the teacher serves the children, the children serve each other and then others within the school, their family, their neighbourhood, and the global village. Parents will often comment that their children enjoy school more because these approaches make them learn and grow better as they are taught how the curriculum relates to real life.

One example is organizing a city-wide Earth Day gathering, in partnership with the City of Vernon and interested businesses, artists, and organizations. The students imagined the gathering, created invitations for schools, and cycled up hill and down to deliver them. They solicited sponsorships, made vegetable soup with a local church, and set up a stage, tipi, and obstacle course for the event. Students discovered that a lack of communication is frustrating: "How can we be expected to be prepared when people don't let us know if they're coming to the gathering or not?" This is only one of many enduring understandings facilitated by this service learning experience.

Challenge-Based Projects in Community Learning

Julie Hearn teaches grade 6/7 students in Maple Ridge, BC. She wants her students to know, right from the beginning of the school year, that they will have control of their learning, which they must treat as a big responsibility. She hangs a banner in her classroom with the words "We are creating ourselves." She then takes her students through several activities to help them see how their thinking evolves through their learning. She believes it's critical for her students to understand that what they know and believe *should* change because of their learning experiences. What they think they know today, might turn out to be completely different tomorrow, and different again the next week.

As a kick-off for a new term and a social studies unit, Julie chose a study of homelessness, an issue that affects communities across the globe. She knew that her students learn best by connecting personally to the content, and hoped that this topic might help them build a greater connection to their own community. Julie uses project-based learning on a regular basis in her classroom, and has focused primarily on projects that emphasize inquiry. She finds the inquiry approach suits her students' curiosity—they enjoy being able to make choices as they learn and to pursue their passions.

Drawing on ideas from inquiry-based learning, Julie decided that the project needed the essential question "Why does homelessness exist in Maple Ridge?" to guide student investigation and inquiry. She also knew that this particular group of students needed many opportunities to be active and connected while learning through their project. Julie started shaping her unit and lesson plans, designing a wide variety of activities and experiences (Figures 7.6 and 7.7) that would readily engage her diverse learners.

Community Connections: Learning in the Field

Julie believes that incorporating the community into a learning experience is necessary in order for students to become well-rounded learners and responsible citizens—outside the confines of the classroom. Every school year, she and her students complete at least one activity that clearly connects the class to their community, whether it is a food drive for the food bank, collecting toys for the children's hospital, or raising money for the local animal shelter. So she took her students on a walking field trip into the heart of the community.

First, she made arrangements to visit four local organizations and meet with a community expert at each location. Supported by the school principal and some enthusiastic parents, the class walked into town on a blisteringly cold Monday in January. The students then divided up into small groups with a clipboard, a map, possible questions to ask at each location, and some paper to record ideas and questions and to make notes (Figure 7.8). They also brought along an iPad to take photographs, record video and interviews, and jot down notes about their observations and conversations. Walking

Figure 7.6 Outline of types of learning activities for Homelessness Unit

Figure 7.7 Learning activities from sources and resources beyond textbooks

Activity	Description
Current Events	Julie selected 10 different newspaper articles (six copies of each article) that centred on the issue of homelessness from across the country and shared them with her students. The articles represented different sides of the homelessness issue. Julie did a mini book-talk on each of the articles and then gave students time to read and reflect.
Reading	Each of the students read the story "Charity" from the book *Two Sides to Every Story 2* (Gross 2011, pp. 28–33). Afterwards, they discussed their inferences and perspectives on the issues raised in the fictional account of a young girl who was interacting uncomfortably with a homeless man.
Drama	Julie divided her students into groups of two. In partners, they role-played a situation where a homeless individual approaches a person walking along the street. Each student was given the chance to act in each role. The most important element of this activity was in the detailed debriefing sessions that the teacher held with her students, asking them key questions about their experiences in each situation.
Film-Making	After their walking field trip in town, Julie had her students create video "Thank you" tributes for each person who made their field trip possible. Students thanked these important people by recounting memorable moments, sharing statistics that they had learned, and expressing genuine thanks to each individual.
Facts and Figures Count	To help her students ground their understanding in firm facts, Julie selected short sections from a high school teacher's guide to integrating homelessness into the curriculum (Hales 2010). Specifically, Julie was most interested in providing her students with the charts and statistics included in this guide. To help them analyze the numbers, she had her students study the patterns and correlations, and seek explanations and causes for changes in the numbers of homeless.

© Portage & Main Press, 2014, *It's All About Thinking: Creating Pathways for All Learning in the Middle Years*, BLM, ISBN 978-1-55379-509-4

Figure 7.8 Record sheet for walking field trip

Community Organization Record Sheet

When you visit each local organization, organize your notes in the categories below (or record a short video journal) describing what you learned — facts and impressions.

Think about these questions when you make your notes:

· What is the purpose of the organization or the agency?

· What problems in our local community did the representative(s) mention?

· How does the organization or agency help the citizens of Maple Ridge?

· What interesting facts or statistics made a real impact on you?

R.C.M.P. Detachment	Food Bank	Addiction Services	Homeless Shelter

---

from one organization to another, students discussed what they had learned from their interview, prepared questions for the next stop, and recorded their observations of people, signs, events, and other details on the streets along the way.

The next day in class, the students documented their most memorable experiences in a journal-style activity. They used relevant facts and figures from their notes, including newly acquired vocabulary, to make subtle distinctions between important ideas, and described the complexity and challenges of being homeless. For each of her students, the ideas and information flowed easily in their writing. Their experiences on their outing gave them an understanding of the underlying issues and of the helpful services available in their community. Julie was genuinely surprised at the level of knowledge and understanding that each student had gained as a result of their interactions and observations. The result was far more successful than any classroom-based activity she could have designed.

Community Connections: Learning from Experts

Julie ensured that her students had frequent access to digital resources so they could take advantage of their class set of laptops and engage in a multitude of research activities, using online databases, encyclopedias, digital news media, and countless websites to compile their information. She noticed that students, while involved in a research activity, were completely silent and stationary, working away on their computers. Julie found this particularly odd and somewhat unsettling. In her personal experience, being active while learning had led her to greater understanding of material over the long term.

The next day, Julie decided to duplicate the previous day's lesson with one significant difference—the students would not be permitted to use the Internet for any of their research. They had to find information by reading textbooks and magazines, phoning family members, looking through the newspaper, and asking each other questions. This time, Julie observed her students smiling, interacting with each other, and discussing ideas to help clarify their thinking. By removing the Internet from the research, she was able to restore student engagement. Since this experience, Julie ensures that research-based learning activities extend beyond the scope of a Google search on the World Wide Web.

For students accustomed to learning in a traditional classroom setting, acquiring information from people in the community can be a powerful experience. Having human experts as learning resources gives students the opportunity to create relationships with people who are connected to and knowledgeable about their topic of study (Figures 7.9 and 7.10). Julie arranged for local residents to visit the class to share their first-hand knowledge, experiences, and connections to the issues of homelessness.

Figure 7.9 Community experts for Homelessness Unit

Effective Essential Questions and Challenge Statements

The essential question for a unit drives the learning in an inquiry classroom. While students can certainly be involved in the process, it is critical that the teacher understand what creates a powerful query. To test the strength and durability of a question, Julie Hearn uses the Q Matrix from Wiederhold (1998) (Figure 7.11A and B). Once she has the big idea or goal for an inquiry unit, she works to create the question that ideally fits in the lower right quadrant on the matrix (marked 4 on the diagram). These questions in quadrant 4 (*How might…?, Why would…?, How will…?*) are open-ended

Figure 7.10 Lesson plan for classroom visitor

Lesson Plan: Guest Expert Interview #2

Focus/Big Idea		
Interview a representative from the Ministry of Social Development to gain information about the issue of homelessness and the services offered by the local government.		
Details		
Before the Interview	**During the Interview**	**After the Interview**
Review questioning techniques with students: • What types of questions get detailed responses? • What types of questions will not get detailed responses? Have students identify and clarify the purpose of the guest expert visit: • What type of information could the guest provide? • What other information would you want to know from this guest? • What types of questions would be most powerful for this expert? Give students time to prepare a list of powerful questions: • Write questions on paper or on iPad to use for interview	• Assemble the students in a close seated group • Introduce the guest to the class • Guest expert talks about their position at the Ministry, their job duties and background • Students pose questions to the guest expert • Students make notes on iPad during discussion • Thank guest for visiting our class and school	• Students post their notes and thoughts from the guest visit/interview to their online course • Students create "Thank you" video and card to send to expert for their time

and leave plenty of room for exploration and discovery within the big idea. Questions that fit into sections 2 or 3 must also be strong questions, and can be equally appropriate, depending upon the subject, the length of the project, the available resources, and the ability and interests of the students.

Julie has found that her students generally lack the skills needed to synthesize their learning, which led them to a weak conclusion when answering an inquiry question that was poorly supported with little or no concrete evidence. She resisted over-stepping her role as facilitator while students sought their answers, yet struggled to accept their inaccurate or undocumented conclusions as good learning practice.

Julie had been introduced to challenge-based learning (CBL) on several occasions, but it was during this Homelessness Unit that she finally picked up the *Challenge-Based Learning: A Classroom Guide* (Apple Inc. 2012) and gave it a more thorough read. One significant difference that she immediately noted was that the challenge element in challenge-based learning really begins at

Figure 7.11A Q Matrix used to test the strength and durability of an "essential question"

Q Matrix

	Is...?	Did...?	Can...?	Would...?	Will...?	Might...?
What...						
Where/ When...						
Which...						
Who...						
Why...						
How...						

Cooperative learning and higher level thinking: The Q-matrix. Wiederhold 1998

the point where inquiry-based learning typically ends. In the CBL model, after acquiring knowledge and deriving meaning from research and learning materials, students subsequently begin a project to meet the given challenge. This extension of the inquiry model was exactly what Julie was looking for to create a more authentic and personal learning experience for her students.

It took Julie several attempts to develop a challenge statement that she could issue to her students for the next phase of the unit. It was critical to her that the challenge be demanding yet doable. She settled on the following challenge for her students:

Challenge: Improve our school's compassion toward homeless people

Julie noticed that the moment she issued the challenge to her students, their reactions indicated confusion and bewilderment. They were accustomed to being asked to make a brochure, or a poster, or even a handout. This time, she was asking them to change somebody else's opinion, and that sounded like hard work. This was exactly what she was hoping for—that the project was a true challenge. Julie assigned the students into groups of three, and set them to work on brainstorming their solution.

Measuring Success: Student Self-Assessment

Once the students were ready to put their ideas into action, they had to first design a method to judge the success of their projects. Julie posed the question:

Figure 7.11B Question Matrix

The Question Matrix, developed by Charles Wiederhold (1995) is a collection of 36 question starters that help promote student thinking. They ask what, where, which, who, why, and how. The questions toward the top of the matrix are knowledge and information questions. The questions in the lower rows require analyzing, synthesizing, and evaluation, and they promote higher order thinking. Students can generate and answer their own questions about any topic. Teachers can use the matrix to ensure a wide variety of questioning in their classrooms.

	Event	Situation	Choice	Person	Reason	Means
	What...?	**Where/When...?**	**Which...?**	**Who...?**	**Why...?**	**How...?**
Present knowing Can you recall what you have seen or heard?	What is...? What happened after?	Where/When is...? What happened when?	Which did...?	Who is...? What was it that...? Can you name...? Who spoke to...?	Why is...?	How is...? How many...?
Past understanding Can you explain or show you understand?	What did...? What was the main idea?	Where/When did...? What do you think could have happened next?	Which did...?	Who did...? Who do you think...? Does every one act in the way... does?	Why did...?	How did...? How would you explain...?
Possibility applying Can you use the new knowledge or show how it connects to other things you know or can do?	What can...?	Where/When can...? Do you know of another instance when...?	Which can...? Which factors would you change if...?	Who can...? Who can you think of that would be able to...?	Why can...? Why can some people... and others cannot?	How can...? How, from the information given, can you develop a set of instructions for...?
Probability analyzing Can you break down the information in a meaningful way?	What would...? If ... happened, what might the ending have been?	Where/When would...? Can you explain what must/might have happened when...?	Which would...? Which choices lead to...?	Who would...? What were some of the motives behind... doing what they did?	Why would...? Why did ... changes occur?	How would...? How is... similar to/ different from...?
Prediction evaluation Can you justify a decision with evidence of reasoning?	What will...? What do you think about...?	Where/When will...? What happened when...?	Which will...? Which is more important... or...?	Who will...? Do you believe what ... said? How would you feel if...?	Why will...? Why was this a success/otherwise?	How will...? How would you have handled...? How effective are...?
Imagination creating Can you create new products, ideas, or a new way of looking at things?	What might...? What might be created by combining... and...?	Where/When might...?	Which might...?	Who might...? Can you see possible solutions to/for...?	Why might...?	How might...? How many ways can you...?

How can you measure the success of your project to improve the compassion your target audience feels toward homeless people?

and asked each group to design a plan to answer it. The students tackled the difficulty of determining whether people actually had a change of opinion, and came up with the following measurement indicators: short questionnaires for students, written reflections for teachers, and photographs to measure student engagement. The following are examples of student-created assessments:

Engaging Movie: The grade 6/7 students proposed to survey the grade 4 students, by asking these questions:

- What is your attitude toward homeless people?
- Do you find homeless people scary? Yes. No. Kinda.

Target the Teachers: They proposed to ask the teachers, after the presentation, to reflect on these questions:

- *What are your thoughts about homelessness?*
- *Did our video change your opinion on homelessness in any way?*
- *Have you ever had an encounter with a homeless person? If you have, how did you feel about it?*
- *What are your thoughts, comments, suggestions about our video?*

Storybook: For the kindergarten class, the students took photographs of these young learners as they listened to the story to assess their level of engagement. They also recorded the comments and questions that the children asked after the reading.

Students' predictions: The day before the students were to present their projects, Julie asked them to predict what the reactions of their audience might be to their presentations. She asked them to outline any problems that might occur when they presented their projects. She also wanted them to predict how successful their projects would be in meeting the challenge of improving people's compassion toward homeless people.

Reflection

When Julie reflects on her students' success with the challenge-based project exploring homelessness, she sees clearly the contrast with past inquiry-based projects. After working on them, her students had often felt flat, spent, and exhausted by their efforts once the learning was finished. This time, they felt an overwhelming sense of pride and achievement, and felt empowered that they had taken on a new learning model and had some successes. The words *hobo*, *druggie*, and *bum* now left students with a feeling of distaste and disgust. They had been transformed, and felt compassion toward homeless people and people who were struggling with addiction and mental health issues.

Figure 7.12 Some students' journal reflections after their walking field trip

"Before I went on this field trip, I thought homeless people were mean, and dirty people on the streets, but now I feel, really sorry for them. They must feel scared, and lonely at times."—*Grade 6 student*

"I feel bad for everyone in the world that don't have families anymore or their life is ruined, I feel bad for the homeless people who don't really have a place to go and a loving family."—*Grade 7 student*

"This field trip was important to me because I had a chance to see what would happen to me in the future. I want to be a successful man who makes wise choices and to be a hard working adult."—*Grade 7 student*

"I have learned to have more sympathy for homeless people. The only reason that most of them take drugs and drink a lot is to get away from something depressing in their lives. At the end of the day, they are people, and were probably born into this world just like us."—*Grade 7 student*

Conclusion

Social and emotional learning is central to our goals as educators of students in the middle years. Adolescence is an ideal time for students to develop self-awareness and a sense of social responsibility. It is critical, then, for teachers to provide young adolescent learners with opportunities to engage with their society beyond the classroom. When developing projects and interacting with community mentors and experts, they recognize the relevancy of their academic skills and competencies, which provide the motivation to respond to future challenges. Issue-based and project-based learning can help our students engage in deep self-investigation while bridging from the curriculum content to the world.

We can facilitate a positive journey of social and emotional learning for students while at the same time cultivating their cognitive capacities. We can help by setting personal intentions, co-constructing inclusive and collaborative class expectations, modelling attentive listening and responsive problem-solving, asking students to develop questions and projects that are meaningful for them and the community, and providing activities that require critical thinking. It is vital, to create opportunities for students to build their trust in themselves, in each other, and in us, their teachers. It takes time for young adolescent learners to believe in themselves, and to accept that others, too, believe in them.

A learning community that embraces social and emotional learning is one where students feel welcomed for who they are and valued for what they bring—learning communities can form both within and outside the classroom walls. We are all learners. We are all teachers.

Chapter 8

Creating Pathways to Self-Regulated Learning

Educators Involved

Lynn Wainwright: District Aboriginal Resource Teacher, SD 38, Richmond, BC

Tammy Renyard: Classroom Teacher, SD 61, Victoria, BC

Eve Minuk: Learning Resource Teacher, SD 38, Richmond, BC

Ken Wayne: Classroom Teacher, SD 62, Sooke, BC

Tammy Orthner: Classroom Teacher, SD 62, Sooke, BC

Sheri Gurney: Classroom Teacher, SD 62, Sooke, BC

Assessment *for* learning (AFL), also called formative assessment, supports students *while* they are engaged in developing skills and understandings. In chapter 3, we described the need to build a class profile in order to set goals for our teaching and still ensure that each student in our class received personalized feedback. We work with six key strategies (Black et al. 2003) for formative assessment, which involves specific tasks for teachers and goals for students (Figure 8.1). Effective lesson-planning for a particular class relies on the information about students' thinking strategies and their understanding of essential information obtained through AFL. This knowledge helps us set focused class-wide goals that apply to *all* students, but does not exclude the specific needs of some individual students.

We ensure that student activities provide practice with goals throughout a unit of study and subsequently measure their progress in a summative assessment. During in-class efforts to provide descriptive feedback to students we ask ourselves *What's working? What's not? What's next?* to have the greatest impact. Students listen, respond, and reflect on our feedback and that of their peers. They learn to identify areas of strength and areas to work on, and to set and revise goals for their own learning from activity to activity. Teaching students how to self-regulate their own learning provides them with essential skills for lifelong learning.

Helping Students Self-Regulate

We need to develop self-regulated learning explicitly and habitually. When planning a unit of study on the topic of residential schools, Nicole wanted to include activities and experiences that would help her grade 6 students improve these essential skills. Like many other students, they have learned that metacognition is important, but they need models for how to apply it. Nicole called upon colleagues Leyton and First Nations Consultant Lynn Wainwright to co-plan a unit. In their plan, they addressed the learning outcomes that would help develop students' knowledge, skills, and attitudes, but also take the students' interests, personal backgrounds, and learning strengths into consideration.

They began to build a context for investigating residential schools by having students take multiple perspectives on the issue. Their plan was to immerse students in the stories of those who experienced residential schools,

Role of the District Aboriginal Resource Teacher

Lynn Wainwright is often invited into classrooms for presentations or collaborations to support the integration of indigenous knowledge and perspectives into the curriculum. She recommends literature and multimodal texts to teachers, including the texts on Indian Residential Schools in Canada for Nicole's class. Lynn's goal and hope is to deepen understanding of this often hidden and painful legacy of our shared history. The critical support that Lynn provides involves creating and establishing a safe environment that respects diversity, hears all voices, and allows students to experience a sense of belonging.

Figure 8.1 Six key strategies for AFL, with teacher tasks and student goals

Strategies	Teachers...	Students...
Intentions	• post and refer to learning intentions where students can see them • may pose them as questions	• refer to learning intentions and inquiry questions during and after learning activities • can verbalize what they are working on
Criteria	• create criteria with students • make and use t-chart where criteria are on the left and indicators and/or examples on the right	• know what the focus of a lesson or task is • are included in developing criteria • refer to criteria in conferences with teacher/peers • offer suggestions for revision of criteria/rubrics • advocate for themselves, using criteria
Descriptive feedback	• offer descriptive feedback to help students determine where they are in the learning process and make adjustments for further success • may do this orally or in writing	• receive descriptive feedback related to learning outcomes and other relevant criteria • listen to feedback that is personalized, based on what they say, do, and produce • work with descriptive feedback to improve their performance (feedback is not a grade or number) • realize that feedback is not a grade or a number
Questions	• use questions that are open-ended • encourage all students to respond to and ask questions • encourage students to develop their own questions	• develop questions related to the topic of study and their personal interests • devise questions that go beyond the literal to the inferential and "beyond the text" • recognize that questions deepen their understanding of learning intentions • recognize that questions extend their learning beyond the stated learning intentions or outcomes
Peer- and self-assessment	• offer opportunities for students to self-assess and give feedback to peers, moving them toward personalizing and self-regulating their learning and success • coach students to use shared criteria when offering praise and constructive feedback • invite students to conference with peers on ongoing projects and tasks	• refer to the criteria to identify the strengths in their performance and to identify personal goals to work on • give feedback to their peers, using criteria to identify strengths and areas to work on
Ownership	• encourage students to own their learning, to feel a shared ownership of the learning community, and to work toward making a difference in their own and others' learning • provide opportunities for students to create and/or revise criteria • create opportunities for students to reflect in their learning • invite students to set goals for learning • periodically ask students to refer back to goals, plans and criteria	• set goals, make a plan to achieve their goals, monitor their learning, and revise goals and plans • refer to the descriptive feedback they receive • can explain the role they had in creating learning tasks and outcomes, and their own understanding of them as well as the skills they have developed

© Portage & Main Press, 2014, *It's All About Thinking: Creating Pathways for All Learnings in the Middle Years*, BLM, ISBN 978-1-55379-509-4

and to have them write poetry to, as, or about these individuals. They provided picture books, poems written by local students of First Nations ancestry from *Duck Soup for the Aboriginal Soul* (Reid and Cook 2000), and the novel *No Time to Say Goodbye* (Olsen 2001) that would fuel their writing.

Since their overall unit goal was for the students to think about their own learning, Nicole and Leyton asked them to generate criteria for the poetry in free verse that they were being asked to write. Their next task was to choose the reading strategies that matched their criteria. When students identified images, feelings, the five senses, and powerful words as criteria, Nicole and Leyton used them as aspects of their teaching strategies. The first lesson with poetry was the anchor for every reading and writing activity after that. The three lessons that follow reflect the pivotal points for our students' success in writing poetry.

Lesson 1 (anchor lesson)

Goal: Students learn to generate powerful criteria for writing poetry in free verse.

[handwritten: intentionally set this]

Setting the context

Nicole and Leyton selected three poems from *Duck Soup* and organized the students into groups of four. They read Jerry's poem *My Grandma* together. In their groups, the students reflected on "What makes this poem powerful?" and shared their criteria supported with examples from the poem. After class discussion, they recorded each group's responses on a T-chart.

What makes this poem powerful?	Example from the poem

Criteria

Together, the class read two more of the student poems in free verse from *Duck Soup* ("Dreams" by Crystal Williams and "orange soda pop" by Whitney James). Leyton and Nicole then repeated the process of looking for examples and defining criteria for powerful work. Within their group, each student circled their top three criteria and shared them, then negotiated down to four "must haves." As a class, the groups discussed the criteria further, considering the relative merits and drawbacks of each, to reach a final list.

Figure 8.2 Class criteria for writing free verse

• Captures the reader's attention	• Makes you wonder
• Emotions	• Message
• Interesting	• Creates an image in your mind
• Descriptive words	• Detailed
• Humour	• Powerful words
• Exciting	• Hilarious
• Colourful words	• Fantastic topic
• Connects to your life	• Feelings
	• 5 senses

Nicole and Leyton wanted to combine these class-generated criteria with the provincial performance standards for writing, but also to allow the students' thinking to set the direction of the unit. They decided to use one teaching strategy several times throughout the unit. They adapted the strategy "Four Quadrants of a Thought" (Brownlie and Close 1991) because it addressed the criteria students identified during their brainstorming session (see Figure 8.3). Teachers and students used the class-generated list of criteria to focus their reading and to set goals for their writing and for assessment—self-assessment as well as assessment by their peers and their teachers.

Figure 8.3 Four Quadrants: Thoughts and reactions in a graphic organizer

Images *Gives the reader a picture in their mind*	**Physical Senses** *Has descriptive, powerful, and/or colourful words*
I see...	I hear...
Language (Imagination) *Makes the reader wonder*	**Emotions** *Shares feelings*
I wonder...	I feel...

Lesson 2

Goals:

- To help students generate ideas and questions about residential schools
- To identify images, words, and feelings in free verse

Leyton and Nicole discussed with the class how the Four Quadrants reading strategy matched the criteria they generated for a powerful poem. They asked students to discuss in groups what they could write or draw in their graphic organizer. Nicole and Leyton then took turns reading aloud from the picture book memoir *Mush-Hole: Memoirs of a Residential School* by Maddie Harper (1993). Using the first two pages, they modelled the process of writing and drawing words, images, the questions that come to mind, and the feelings of characters in the Four Quadrants graphic organizer on the white board. Then students added their own ideas based on the next pages of the text. A few students were asked to add their ideas to the shared graphic organizer. This was an opportunity to show the many different ways one can process information and represent ideas. Leyton and Nicole referred to the criteria list when they asked the students whether and how *Mush-Hole* met any of the criteria of "What makes writing powerful?"

Continuing to move through the story, Nicole and Leyton occasionally stopped and students shared their responses within their small group, explaining why they chose the detail they did and how it met the criteria. They asked students to ensure that they had more than three items per quadrant by the end of the story.

Students could then choose to write either *as* a character in the book, *to* a character in the book, or *about* a character in the book. They referred to the criteria to consider how to make their writing more powerful.

To further nurture students' self-regulated learning, Nicole asked them to reflect on which criteria they believed they could better address in their poem. They finished the lesson by reading out pieces. Some students had already written in free verse form, while others wrote prose pieces. After each student read their work, the class identified which criteria they had heard in the piece. This activity required students to be actively engaged during the lesson as they identified key images, words, questions, and feelings and then personalized and transformed them as they wrote their own pieces.

As Nicole worked with Lynn to explore other aspects of First Nations culture and the students engaged in various inquiry activities, they used the criteria and the Four Quadrants graphic organizer several more times, and each time they ended by writing a poem in free verse.

Lesson 3 and on

Goals:

- ⊙ To fuel student writing
- ⊙ To practise collecting ideas for writing

Strategies: "Four Quadrants" and "Reading like a Writer"

As students read or listened to a story, poem, or article, or responded to an image, they wrote and drew in their graphic organizer, using descriptive phrases, images, sensations (5 senses), and emotions. Then, as the text was read several times, they shared their writing with a partner and added to their organizers any ideas that came out of their discussion. After a subsequent discussion with the whole class, more ideas were added to the class example.

Final Lesson

Goals:

- ⊙ To process the ideas and apply the knowledge strategy
- ⊙ To have students write their own free verse

With the class, Nicole and Leyton reviewed the criteria that describe free verse:

- does not follow classic rhymes or meters
- may use poetic techniques of key words, patterns, and repetition
- may express powerful ideas in prose, but is formatted on separate lines
- may repeat words or lines in stanzas, with varying appeals to the senses
- usually uses language that evokes strong feelings
- usually uses descriptive phrases that call up strong images

It was not long before the students had written six poems. Leyton and Nicole asked them to select their two strongest ones and to conference about them with two other students and one teacher, and to then rework their pieces based on the feedback they received.

For the end-of-unit celebration, Lynn Wainwright returned to lead the class through celebration activities and to share their favourite works (see Figure 8.4 for examples).

Figure 8.4 Examples of students' free verse

Mush Hole
by Augustine

A jail of terrors is now my home.
I have tried to overcome my fears
And luckily I managed to survive
In this mush hole.
I am not the only one here
There are many other kindred spirits
Trapped.
We learn many traditional things
But none of the things we learn
Have anything to do with real culture,
My spiritual self.
My traditions are now worn out,
Left in the cold,
Abandoned by its children,
Us the First Nations people.
The Europeans
Have taken our culture to the ground.
Our culture said "time out"
And gave up,
At least for now.

Residential Schools
Roman Klima

Residential schools are places
Of terror and tremor
It's like going to a jail cell
Locked in
No where
To go.

It's a vast emptiness of
Terror and horror
With Nuns as powerful
As mountains.

Trying to get past
Them is like trying to get up
A straight hill
With no ledges.
There is no way out

But for now residential schools
Are closed and
First Nations hope
It stays that way
Forever

My Feelings
by Travis

I feel good when I'm with my family, but
feel the same as you because my mom
has lots of hard times in her
life like drugs and alcohol. Then it
started to infect me inside my heart
how bad and confusing my life is.
Now I'm sad because my mom is
Gone and I'm not with her.
I feel so miserable and scared for
Her. She's in Vancouver right now
But, I don't know where she is and that
worries me. I've moved to lots of
other schools. Lots of the kids are
cruel and, even some of the teachers
can be. But your school was probably
more cruel. It must have been painful
terrifying from the horror that came from the belt
or stick in those long years. It must have been lonely at the school
and when you ran away and went to skid row! I feel sick
to my stomach that they did all that. You probably ran
away from the terror and horror of that prison school.
I hope you feel better about your native self. I'm
native too. My name is Travis, and I'm in grade six.

Building Criteria with Students

If we want students to self-regulate and co-regulate their learning, they need to become engaged in defining criteria and monitoring their learning against these criteria. Start by building criteria with students for a task that is familiar and comfortable for you. In the previous example, Nicole and Leyton chose free verse poetry because they could show student samples and use picture books to support students' brainstorming. As you became more comfortable with building criteria with your class, build criteria that involve communication, collaboration, and critical thinking. These competencies are less obvious to students and yet, when developed, make a significant difference for students in their learning.

For example, before starting a Literature Circle, as part of a Humanities unit on the theme of displacement, Nicole's students were to determine the criteria for a powerful Literature Circle discussion.

To build class-generated criteria:

- Provide the focus question on which students must collaborate to establish their criteria: "What makes a powerful discussion in a Literature Circle?"
- Ask that each student record their response on a separate strip of paper. Then ask them to share their responses in groups of 4 or 5 and decide collectively which are most important, and how they can be categorized with a descriptive heading.
- Have the groups return to full-class discussion, and share their category headings with their corresponding criteria. On the board or chart paper, resolve the most appropriate categories and negotiate the assignment of the criteria to achieve consensus—a messy, but crucial, process for students to participate in, because they are then more willing to take ownership of the criteria and of the processes of collaborative learning.
- Format the results (categories and criteria) and provide a copy for each student as reference in their notebook (Figure 8.5).
- Teachers can sit with, or in proximity to, student groups to listen in and assess how well they are developing their skills in reference to the criteria.
- Most importantly, have students self assess and set goals using these criteria.

Figure 8.5 Class-generated criteria for Literature Circles

What makes a powerful Literature Circle?			
Reading strategies	**Talking strategies**	**Taking responsibility**	**Cooperation and Teamwork**
• Make images • Make connections • Ask questions • Look in the back of the book for help	• Everyone participates in discussion • One speaker at a time • Take turns speaking • Wait until it's your turn to speak • Speak clearly; make eye contact • Pay attention to other speakers • Piggy back on someone else's ideas • Ask questions • Listen to others while they speak • Listen to everyone's ideas before making a group decision	• Be on task • Finish assigned reading and understand it • Take care of your personal belongings • Check over your work with your group • Do not spoil the ending of the book	• Be *co-op-work-ative* • Help each other • Encourage others • Work as a team • Respect others' ideas; do not judge their thoughts and feelings

Alternative ways to generate criteria

1. Have a group of 4 or 5 adults model a Literature Circle discussion for students to watch, listen to, and describe what they see and hear as desirable criteria. This is a "fishbowl" approach to criteria building (Schnellert, Datoo, Ediger, and Panas 2009).
2. Have a group of 4 or 5 older students who are familiar with this process model the discussion to introduce new students to how the process works.
3. For more examples of criteria building see *Setting and Using Criteria* (Davies, Cameron, and Gregory 2011) and *Student Diversity* (chapter 4) (Brownlie, Feniak, and Schnellert 2006).

Making Shakespeare Accessible

Some students could plot their interest in reading on a continuum from non-reader to voracious reader. In Tammy Renyard's English 9 class, she has heard struggling readers say that they've never read an entire text. In fact, they pride themselves on the strategies they use that allow them to be successful *without actually reading*—they are masters of fake reading! Tammy's goal, therefore, is to actively engage her students with text by asking herself: "How do I structure student learning so that fake reading is not possible? How do I empower students to recognize their strengths in language arts? How do I deeply engage students in text?"

One text that she likes to use is Shakespeare's *A Midsummer Night's Dream*. Tammy knows that if she can successfully introduce Shakespeare and have students deeply engage in the learning, they might shift their attitude about literature, which might change how they view themselves as learners.

Unit Goals

- Introduce a complex text through a variety of formats (play, graphic novel, read-aloud, movie, puppet show).
- Recognize and use learning modes that work best for students.
- Uncover the themes of *A Midsummer Night's Dream*.
- Examine the characters.
- Write in the role of at least one character and explore motives, feelings, and plot.
- Use images that capture the important events and ideas in the play.
- Develop a mind map (Bennett and Rolheiser-Bennett 2001) that demonstrates their understanding of the elements of the play, and the interconnections of characters, plot, and theme.

Act I: Introduction to the Play

On the day she introduces the *Dream*, Tammy gives pairs of students strips of paper that contain basic information about the play (characters, setting, plot, and theme). She asks each pair to organize the strips in a way that makes sense to them. Through this process, the students activate any background knowledge about the play, the genre, or stories in general as they discuss the details they have in hand and try to see how they fit together. Then, students are asked to share something they notice or a question they have about the play and write a personal prediction based on details they note.

In the subsequent class, students participated in the Susan Close strategy GOSSIP (Go Out and Selectively Seek Important Points). They brainstorm and write what they already know about the play in one quadrant. They share their ideas and those of others with new partners—the gossip. This sharing allows students to cover the main elements of the play—the characters, setting, and plot—and gain some idea about possible themes. Tammy suggests to the students that, with the knowledge they now have, they will discover how they can best read and understand the text and enjoy the play. For example, the students track their thinking during the reading of each Act of the play. The graphic organizer (Figure 8.6) encourages the class to focus on what's important and why (Harvey and Goudvis 2007; Close 2014) and on images and details, then to write a one-line summary of each scene in each Act. Class can continue making similar graphic organizers for each subsequent Act.

Figure 8.6 Graphic organizer for students to track reading of Acts

A Midsummer Night's Dream

What's Important		Why
Act I – Scene I Setting:		
Act I – Scene II Setting:		
Image	Detail	
Act I – Scene I: What happened? (one sentence summary)		
Act I – Scene II: What happened? (one sentence summary)		
Connections: What connections are you making to the text?		
Prediction: What I think will happen next		

Proceeding through the Acts

Introduce the play with a different focus for each Act. Stop students periodically throughout the reading to discuss what's happening, what's important and why, what they are noticing about characters, what questions come to mind, and so on. At the end of each Act, have students work as partners to consolidate their understanding. They might also use their graphic organizer to keep track of their thinking and to reflect on what they notice about their own thinking and learning during that class. Their observations and reflections become more important as the teacher introduces the different formats and modes based on the work. Invite them to select one character's part to read aloud, but reassure them that the role can be small and read out loud with a partner.

> **Note:** Prior to this unit, several months of strategic scaffolding have created an atmosphere and community of safety so that students feel comfortable reading out loud. After having worked with partners, small groups, and the full class prior to this, the students know they will have time and support, if needed—for example, shorter selections to read, smaller roles, and text photocopied so they can practise before reading out loud.

Mini-Task

With Act I, work with the class to generate criteria for writing a letter (voice, language use, details from text). Ask students to assume the role of a character and to write a letter explaining what's happening in their life at this time. Follow up by asking students to reflect on their writing: *"What did you notice about your learning when you were in the role?"* When students begin to understand when their learning is strong, they will be able to replicate or seek out similar opportunities.

Act II: Graphic Novel Format

Have students work with a partner to navigate the text. Prompt them again to reflect: *"What are you noticing about your understanding of the text when we use the graphic novel?"* Discuss whether they prefer the format used for Act I or the graphic novel format and why. Invite students to report out, using the response frame *"We think the read-aloud or graphic novel format is more accessible because_____."* It's important, if not critical, to continually encourage students to be conscious of their learning style. Have them continue to track their understanding of the text on their graphic organizer (Figure 8.6).

Act III: Movie Format

Using the 1999 version of the movie, have the class start at Act III. Pause the movie frequently to allow students time to interact with their partner. At the end of the Act, pose the following questions:

- What did you notice about your learning? Think about our three formats we've worked with so far—print, graphic novel, movie—and talk to your partner about which text you found most accessible and why.

- Directors make many decisions about how to make a play or story come to life on the screen. Which parts did you think were well done? Which parts seemed odd to you?

Mini-Task

Go back into the play (print text) to find and list the best insults. Find a partner and exchange your insult lists. As a class, continue to break down some of the insults and character motives, and discuss whether or not these would be considered insults today.

Act IV: Student Choice

Ask all students to reflect on their learning style, and decide how they want to work with Act IV. As they select, put a quick tally on the board. Then allow them to finish Act IV in their own way—read aloud in a group, read aloud the graphic novel, or finish the movie. Have students again reflect on what they noticed in the different versions, and then complete their graphic organizer.

Mini-Task

Have each student select a paper strip bearing the name (in one ink colour) of a character in the play. Then all students search for others whose character is written in the same colour ink to form a group. The group must then find the act and section in the play where their characters interact and take on the roles in a mini performance. The catch? Their character is a gingerbread cookie that must be iced to look like the character. They will be behind a draped table to perform, and they can use their text for support. This strategy (or your own version) not only honours students' creativity and adds novelty but also allows students a sense of safety because they are "hidden behind the cookie," if you will.

Generating criteria for the summative assessment

Present students with examples of mind maps to discuss how effective they are. Ask them to refine a set of criteria for creating effective mind maps. This activity should precede—and scaffold—any summative assessment activity in which students have to create an individual product.

Final independent task

- Write a few paragraphs on your understanding of Shakespeare's *A Midsummer Night's Dream*.
- Write a few paragraphs about which format best helped you access the text, using examples from Shakespeare's *A Midsummer Night's Dream*.

Teacher Reflection

Student learning and engagement were extremely high throughout the unit. Students were able to reflect on their learning styles and explain why certain approaches were easier while others were more challenging. More than half of this class had been identified as having learning needs; in fact, several students had not successfully completed English 8. Although Tammy would base their marks on their final independent tasks and their personal reflections, she asked her students to write the same final test as used by other teachers who taught the same course and play. Students were surprised by and proud of their results. Her process of engaging her students through active participation in varied formats of the text—combined with the metacognitive question *"How best do I learn?"*—led to deep and meaningful learning.

Engaging Students as Critical Thinkers

In our teaching, we involve students in building and using performance criteria from the beginning of a unit of study. When we develop and use the same criteria for both the formative and summative assessments, students become connected to the course content and engage as strategic learners. When students do not know the targets for their learning, they cannot meet them. Learners figure out what criteria are relevant to a particular task, makes plans in relation to those criteria, and monitor and reflects on their success as they engage in a task over time. To help students become self-regulated learners, we invite them to create criteria and to find evidence of these criteria in samples of their own work. Most importantly, we want students to assess their own work and adapt what they do, keeping both external and internal criteria in mind. As they develop more fully as self-regulating learners, they rely less on teachers and seek out other human sources and resources to clarify and extend their ongoing learning.

Rubrics and Timelines in Social Studies

In Linda, Leyton, and Eve Minuk's social studies unit, one of the learning tasks was to create a critical timeline of the actions of Napoleon Bonaparte and decide whether or not his actions were heroic or not. Students engaged with diverse texts to determine the most important information to place on their critical timeline. Numerical values were associated with the information on a scale from minus 5 to plus 5 with plus 5 being the most heroic.

The criteria developed with the students in this example were to help them determine importance, use evidence from resources to justify their interpretations, and become more metacognitive. Students developed their competency in these areas over time through a variety of activities and tasks. It's important for students to know the criteria—and work with a rubric—so that they can receive feedback, self-assess, and adjust their actions to achieve increased success. A rubric offers gradations of competence and gives all learners areas for improvement.

Lesson 1—Previewing Text Features

Connecting

- Students look at the texts for this unit and preview them to predict key learnings. They had previously learned to look at text features (titles, subtitles, illustrations, maps, charts, and other text inserts) in order to predict the content.
- They share their thinking and create a list of predictions.

Processing: Reading to determine importance

- With a shared text, ask student partners to make predictions while developing a Tchart with three of their predictions on the left side and corresponding evidence on the right.
- After modelling an example, have students read the text, putting sticky notes beside the five most important events or actions. (In this lesson, students were weighing the importance of Napoleon's actions based on how they affected the people of France positively or negatively.)
- Have student pairs merge into groups of four, to share and discuss what they believe to be the four most important ideas, events, and facts. Each student takes one of these and draws on a sticky note an image representing this event.

Transforming/Personalizing: What's important and why?

- Students place the images on their paper and respond to the prompts: *"What is important?" "Why is it important?"* Students link their answers to the text.

Lesson 2—Building Criteria

Connecting

- Gather several samples of critical timelines for historical events. Have students (in groups of four) examine them in response to the question: *"What are the most powerful aspects of these illustrated timelines?"*
- When they have finished, combine two groups (eight students) to discuss and compare their criteria and propose different category titles (up to eight) for grouping all their criteria.
- Invite the groups to report their results to the whole class, and record the range of responses, including all overlapping details, until the next step.
- If necessary, ask students to point out the overlapping details. Then ask them to negotiate and agree on final titles for the essential categories. Suggest that they come to an agreement on four categories to frame the performance rubric within which they will define the progression of performance criteria and refine the phrasing of description points on a four-point progression of criteria.

Processing

To assist them in organizing their thoughts on paper, provide a template with appropriate boxes using these instructions:

1. In small groups, examine the timeline samples. Record the features—format, symbols, people, images, essential text—and other details that you think are significant enough, even critical, in the timeline sequence for the topic.
2. Review your notes with your group to see how you might sort the significant features into categories. Name the categories and re-list the features under the different category titles.
3. With students participating as a class, discuss the categories and features to refine the descriptions and re-phrase them as criteria for reference as each student develops their own timeline.

Transforming / Personalizing

- Draw five columns on the board from left to right with the headings: Column 1: Criteria; Column 2: Attempted / Good start; Column 3: Complete / Almost there; Column 4: Proficient / You did it; Column 5: Distinguished / Woohoo!
- Finish the table framework for the rubric. Down the first column, write the four criteria: Key events; Explains impact of event on society; Images connect to key event; Communicates unity of overall message.
- Have students place their sticky image on the board under the heading they think it best fits, and share out why they placed it there. Have a recorder jot down the reasons, which can become the descriptive criteria for the levels of performance. Allow students to move their image if they change their mind.
- For the next class, draft a rubric of the class-created criteria (Figure 8.7).

Numeracy Circles: Tackling Problems Together

Ken Wayne, Tammy Orthner, and Sheri Gurney from Sooke School District are three teachers who take every opportunity to collaborate and develop their practice. Ken was teaching grade 8 and 9 math and science while Tammy and Sheri were both generalists in grade 7, when, as a group, they collaborated on this math unit based on backward design principles.

For years, Tammy and Sheri had been successfully teaching Literature Circles, based on Faye Brownlie's model in *Grand Conversations, Thoughtful Responses* (2005). They loved the reading choices offered to their students, the variety of levels to maximize individual success, and the learning that took place through rich conversations about shared text. Could they recreate this valuable, collaborative learning environment in a math setting? Would they be able to develop something that would be successful at all three levels—grades 7, 8, and 9?

Figure 8.7 Class-created criteria in assessment rubric for critical timeline project

Name: _____   Date: _____

Rubric for a Critical Timeline

Performance Indicators
(Observable descriptors indicating extent to which a criterion is set)

	Attempted	Complete	Proficient	Distinguished
Key events	Lacks evidence of care taken in selecting key events Demonstrates insufficient grasp of the content	Some relevant events; may lack range of scores and impact	Includes relevant events from French Citizens' point of view	Evidence of great care taken in selecting most relevant events that show great range of impact on French society
Explains impact of event on society	Lacks explanation of the impact the event had on society	Inconsistently explains impact events had on society	Clearly explains the significant impact events had on society	Clearly and concisely explains the significant impacts that events had on society
Images connect to key event	Few or no images used to represent events or their impact	Some images connect to the key events and add to the overall timeline	Some images symbolize impact of key events	Images vividly represent how key events impacted society; may include icons
Overall unity/ message	Impacts of some events are communicated, but relationship is unclear; may be out of order	Minimal sense of cohesion; some events may not seem related; impact is lacking logic	Attention given to making timeline an effective tool for communicating how specific events are related to French society and one another	Strong sense of cohesion: the timeline is an effective tool for communicating the impact of events during the Napoleonic Era on French society
	Teacher Evaluation: ____ / 4		Self-Evaluation: ____ / 4	

Minuk, Schnellert, Watson: January 2008

As a team, they identified the math topics and processes that their students struggled to learn. Across all three grade levels, students faced the most difficulty when answering mathematical word problems. It appeared that some students tackled the problems without forming a plan of attack and that they did not, in fact, understand what the "problem" was. The teachers resolved to teach the strategies that could help their students systematically break word problems down in order to help them understand the mathematical concepts and processes being asked of them and, thus, work out a solution. They planned to emphasize different ways to solve problems, to have students work in groups to share their questions, their findings, and their "ways of knowing." Through this sharing, students could help each other over stumbling blocks, share the paths they took to reach an answer, and apply new learning to their own work.

The three teachers recognized that their diverse students all brought different abilities, background knowledge, and ways of expressing their learning into the group. Nevertheless, they wanted their students to have success in mathematics by learning several strategies and plans that would carry them through a lifetime of math-related problem solving. They hoped that, through Numeracy Circle discussions, their students would begin to understand the advantages of working together and see how they could use each other as valuable resources.

Rationale

As the teachers began to plan the Numeracy Circle unit, they isolated some difficulties their students had when solving word problems and listed their needs:

- Students need to identify what the question is asking.
- Students need to access their background knowledge in order to connect it with their understanding of the problem.
- Students need to estimate the answer in order to verify their answer.
- Students need to express their thinking in pictures, numbers, and words.
- Students need to share their thinking and strategies with others in their group.
- Students need to self-assess their level of understanding before and after Circle meetings.
- Students need to discover more than one strategy for solving a problem.
- Students need to reflect on their learning.

In order to respond to these expectations for their students, the teachers realized what they had to do

- Immerse students in a variety of word problems similar in concept, but differing in difficulty.
- Expose students to multiple strategies for solving problems.

- Directly teach the steps in each problem-solving strategy, using a graphic organizer that the students could use for meetings of the Numeracy Circles.
- Provide opportunities for students to show their learning in different ways.
- Create an environment where students feel safe to talk, make mistakes, and recognize that it's okay not to know the answer.
- Conference with students about problem solving and use their responses to identify gaps in their learning and to guide their subsequent teaching.

Literature Circles as a Gateway

Tammy and Sheri's favourite part of their English program is teaching their classes through Literature Circles. Using a variety of novels, they tried to meet their students' interests and varied reading levels. Students would read at their own pace, but meet bi-weekly to discuss the connections they were making. Through these conversations/ discussions, the students could delve more deeply into the meaning of their book, its characters, and the plot. By sharing the connections they were making, the students left the Literature Circles with new understandings. The teachers wanted to emulate the success of this approach as much as possible for their Numeracy Circles. But they decided not to have six levels of text, as in the Literature Circles, and instead to offer their students a choice from two or three word problems at varying levels and addressing the same concept, and allow time during class to complete their question using the graphic organizer (Figure 8.8).

For the Numeracy Circles, they organized their students into groups based on which question they had chosen. Within their group, students described to other members the strategies they used to solve the problem. For the students who had not solved the problem completely, the members of their group would help them reach an understanding of the problem and how to solve it. The Numeracy Circles supported students to reach a deeper understanding.

The teachers recognized that their students could answer questions involving just numbers, but with word problems—even when the same concepts were being addressed—the students seemed stumped. Arthur Hyde had found that when the students looked at the problem with specific questions in mind, they found it easier to understand and solve (Hyde 2006). Tammy, Sheri, and Ken adapted his questions to create their own graphic organizer for problem solving in their Numeracy Circles:

1. What do I know for sure? (What is happening in the problem?)
2. What will the answer tell me? (What am I trying to find out?)
3. Are there any special conditions and rules that I need to know, or do I need background knowledge?
4. About how much would the answer be?

Figure 8.8 Graphic organizer for problem-solving strategies in Numeracy Circles

Numeracy Circles

Name: _____

THE BIG 4: Questions to ask to get a handle on any word problem

What do I KNOW for sure? What is HAPPENING in the problem?	What will the answer TELL me? What am I trying to FIND out?	Are there any special CONDITIONS and RULES that I need to know, or do I need BACKGROUND KNOWLEDGE?	ABOUT HOW MUCH would the answer be?

This is how I solved the problem using pictures, numbers, and words:

☐ ORIGINAL COLOUR   ☐ NEW UNDERSTANDINGS COLOUR

"You should leave your Numeracy Circle group smarter than when you entered it!"

REFLECTING ON MY LEARNING (or Why I am smarter after my meeting)

_____

_____

_____

© Portage & Main Press, 2014, *It's All About Thinking: Creating Pathways for All Learnings in the Middle Years*, BLM, ISBN 978-1-55379-509-4

Students who don't understand what the question is asking of them have a real struggle to respond. Hyde's model requires them to start pulling facts out of the problem:

"What do I know for sure?" From the answers, students can then isolate what the answer should tell them. *"What am I trying to find out?"* Responses to these two questions together give the students a solid base—what information they have and what information they need to find out. The third question *"Are there any special conditions…?"* focuses on what skills or mathematical concepts they need to apply in order to successfully solve the problem. The fourth question asks students to estimate the answer by drawing on all the information they have identified and any background knowledge they have. Their estimated answer is an important last step because it can help students reflect on the method they plan to use to solve the problem, which gives them a point of comparison for their solution.

After working through the process, the students asked more specific questions, and could self-assess to determine where they needed redirection. They gained more independence because they were able to record something on their organizer (no longer just a blank page), and that independence led to increased self-confidence.

The teachers allowed their students to solve the problems using any method or strategy that worked for them. The emphasis was to solve the problem as best they could while explaining their thinking through pictures, numbers, and words.

Learning Intentions

Ken, Tammy, and Sheri developed their lesson plan with this essential question in mind:

> *"Why is it important that I be an active problem-solver who can explain my thinking?"*

They then broke down the question into three parts, which became the learning intentions:

- How does explaining my thinking lead to a deeper understanding?
- How does finding patterns and relationships help me to choose appropriate strategies?
- Why is it important for me to be an active problem solver?

Lessons 1 and 2: Modelling how to work through a problem

- Lesson 1: Introduce students to the graphic organizer (Figure 8.8) to help guide them in solving any problem. Model each step using a think-aloud with a word problem.
- In Lesson 2, use a different word problem and ask students to describe their thinking as they work through the steps together.

- Ask students, together as a class, to reflect on how the steps can help them understand what they are being asked to do.

Lessons 3 through 8: Gradual release

- Using a common math problem, students work in groups, then pairs, and finally individually to solve varied word problems using the graphic organizer.
- After each problem, bring the class back together to complete a graphic organizer collaboratively as a class. Encourage your students to write or highlight new understandings in a different colour on their own organizer. Emphasize the varied strategies that students offer.

Lessons 9 through 14: Numeracy Circles

- Ken, Tammy, and Sheri moved on to Numeracy Circles where students engaged in small-group discussions based on the "just right" problem they selected to solve.
- To ensure the students' Numeracy Circles had successful meetings, the teachers made frequent references to Literature Circle meetings in order to elicit from their class the criteria they followed for successful group conversations. They also posted the criteria in the classroom as constant reference, if needed, during the Numeracy Circle meetings.

> A great source for differentiated word problems related to the same big idea is Marion Small's *Good Questions: Great Ways to Differentiate Mathematics Instruction*, 2012.

- Students chose their "just right" question, completed the graphic organizer to the best of their ability, and shared what they had done in their Numeracy Circle meeting. Students added to their organizer any new strategies or new ways of thinking that arose from the discussion.
- While the Numeracy Circle groups were meeting, Ken, Tammy and Sheri circled around the room to listen in, to help further discussion, and to encourage and reinforce their expectations. At this point, they also noted the teaching points they would bring to the closing class discussion.
- They gave their students time to write (on their organizer) their reflections on the Circle discussion process for collaboration in solving mathematical story problems—and to articulate their new learning.
- The teachers ran their Numeracy Circles in conjunction with the regular math curriculum, and the story problems chosen for Circle time reflected the concepts being dealt with in the curriculum.

Assessment

- The teachers' expectation was that students would be able to apply the strategies they learned to any problem, at any point, in any grade.

A true assessment, then, would demonstrate whether students had internalized strategies and were able to apply it on their own. Ken, Tammy, and Sheri found in subsequent tests and assessments for units of study that their students could independently attack word problems using the questions on the graphic organizer.

- After the Numeracy Circles, students handed in their finished graphic organizer when they had completed their reflection.
- Use the *BC Performance Standards for Numeracy* <www.bced.gov.bc.ca/perf_stands/numeracy.htm> or your own region's rubric (many provinces use the numeracy rubrics found through your jurisdiction's connection to WNCP <www.wncp.ca>) in assessing the students' thinking, solutions, and explanations.
- During the Numeracy Circles, the teachers assessed their groups formatively, by providing immediate feedback and redirecting them as necessary to move the students forward in their discussions and efforts to reach solutions.

At the end of the unit, Ken, Tammy, and Sheri were thankful for the time, the professional development, and resources allotted for their inquiry. The process had allowed them to collaboratively develop a tool that helped not only their students but others to approach, understand, and solve word problems successfully. The students enjoyed the Numeracy Circles and appreciated the independence and confidence the circles afforded.

Conclusion

Formative assessment approaches such as criteria-building, using a rubric to self-assess and give feedback, asking students metacognitive questions, and using peer-assessment can nurture students' self-regulation of their learning. We want students to be able to describe how they work from their strengths to build a plan that meets their particular learning needs. By becoming self-aware, students will be able to adjust their learning to meet new criteria. When students can select, use and adapt appropriate thinking strategies to aid in the achievement of their goals, they become their own teachers.

Chapter 9

Creating Pathways Using Diverse Texts

Educators Involved

Sue Gall: Classroom Teacher, SD 38, Richmond, BC

Starleigh Grass: Senior Policy Analyst, First Nations Education Steering Committee, British Columbia

Kristi Johnston: Classroom Teacher/Teacher-Librarian, SD 75, Mission, BC

Andrea Hart: Classroom Teacher, SD 61, Victoria, BC

Tammy Renyard: Classroom Teacher/Vice Principal, SD 61, Victoria, BC

Should all students be expected to engage deeply with the same text? What values are we projecting to students when we use only one text, at one reading level, with one particular perspective? What is our responsibility to our students?

What is a text?

The definition of literacy is expanding hand in hand with the definition of a text. At one time literacy referred to the ability to read printed words on a page. However, literacy now encompasses the ability to understand many types of media in a variety of contexts. We now have science literacy and environmental literacy and many, many more. These kinds of literacies recognize that thinking and learning in a discipline is based on how one acquires, creates, and shares information in specific ways—using texts as diverse as talk and action, tools and artifacts, ecosystems and cultures. Expanding our definition of "text" enables us to ensure that our students are literate in a multimodal world (NCTE 2007).

This expanded definition of text allows teachers to increase the scope of materials and resources that our students can access in order to grasp the concepts introduced in any curriculum. In today's media-rich environment, we have to equip our students with the ability to understand, work with—and create—a variety of texts, including audio, visual, and tactile media. Teaching skills and strategies, such as inferring or connecting, helps students access all texts, but students also need to be taught specific strategies like deconstructing the point of view in a video. When we build in metacognitive opportunities as well, we increase the likelihood that students' awareness of the skills and strategies that they are building will transfer across texts.

The Power of Text Sets

By offering a class many types of text on a theme, we can reinforce learning for all students. A thematic set in multiple media allows learners to choose types of text that support their strengths and build different literacies. A website, for example, might have a helpful infographic of the product lifecycle of a plastic water bottle. By including infographics as a type of text, we can incorporate information that might otherwise not be accessible by all students.

Students choose the type of text they prefer and form groups based on that text. In each group, the students work cooperatively to explore an inquiry question through their text, and communicate their insights to the others. Some individual students, after contributing to one group's collaborative inquiry activity, might move into a different text group. When they all come together as a class and communicate their insights to the other groups, they all benefit from one another's experiences of multiple texts.

In earlier chapters in this book, we introduced literature, information, and numeracy circles. These are also text sets. A Science teacher, for example, might include a variety of nonfiction books on a topic in order to show the dynamic nature of scientific knowledge and inquiry (Ebbers 2002).

Offering students choice in texts gives them ownership over their learning and increases their motivation and engagement, all leading to positive attitudes toward reading (NCTE 2007). Working with text sets increases students' agency, provides opportunities for scaffolding participation, and increases student confidence (Cumming-Potvin 2007).

By choosing one text from texts of different types and language levels, students can work more independently and participate in their learning from a position of strength. By researching a range of media for thematic text sets, teachers help equip students with the skills and strategies to navigate and make personal decisions within their text-rich world.

Culturally Responsive Teaching

Two of the core assumptions in culturally responsive teaching are that "culture infiltrates everything and cannot be ignored if one is to be an effective educator," and "cultural diversity is a strength" (Gay 2010). Text sets that represent multiple cultures heighten students' awareness of aspects of their cultural identity. By including texts that reflect the diversity within our classroom, we provide opportunities to build cultural congruity because students can find "matches, intersections, and bridges" between the materials and activities in the classroom and their lives outside of the classroom. Gay recommends that educators habitually build diversity of learning materials into content areas such as math and science where many minority students struggle the most (Gay 2002).

When students regularly see themselves represented in the texts they use, their engagement increases (NCTE 2007). Pairing culturally diverse texts with culturally responsive teaching can lead to high levels of engagement and inclusion in classrooms. By bringing culture to the forefront and highlighting diversity as a strength, teachers provide an environment that helps students understand the importance of different perspectives and cross-cultural communication, and these help to build positive self-concept.

Universal Design for Learning

Universal Design for Learning is an instructional framework that guides teachers to plan for and capture the strengths within the diverse composition of every classroom. By assembling text sets of varied formats, teachers provide students a choice in the type and format of resources that best suit their individual learning needs. Students' exploration of an inquiry question through "reading" varied resources—whether individually or as partners, whether in small-group or whole-class discussions—fosters the kind of collaborative environment that includes all learners and scaffolds the learning.

See chapter 4

Literature Circles and Thematic Teaching

There are times when using a single text with the whole class can be helpful. For instance, novel studies might use one common text to build students' background knowledge and develop a common language and common purpose for reading more widely about a particular topic. In this way, teachers can introduce anchoring strategies before moving their students into Literature Circles or Information Circles.

As an example, Nicole began a unit with the whole class on the theme of "displacement," using the novel *I Am a Taxi* by Deborah Ellis (2006), before moving on to the text set of novels for Literature Circles. Having this common focus supported students by activating their background knowledge before they chose from the wider range of short texts — picture books, newspaper clips, videos, YouTube clips, music, and information books. Offering such a variety of texts accommodates the students who need more accessible texts in order to learn content and keep up with their peers. We can no longer teach to one type of learner, and diversity in the range of texts we offer our students provides greater opportunities for including all students in the learning.

Sue Gall, a grade 6/7 teacher at Ferris School, has been working with Nicole for several years, sharing a passion for literacy and social justice issues. When planning a new unit, they often call Kidsbooks (a bookstore in Vancouver) for help in gathering texts related to their theme. Together they developed the list of titles for the resources they needed for four thematic units. They decided on 8 to10 novels, and divided the books between them to read over the summer to make sure the resources would meet the interests and reading levels of their students. The list (Figure 9.1) included at least one picture book and a graphic novel as accessible titles (A) and a challenging novel (C) to address the range of learners. The number in parentheses following each book title indicates the number of copies of each title. Nicole and Sue created a school-wide novel rotation plan (Year 1 and Year 2 columns of titles) to ensure that the same novel would not be used in consecutive years, which is especially pertinent for combined grade classes.

Figure 9.1 Text sets on theme of "displacement" for Literature Circle in combined grade 6/7 class, including a two-year rotation plan

Year 1	Year 2
Kogawa, J. *Naomi's Road* A (3)	Naidoo, B. *The Other Side of Truth* C (6)
Porter, P. *The Crazy Man* A (6)	Myers, W. D. *Darnell Rock Reporting* A (6)
Olsen, S. *No Time to Say Goodbye* A (6)	Carlson, N. S. *Family Under the Bridge* A (3)
Walters, E. *War of Eagles* C (6)	Banning, G. *Out on a Limb* A (6)
Williams, L. E. *Behind the Bedroom Wall* A (6)	Key, W. *Alabama Moon* A (6)
Walters, G. *Fouling Out* A (6)	O'Connor, B. *How to Steal a Dog* A (6)
Watts, I. *Goodbye, Marianne* A (6)	Walters, E. *Shattered* A (6)
D'Adamo, F. *Iqbal* A (30)	Ellis, D. *I Am a Taxi* A (30)
Fine Arts (Drama)	**Fine Arts (Drama)**
Burdett, L. *Hamlet*, Shakespeare Can Be Fun series (30)	Burdett, L. *Romeo and Juliet*, Shakespeare Can Be Fun series (30)
Theme: Identity	**Theme: Perspectives**
Cummings, P. *Red Kayak* C (6)	Boyne, J. *Boy in Striped Pajamas* A (6)
Spinelli, J. *Flipped* A (6)	Naidoo, B. *Burn My Heart* C (6)
Spinelli, J. *Stargirl* A (6)	Cummings, P. *What Mr. Mattero Did* A (6)
Koss, A.G. *Girls* A (6)	Choldenko, G. *If a Tree Falls During Lunch Period* C (6)
Bunting, E. *Blackwater* A (6)	Choldenko, G. *Notes from a Liar and her Dog* A (6)
Walters, E. *Alexandria of Africa* C (6)	Hayes, R. *Mixing It* A (6)
Singer, N. *Feather Boy* A (6)	
A = accessible; C = challenging; (#) number of copies of the title	

First Nations Community-Generated Texts

Starleigh Grass highlights community voices, both in her own classroom practice and when she works with community organizations on curriculum materials. When planning a lesson on "persuasion," Starleigh includes several articles from a local First Nations publication that illustrate different approaches to persuasion and information-sharing. By providing texts created by a local First Nations community, Starleigh supports her students in imagining different ways that they can participate in public dialogue and decision making.

School-based Aboriginal support workers as well as school librarians can offer teachers information about community-generated texts of local First Nations. Many local band offices, tribal councils, or other organizations publish articles, community reports, and interviews in newsletters or newspapers, some of which are accessible online. Such resources can provide useful curricular connections for teaching students how to read and write relevant and personal nonfiction.

Local rights and title court cases provide another source of similar texts. Leaders in Starleigh's nation, for example, led a court case for rights and title to their land, and the court decision was published online—along with appendices submitted by the plaintiff, the Tsilhqot'in Nation. These appendices included compilations of oral history from Elders on such topics as traditional land use, boundary maintenance, early contact, and settlement. The instructional possibilities for including such materials in a unit of study are infinite. Using current texts from *recent* community, legal, and organizational sources ensures that we do not "freeze" indigenous people in the distant past.

> Aboriginal texts create an inclusive environment that respects and honours diverse voices and that can contribute to closing the achievement gap.

Sample Lesson

Our middle years students need to learn about important issues from the past that still impact us today. Starleigh teaches about Aboriginal persons' experience in residential schools. The Truth and Reconciliation Commission <www.trc.ca/> features first-person accounts of residential school survivors. On the ArtsLink website <artslink.ca>, teachers and students can freely access short biographies of ten artists who are residential school survivors. Their biographies reveal the negative impact that residential schools had on them and how their art is helping them heal. The material provides a lead-in to other readings on residential schools.

Most of the readings on the ArtsLink site are not overly graphic; however, some sections are upsetting. Three pieces suitable for grades 4 to 7 are based on true stories: Shirley Sterling's novel *My Name is Seepeetza* was authored by a residential school survivor from the Nlakapamux First Nation in British Columbia; Christy Jordan-Fenton's novel *Fatty Legs* and *A Stranger at Home* were authored in collaboration with her mother-in-law, Margaret Pokiak-Fenton (Oleman), an Inuvialuit from the High Arctic. *Fatty Legs* documents Oleman's time at residential school and *A Stranger at Home* documents her difficulty reintegrating into her family and community after residential school.

It might be wise to have a school- or community-based Aboriginal support person available for students who might become upset. The Truth and Reconciliation Commission also has a 24/7 helpline (1-866-925-4419) available for survivors and their families. Although the stories of residential schools are a sensitive and, at times, uncomfortable topic to teach, the 2010 *Urban Aboriginal Peoples Study* <www.uaps.ca/> found that more than half of non-Aboriginal people interviewed had never heard of residential schools. When Prime Minister Harper offered the federal government's apology for residential schools in Parliament in 2008, the speech included a commitment to educate all Canadians about residential school history so that everyone can be a part of the reconciliation and the healing. As educators, we all have a responsibility to see that commitment through.

Introducing the topic

Before introducing the text set, post the following questions on the board:

- Why do we study residential schools?
- How did residential schools impact individuals?
- What does "to heal from residential schools" mean?

Have the students record these questions, then brainstorm with a partner to come up with possible answers to these questions. Ask each team to share with the rest of the class their answer to one of the questions.

The first text

- Ensure that all students have Internet access to the ArtsLink site to find the biographies. Have them work as partners to read the introductory paragraph of three different artists, then choose one artist and use the information, including artwork and videos, from the biography to answer the three questions presented in class.

Sharing with another group

- After students have had sufficient time to read a biography and record their answers, have them meet with another group that has read a different biography. Have them compare: How are the answers the same? How are they different?

Whole-class discussion

- As a class, compile a list of the answers to the three questions. Because not all texts explicitly address the first question, discuss possible answers that could be inferred from the biographies.

Reflecting on new understandings and moving inquiry forward

- Have students reflect on how their understanding of residential schools changed as a result of reading the biographies and participating in the class discussion. When they write out their reflections, encourage them to refer to specific details from the interview or the class discussion. Ask students to end their reflection with three questions that they still have about residential schools.

Critical Literacy versus Critical Reading

Critical literacy is the practice of reading texts to look for underlying messages. The important aspects are (a) being able to have a discussion with others about the different meanings a text might have and (b) teaching learners how to think flexibly about a text—that is, to develop critical literacy (Goatly 2000).

When Starleigh seeks texts created by First Nations communities, it's because she wants to add diverse and authentic voices, so her focus on critical literacy is appropriate to the intended purpose. The intent of her text set is not to prove or disprove the residential schools experiences described, but to help students understand those experiences. Starleigh redirects the conversation toward critical literacy by asking students what they think the writer wants readers to understand, or what they think the underlying message is in the text. This approach usually allows a shift from initial resistance to a fuller discussion of the ideas and issues presented.

Information Texts: Synthesis and Inference

While teaching her Humanities 9 class, Linda discovered that the students could make personal connections and find relevant ideas in their texts but, as a group, they found it challenging to make inferences, a thinking skill they needed to develop. She invited Leyton to help her plan a lesson for her class, using accessible text material that would both meet the needs of all learners and improve their awareness of how to make broader connections and inferences. Together, they created a lesson in which they used three nonfiction articles with a common theme. The students had to navigate the ideas and connections between the three pieces of text.

Short pieces of content-rich text are most effective when launching a lesson to build students' knowledge and develop thinking skills. Leyton chose "Pasteurization," "The Printing Press," and "The Wheel" from *The 10 Most Revolutionary Inventions* (Cutting 2007, *The 10* series, ed. Jeffrey Wilhelm). This series (like Scholastic's Power Zone, Nelson's BoldPrint, and National Geographic's Global Issues) is designed to be both accessible and engaging for diverse learners in a middle years class.

These articles related to the Industrial Revolution, the social studies topic of the current unit of study, which meant that the students could access their background knowledge. In the full lesson sequence, Linda and Leyton not only accessed students' prior knowledge and built from their strengths, they also extended the students' capacity to work with key ideas by making connections, making inferences, and synthesizing information. Lessons like this can be planned around any big idea in any content area by seeking and using accessible, engaging texts that offer students variety beyond the single textbook.

Connecting
Three Pieces of Tape

- Provide each student with three pieces of masking tape.
- Ask them to think of three big ideas from the unit under study, and to write one idea on each piece of tape.
- As students are jotting down their ideas, circulate and check with students about their draft ideas.
- Have students stick the three strips on their arm.
- Have them get up and stand near other students with similar words on a piece of their tape.

Figure 9.2 Graphic organizer for Three Pieces of Tape activity

Name:_____ Date: _____ Block: _____

Working with 3 Texts: Big Idea Tape

Stick tape here!

Make a prediction...

Yea, this works! ☐	Nope, this predicition doesn't really fit ☐

Text 1:

	Important information	Big idea(s) so far
Partner 1		

Text 2:

	Important information	Big idea(s) so far
Partner 2		

© Portage & Main Press, 2014, *It's All About Thinking: Creating Pathways for All Learnings in the Middle Years*, BLM, ISBN 978-1-55379-509-4

Figure 9.2 Graphic organizer for Three Pieces of Tape activity (continued)

	What do the 2 articles have in common?	Together decide on **1 big idea**
Partner 2		

Text 3:

	Connect	*Self*	*Text*	*World*	*Media*	**Evidence**
Partner 3	I am connecting this text to	☐	☐	☐	☐	
	I am connecting this text to	☐	☐	☐	☐	
	I am connecting this text to	☐	☐	☐	☐	
	I am connecting this text to	☐	☐	☐	☐	

Explain: Pick a big idea that connects all three texts. Use evidence from your organizer and the tedxt to explain your thinking.

- Have students form groups of 2 or 3, based on their common ideas.
- Ask them to talk about how their words go together, and what they were thinking when they wrote the strips.
- Prompt them to discuss what their other words are, and how they relate.

Processing
Should I Stay or Should I Go?

- Have students return to their seats and distribute the graphic organizers.
- Split the class into three sections named for one of the three texts (i.e., back third, middle third, front third of room). Within their section, pair the students.
- Say to the students: *"With your partner and using your three strips of tape, discuss what you think we will read about today."*
- Have students decide on their best guess for the topic and place the piece of tape in the Big Idea box on the graphic organizer (Figure 9.2).
- Have the students refer to their tape and write their prediction in the next box.
- Put the same text face down on the desk to both Partner 1 and Partner 2. (Article #1 to pairs in back section of room; Article #2 to pairs in middle section, and Article #3 to pairs in front section). Have students flip over text, record the title on the Text 1 line, then read the article to find three pieces of evidence to support their prediction.
- Students then either:
  - check off the "Yea, this works!" box, then fill in important information on the organizer or...
  - if the article does not relate to their prediction, check off the "Nope, this prediction doesn't really fit" box.
- Then prompt students to find three important pieces of information from the article and fill in the organizer.
- Partners share which information they thought was important and together they brainstorm what they think the big idea of the article is and record it on the organizer. This ends the first round.
- Ask the partners to decide which of them will stay at their seat and who will go on to a new partner. The "goers" get up from their desk and find a new partner ("stayer") with a text that is different from theirs.
- The stayers, referring to their organizer, explain to their new partner what their prediction was and what they learned from their article,
- The goers take their turn referring to their text and their organizer.
- Stayers and goers trade texts (but keep their organizers).
- Ask students to read their new text silently, and record three important pieces of information, and what they think the big idea is in this new text.

- Then ask the students to talk about, decide, and write down the main idea shared by the two texts.
- Ask goers to find someone else with a text they have not read yet (they take their organizer and the text they have just read with them).
- With their new partner, they take turns sharing a big idea from one or both texts and offer the evidence to support their decision about the big idea.
- Partners switch texts (Text 3), and this time they look for three connections (Text to Self, Text to Text, Text to World). Ask the students for examples of these three kinds of connections to focus their reading.
- Students read their texts, looking for connections.
- Ask students to review their connections to see whether one or more relate to the big idea. If yes, circle it. If no, make one more connection that does relate to the big idea of the text.
- Ask students to take their best connection, and support it with evidence from the text explaining how it relates to the big idea.
- Ask students to share with their partners by having them quote the text when explaining their big idea and evidence. This may require teacher modelling.

Transforming/Personalizing
Marshalling evidence

- Ask students to pick one big idea that connects all three texts.
- Prompt them to use evidence from their organizer and the three texts to explain their thinking. They do this in the Explain box on the organizer.
- When working around the room, prompt students, with questions or suggestions like: *"How can you connect this back to the big idea?" "Try using quotations," "Can you add examples from other texts?" "Try to link all your ideas together."*
- Ask for volunteers to share what they think the big idea is and why.
- Give each student one final piece of tape on which to write what they believe to be the big idea of the day.
- As they leave the class, they put their big idea strip of tape on the white board near other similar ideas.
- If time permits, students can reorganize the pieces of tape creating a visual mind map of student-identified key ideas.

In just one lesson students began to make inferences by finding and supporting a big idea. Using a sequence that includes a set of accessible texts connected to a big idea and student partner talk to support meaning-making can effectively scaffold student skills development.

Graphic Novels Expand Our Repertoire of Text

Kristi Johnston, an English teacher and teacher-librarian in BC's Mission School District, is passionate about developing the literacy skills necessary for her students to be successful in the 21st century. At the middle school level, many students spend much of their out-of-school time in a visual world, playing video games, and spending time on the Internet. The National Council of Teachers of English has begun redefining what it means to be literate in the 21st century. Because of technology, the NCTE has developed position statements that illustrate how a literate person in the 21st century must possess a wide range of literacies. The NCTE supports and profiles graphic novels as an important tool that will help students develop 21st-century literacies (NCTE 2007 and ongoing).

Using Graphic Novels

Kristi uses graphic novels as part of whole-class instruction, allowing students to choose a graphic novel for a Literature Circle. She found |two resources invaluable in her planning: *In Graphic Detail* by David Booth and Kathleen Gould Lundy (2007) and *Teaching Graphic Novels* by Katie Monnin (2009).

Some key elements of instruction when introducing graphic novels:
- Some students may be unfamiliar with graphic novels, so it can be helpful to demonstrate how to read them, discussing how the text and features of graphic novels work together to tell the story.
- Discuss the similarities and differences between print-only novels and graphic novels so students can recognize that both share the same elements of fiction writing—although differences are evident in the text features.
- Students should be made aware of how to make inferences about characters from their facial expressions and body language.
- Note how the use of colour depicts the tone and mood of the setting.
- Consider the varied vantage points from which the story is told—close-ups, overhead shots, panoramic shots.
- Discuss how character interaction is conveyed through text in speech bubbles and thought bubbles—plus bubbles for sound effects—to carry the story line.
- Ensure students notice how the size and appearance of the type fonts help to convey meaning.

Lesson 1

- Have enough copies of Figure 9.3 for all students.
- Have students sit in pairs to encourage collaborative discussions.
- Distribute a graphic novel to each student (pairs may get the same book), asking them to look through the novel, then begin to read for about 10 minutes.
- Circulate as the students are reading, and give each student a copy of Figure 9.3.

Figure 9.3 Lesson 1 handout for students

Introduction to graphic novels

With your partner, discuss the question "What is a graphic novel?" Then, write down your definition.

Our definition of a graphic novel

- With your partner, examine and compare a graphic novel with a print-text novel.
- Write 5 things you notice about each book.

Graphic Novel	Print-Text Novel

- Ask the students to have a 2-minute conversation with their partner about features they have noticed while reading the graphic novel.
- Direct their attention to the handout and the question "What is a graphic novel?" Give the partners 5 minutes to discuss, jot down ideas, and write their definition.
- Have one member of each pair stand up and share their definition with the rest of the class. As the ideas are shared, write the responses on the board. When finished, ask the class to pick out words and phrases that are repeated, and underline them in red.
- Then, ask the students, again as partners, to use the common words and phrases previously underlined to create a new definition of a graphic novel.
- Have the other member of each pair stand and share the new definition with the class.

These collaborative discussions encourage each partnership to build on the ideas presented by their classmates. Some student definitions of a graphic novel:

> A graphic novel tells a story using both words and pictures. It has characters, setting, conflict, and a plot. Speech is delivered through bubbles rather than quotation marks. A graphic novel is like reading a movie.

> A graphic novel is like a longer version of a comic book. It tells a story and has characters, setting and plot. Sometimes they are in colour and sometimes they are in black and white. It is important to look at the pictures because they help tell the story. Graphic novels also have sound effects.

- Ask each pair to review their graphic novels and fill in the bottom half of Figure 9.3 with five things they notice about their graphic novel and five things they notice about a print-text novel.
- Have students focus on text features, and make observations about how each text is formatted. Use a document camera for students to show the page where their particular text feature is found.
- This lesson leads into the next day's lesson on the terminology used to describe elements of graphic novels.

Lesson 2

- To review the previous class, distribute copies of Figure 9.4A to the student partners, and ask the students to write five similarities and five differences between a print-text novel and a graphic novel. A Venn Diagram would also work well with this lesson.

- Using P1/P2 partner talk, ask pairs to share one of their similarities and one of their differences. As P1 is sharing, P2 is listening for any new ideas that could be added to their chart. P2 is instructed to put a star beside the new ideas that are added. Giving P2 a job while P1 is sharing ensures that everyone is listening and being accountable.

- Figure 9.4B is an example of a completed comparison.
- Choose the six most important features most evident in the graphic novels the students are reading, and distribute Figure 9.5.
- Go through each feature and, using a document camera, show an example of the feature. Rather than giving the students the definitions, provide the term and point to an example on the graphic novel page that is projected on the screen.
- Ask each pair to have a brief discussion and then write a definition. Choose a pair at random to share their definitions. Encourage students to add to their own definition, using some of their classmates' responses.
- Once students write down all the definitions, have them find examples of each feature in their graphic novels. If students find a feature not discussed, or a unique feature, have them bring it up to the document camera to share with the rest of the class. For example: speech bubbles outlined in red to show anger; jagged speech bubbles to show that a character is shouting; speech bubbles written in italics to indicate the character is whispering; caption boxes in different colours signalling a flashback scene.

Students will be actively engaged in this activity using many higher-level thinking skills to draw conclusions about what they see in their graphic novels. At this point in the lesson, the students are eager to start reading the graphic novels.

Figure 9.4A With a partner, discuss and note down five similarities and five differences between print-text novels and graphic novels

Similarities and differences between print-text and graphic novels

Similarities	Differences

© Portage & Main Press, 2014, *It's All About Thinking: Creating Pathways for All Learnings in the Middle Years*, BLM, ISBN 978-1-55379-509-4

Figure 9.4B Example of a completed comparison

Similarities and differences between print-text and graphic novels

Similarities	Differences
• Both have speech, dialogue, conversation	• PT: character's speech is in quotation marks • GN: character's speech is in speech bubbles
• Both have chapters, page numbers	• PT: you read from left to right • GN: you read from left to right, and up and down
• Both have a plot/storyline	• PT: story is told in paragraphs • GN: story is told in boxes
• Both have characters	• PT: you have to imagine what the characters look like, from descriptions, • GN: you can see what the characters look like in the art
• Both have a setting	• PT: you have to imagine what the setting looks like, based on the author's description • GN: you can see the details of the setting by how it is drawn
PT = Print-text novel GN = Graphic novel	

Figure 9.5 Structure and terminology of a graphic novel

Panel
Each individual "box," most often a rectangle or a square, is one panel that contains a scene with visuals and text and helps tell the story of a graphic novel.
Floating Panel
A smaller panel that "floats" on top of another panel. It is like a "zoom shot" of the larger visual. Floating panels may focus in on one character's face or on a part of the setting and give the reader more detail.
Gutter
The space between the panels — the "glue" that holds the story together. The gutters give the reader a chance to process the information presented in each panel.
Word Balloon
Also known as a "speech bubble." The bubbles have a "tail" that points toward the character's mouth and contain his/her speech.
Thought Bubble
These bubbles look like clouds and contain the character's thoughts. The tail on these bubbles points toward the character's head.
Caption Box
These boxes are shaped like a rectangle, and are usually placed at the top of a panel. The caption boxes provide information about setting, time, and place, rather like a narrator in a play.

Lesson 3

Place a varied collection of graphic novels on display, and ask students to make their choice in pairs. The following are great choices for a Literature Circle using graphic novels, and they cover many different genres and reading levels.

- *The Olympians,* a series by George O'Connor: *Hera, Athena and Hades*
- *American-Born Chinese* by Gene Luen Yang
- *The Lightening Thief* by Rick Riordan
- *Mercury* by Hope Larson
- *Good-Bye, Marianne* by Irene N. Watts

Other excellent sources for Social Studies/Humanities teachers:

- Time Line Series by Scholastic: *Set in Stone* (Mesopotamia); *The Golden Scarab* (Ancient Egypt); *Gladiator* (Rome); *Beware the Vikings, Rebel Prince* (Medieval England), *Master Leonardo* (Italy).
- BoldPrint Graphic Novel Series by Oxford University Press. Edited by Joan Green and Kathleen Gould Lundy (This is the series used for the lesson.)

- Have students read for about 30 minutes, then engage them in related activity using:
  - Tell me 3 things you have learned so far about the main character.
  - Describe 3 to 5 facts about the setting.
  - Write down 5 important events that have happened so far in the story.

  Provide the students about 15 minutes to complete this activity.
- Ask the students to walk around the classroom and share their thinking about their graphic novel with 2 other classmates. The person who is listening has the opportunity to ask 1 or 2 questions about the character, setting, or plot.

This activity gets them talking to others about their graphic novel in preparation for upcoming Literature Circles. Jotting down one question they were asked is their ticket out the door.

Lesson 4

- Provide students time either to finish reading the graphic novel from the previous day or to read another choice from the collection.
- Students read again for about 30 minutes, which should give everyone in the class enough time to finish at least one graphic novel.
- Pose the following question to the class: *What are some ways that you as a reader learn about a character?*
- Allow each pair 2 to 3 minutes to discuss this question, then P1/P2 partners share out to the class. Record their responses on the board.
- Ask students to group their ideas into 2 categories. Ask each pair to think about one of the characters in their graphic novel, and discuss how they are learning about their character's personality. After a brief discussion, choose random pairs to share their thoughts.
- In preparation for Lesson 5, choose some examples of character personality traits from some of the graphic novels shared with the class. This allows the assignment to be modelled for the students.
- Using the document camera, read a few pages to the students and ask them to make inferences about the character's personality based on their speech, their thoughts, and their actions. As part of the inference, the students have to explain their thinking to the class to justify their response.
- Through questioning prompts, scaffold the students' vocabulary development regarding personality traits and focusing specifically on facial features and body language, which are significant in a graphic novel when making inferences about characters.
- Prepare a vocabulary list of personality traits for the students to use to complete the assignment in Lesson 5.

Lesson 5

- Review last day's discussion about how readers learn about a character. In their P1/P2 partners, ask the students to respond to the following instructions:
  - ◆ List 3 ways a reader learns about a character's personality.
  - ◆ Give 3 examples of words to describe a character's physical characteristics.
  - ◆ Give 2 examples of a personality trait.
- Choose random pairs to share their responses.
- Give each student a list of the character traits. Instruct each pair to go over the list and put a star beside two words they have never heard before or words they may not be able to define. Ask one partner to stand and share one word. If one of their words has already been shared, then they offer their second choice. Invite the class to define any unknown words first. If the definition is not correct, provide it. Write the words and their definitions on the board for reference. Encourage students to use the dictionary to find definitions of any other words they are unsure of.
- Make sufficient copies of the handout, Figure 9.6
- Refer to last day's lesson when students were asked to make inferences about the character's personality based on their speech, their thoughts, and their actions. Provide another model using a graphic novel and the document camera. Choose one character and ask the students to look at the character to decide which 3 or 4 physical characteristics will be really important to include in the description.
- Choose random students to share their responses and record them on the board. Invite a student volunteer to draw the character based on the responses from the class on the board. To prompt more specificity in the drawing, ask the following questions:
  - ◆ *If this character went missing, would the police be able to find him based on the description you have provided?*
  - ◆ *Would a police sketch artist be able to create an image of the character based on the information you have provided?*

The student who is drawing may ask for more clarification and descriptive feedback to help accurately portray an image of the character. This activity will help students understand that saying a character is short, has brown hair, and is wearing jeans and a T-shirt is not enough. Prompt the students to discuss the importance of including distinguishing features such as ethnicity, physical stature, hair length and style, and whether the character has any scars or tattoos. This discussion will help them develop specific and detailed descriptions of the characters in their graphic novel.

- Distribute copies of Figure 9.6.

Figure 9.6 Lesson 5 handout for students

Getting to know the characters

Name: _____ Title: _____

Main Character _____

My drawing of my character's physical appearance	My character's personality traits + example from graphic novel
	Trait #1
	Trait #2
	Trait #3
Now that you know something about the character, explain why you would or would not like to have him or her as a friend. Use the personality traits as your evidence.	

- Ask students to choose one character from their graphic novel, and write or draw their character's physical appearance in the left panel, labelling specific details.
- Then ask students to write in each of the other panels a word to describe a personality trait of their character. Below that trait, students should draw examples from their graphic novel that justify their choice. Remind them to make inferences based on the character's speech, thoughts, and actions.
- Invite the students to put their drawings under the document camera and ask for feedback from their classmates. Figure 9.7 offers an example of one student's work. Prompt the students with questions to encourage specificity. Students' collaborative descriptive feedback can result in strong and detailed character descriptions from their peers.

Although graphic novels are a different literature format, they do contain all the elements of print-text fiction such as plot, setting, characters, and conflict. Students will use higher level thinking skills to make meaning and develop deeper understandings as they work through a text where images and words work together to tell a story. Graphic novels are one way teachers can incorporate visual literacy instruction, increase reading engagement, and provide all students, regardless of their reading levels, with a positive reading experience.

Integrating Diverse Texts

Andrea Hart and Tammy Renyard from Victoria School District use diverse texts to increase student engagement and learning. They believe it is critical for students to make content connections with texts commonly used in everyday life. To bring the outside world into the classroom, they use YouTube videos, newspaper and magazine articles, pictures, and more. They want students to interact with a variety of texts in order to make sense of and synthesize information related to big ideas in their world and the disciplines they are learning about.

Although Tammy (Humanities) and Andrea (Science and Math) teach in different content areas, they use similar teaching strategies to engage students in their learning, regardless of grade or content area. They engage in collegial conversations about their practice, co-plan and share learning sequences and teaching strategies debriefing both when things go well and when things take an unexpected turn. They find this process critical for their professional development and appreciate the shift that comes in their practice when they are able to see their work through each other's eyes.

Andrea and Tammy know how important it is for students to step outside traditional textbooks and novels to look at the content they are learning in a more global way. Thus, they ask their students to interact with, make connections to, and ask questions about the concepts and issues they

Figure 9.7 Example of student work for Getting to know the characters

Name: _____Hera_____   Title: _____Hera_____

Main Character _____

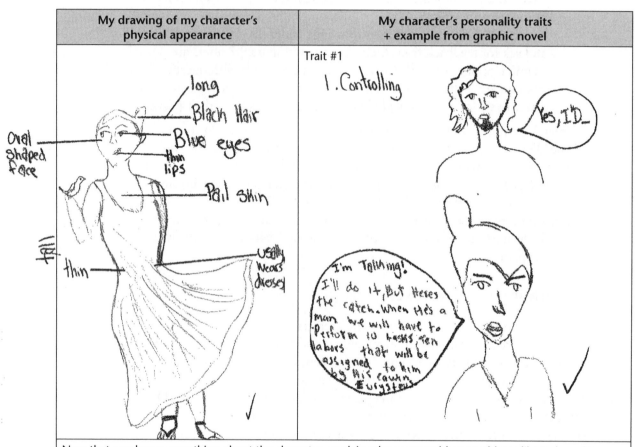

Now that you know something about the character, explain why you would or would not like to have him or her as a friend. Use the personality traits as your evidence.

encounter. Students experience the world differently today, because they are interacting with unlimited content and resources available in sound bytes: media, tweets, YouTube clips, and Facebook posts. It is critical for teachers to honour and explicitly teach students how to use these texts, and help them navigate the amount of information available.

Integrating Real-World Texts in Science

It is challenging to find text that can capture students' attention, be open enough for students to ask questions, and provide an authentic application of the content to be learned. However, even small efforts can make a difference to help students connect to and engage with texts that are interesting and interactive. For example, for the topic of the circulatory system, students can read an article from <www.howstuffworks.com> about athletes using performance-enhancing drugs to increase the amount of oxygen in their blood. For the urinary system, they might view a YouTube clip of the pickle-eating champion patient and read an article from <www.livestrong.com> about the consequences of eating too many pickles. Invite students to ask a wide variety of questions as a result of reading these articles to help them develop an inquiry mindset. Some questions Andrea's students asked include: *"How does a high-sodium diet affect homeostasis?" "What is the reaction that salt creates in your body?"* and *"Does high blood pressure cause heart attacks?"* The inquiry questions that students create will guide them to find more texts on the topic and to build understanding in areas of interest. Most importantly, tapping into these kinds of resources helps our students think about science in relation to their lives and the real world.

The Circulatory System and Homeostasis: How Diverse Texts Can Be Used

In this example Andrea had students creating diverse texts using online tools. While studying body systems, students were asked to consider the guiding question:

"What lifestyle choices help body systems maintain homeostasis?"

- **Part 1:** After building common background knowledge about the meaning of *homeostasis*, students were grouped in teams to study two body systems. After studying two body systems with access to a text set compiled with the teacher-librarian, students had to make connections between the systems and see how they work together to maintain steady levels in our bodies.
- **Part 2:** To help students show their understanding through images, Andrea introduced students to <glogster.com>, an online tool to create an ideagram. Students had to show their understanding of homeostasis of blood oxygen levels by including three big ideas about the topic, including relevant quotes from texts they read, an image that showed

their understanding of homeostasis, any personal connections, and a headline for a newspaper or magazine article about blood oxygen levels.

- **Part 3:** Students had to use the guiding question of the unit. Students were required to explain and represent how personal lifestyle choices relate to maintaining healthy blood oxygen levels and why these choices make a difference.
- **Part 4:** Building in metacognitive aspects, students personalized their learning with an "I-statement" to consider how their thinking had changed as a result of their research. Sentence frames such as "I used to think ____, now I think ____", "I've realized _____", and "now I know _____" provided the prompts that some students needed.

In the content areas, drawing on diverse texts can support students to be more active in their learning. For example, in a sequence exploring the urinary system, Andrea:

1. asked students to assume the role of a doctor and watch a clip of their patient, Arnie "Chowhound" Chapman, champion competitive pickle eater. Arnie has come to them complaining of feeling unwell and the students' task is to create a presentation explaining what the problem is and what Arnie can do about it.
2. provided students with an article about the formation of urine using a two-column journal with the headings "What's important" and "Why" as their processing tool. In the left column students wrote main ideas from their reading and in the right column, the reasons why they thought it was important.
3. used YouTube clips to teach them about the parts of this system. She paused the video at appropriate times to give the students time to talk with a partner about what was important information and to jot down an image and key details to hold onto their thinking.

The urinary system is complex and before students could move on to their final task, they used the iPad application "Educreations" to get some feedback about their understanding of how to demonstrate their learning in a final task. Working in groups, students created a short presentation and showed their work to Andrea.

For both the homeostasis and the urinary tract examples, Andrea co-created criteria with her students to determine what their final demonstration of their learning should include. Criteria should be designed so that students are assessed on their ability to show their understanding of the content as well as their capacity to synthesize and justify their thinking. In this way, the task becomes about thinking in addition to the key content. Co-creating criteria also opens up the conversation about the continuum of understanding. Students are evaluated on the degree of sophistication of their thinking, and they can choose to make changes in the current assignment based on the feedback they receive.

Stop Cyberbullying Unit

In Tammy's English class, students explored the concept of courage and strength from within. She used Faye Brownlie's *Grand Conversations, Thoughtful Responses* (2005) to structure the format of Literature Circles. Tammy selected the novels to provide a variety of reading levels:

A = Accessible and C = Challenging.

Literature Circle Novels

- *Iqbal* by Francesco D'Adamo A
- *Deathwind* by William Bell A
- *Shattered* by Eric Walters A
- *Half Brother* by Kenneth Oppel A
- *Kiss the Dust* by Elizabeth Laird A
- *Hunger Games* by Suzanne Collins A
- *Compound* by S. A. Bodeen C
- *The Graveyard Book* by Neil Gaiman A
- *A Long Way Gone: Memoirs of a Boy Soldier* by Ishmael Beah (Nonfiction) C

Before starting the Literature Circle, Tammy discussed with students what it meant to be courageous or to demonstrate inner strength. It was important to help students develop some background knowledge so that they could make connections to other texts, to themselves, and to the world. These titles were part of a larger thematic text set for the unit:

- Article: "Stop cyberbullying before it starts," a nonfiction piece on the facts of cyberbullying.
- Video clip: Jamie Rodemeyer's story about suicide.
- The Memory Project, WWII: Connected to Remembrance Day, this project provides an online collection of primary sources on Canadian veterans. Students each sought out one living veteran to find out their story and wrote a letter to him or her. Class discussion on courage in times of war.
- News stories on natural disasters where people step up and do extraordinary things.
- Short story: *The Sniper* by Liam O'Flaherty
- Student choice : Students bring texts that they believe show examples of courage.

Learning Intentions

- Educate your parents about the dangers of cyberbullying
- Describe a time you took a stand or a time where you wish you had taken a stand.

Connecting

- Ask students to move to one side of the room if they know someone who has been bullied in school or to the other side if they do not.
- Ask students to move to one side of the room if they have been personally bullied and to the other side if they have not. (Safety and a sense of community have been established in the classroom.)
- Ask students to move to one side of the room if they have been cyber-bullied and to the other side if they have not.
- Ask students to move to one side of the room if they have bullied someone or said something online that they would not normally say to someone. Students move to the other side if they have not.
- Share Jamey Rodemeyer's story (September 21, 2011) through either a YouTube clip or a newspaper article (a young American who committed suicide because of abuse and ridicule over sexuality). Have partners discuss what struck them about the story and make connections to others situations or personal experiences. (A recent Canadian example is the case of Amanda Todd.)
- Ask students to work with a partner and work out some ways that could put an end to bullying. Invite partners to share their solutions and their reasoning or justifications (e.g., My partner and I suggest _____ because _____).

Processing

- Using the article "Stop cyberbullying before it starts" <www.ncpc.org/resources/files/pdf/bullying/cyberbullying.pdf >, ask students to create a two-column note-making sheet. On the left, the students track key ideas about what is important; on the right, they list their questions or thoughts about the significance of their notes.
- Read the article to the class, stopping along the way to have students record their thinking and discuss with a partner new ideas, surprises, and connections.
- Have students share their notes with a partner. Then in a group of four, discuss information they find important for parents to know.

Transforming / Personalizing

- Assign students to create a poster/brochure to educate parents about the impact and the dangers of cyber-bullying.
- Generate criteria with the students, which might include:
  - relevant facts
  - ideas about what parents could do
  - a "Did you know…?" section
  - persuasive language
  - images that represent significant ideas that grab readers and draw them in (that show understanding of the content)

- Ask students to describe a time when they took a stand or a time when they wished they had taken a stand, focusing on one specific example, using relevant details, and capturing the emotion of the situation.

Process of Literature Circles

Students are expected to:

- participate in two Literature Circle conversations per week.
- complete three double-entry journals per week.
- submit their best image/detail journal for a chapter. Students could hand in multiple entries for feedback, then select their best for the summative assessment.
- submit their best "What's Important and Why?" for a chapter. As with image/detail, students could submit for feedback, then select their best for grading.
- prepare their final assignment: a mind map for a novel of their choice or a mind map incorporating multiple novels.

Literature Circle criteria

Co-create the criteria for a Literature Circle with your students by first modelling a Literature Circle conversation or discussion with other members of your team. Ask students to notice the interactions, the kind of information shared, what worked best and what didn't work. From this fishbowl model, create criteria—which might include:

- Come prepared for the discussion
- Listen respectfully
- Initiate conversation
- Attend to the topic
- Participate actively in the group
- Ask questions
- Piggyback on the comments of others

- Allow all members of the group an opportunity to participate
- Disagree constructively and respectfully
- Support opinions with evidence
- Make connections: personal, text to text, and text to world.

Double-entry journal

The goal of the double-entry journal is for students to share their thinking and understandings about their novel, which allows the teacher to step inside students' interaction with that novel. A graphic organizer can support students in organizing their thoughts and responses by including a quotation selected from the text (connection, something funny, exciting, confusing, poignant, or well-written), the chapter and page, why the quotation stood out as significant, and how this connection helps them understand the novel.

When students actively participate in a Literature Circle, they can identify acts of courage and discuss the other issues affecting society that occur in their text. Students will become more skilled with their justifications and better able to support each other in Literature Circle conversations. Students will acquire a solid understanding of the concept of courage by identifying and justifying characters who demonstrate qualities of courageousness.

Final task for the Literature Circle unit on courage

Prompt students to share examples from their books that, in their opinion, relate to the theme of courage or strength from within. To introduce students to the culminating mind map activity, have them work together to describe their criteria for a mind map. Use the list below, adapted from *Beyond Monet* as a model.

- Central image meaningfully illustrates the key idea.
- Ideas radiate out from the central image, from complex to least complex.
- Ideas have key images or words, show understanding (may show humour, use of metaphor, shows understanding of the content).
- Colour or code links are used to show connections; colour supports the connections, and make it easy for the reader to identify the connections.
- Depth of coverage shows a solid grasp of the novel (Bennett and Rolheiser-Bennett 2001).

In their final mind maps, students will demonstrate deep understanding of their novel and provide evidence-based examples of courage. See Figure 9.8 as an example of one student's representation of the book she read.

Teachers could ask their students for feedback on the unit with a question prompt like:

"What did you notice about your learning during Literature Circles?"

Reflections

Andrea (Science) and Tammy (English) noticed that students were more empowered and took greater ownership when choice was offered using real-life texts and examples. Students brought in articles or novels related to the big ideas or themes because they personally related to the content. They were also better able to make personal connections and apply the learning to their own context because they were actively involved. Their ability to recognize out-of-school connections increased. Their students came to realize and experience the potential for accessing information and learning beyond one textbook or one novel.

Andrea and Tammy both stress the importance of students being able to pull ideas and opinions from a variety of texts, using evidence, and synthesize and justify their thinking in a variety of ways—journals, presentations, conversations, using online tools, mind-mapping, and more. When students

Figure 9.8 One student's Mind Map for *Half Brother* by Kenneth Oppel

Josephine

Characters

Ben had a fight with Jennifer because Jennifer didn't want to be close to Ben

Richard trying to keep Zan for Ben. But Helson fighting for Zan to stay with him.

Richard trying to give Zan a better home, but Ben & his mom are treating Zan like a family member.

Peter & Ben getting mad at Richard for making the learning Chair to Zan when he is uncooperative.

Conflict

Theme

Jennifer — Peter — Ben — Zan
Dad (Richard) — Mom

Settings

Victoria B.C
Ben's house
Nevada
Toronto

Zan — Family — Drama — Ben — Jennifer — Comedy — Family — Romance — Ben Jennifer — Ben & Helson

Half Brother

Plot!

Ben's dad making him move to Victoria B.C.

Ben's mom and Zan coming home for the first time.

Ben not making friends with Zan.

Ben making friends with Tim but gets in trouble which makes Ben's dad disappointed in him.

Ben gets used to Zan.

Ben's family makes friends with the Godwin family and Ben gets a crush on Jessica.

School begins & Ben wants to change his personality.

Zan starts to learn his first word ASL

Zan learns to sign his first word hug

Zan left one of the students at Xplar

Its the summer and Zan won't have to go to Egot and Ben has nothing to do.

CBC television came over to Ben's house to see how the Zan project was going

Richard making Zan go to Nevada for a better home

Ben having to stay away from Zan for 2 months

Ben's dad letting Zan go to keep Helson

Ben and his mom stay from home to Nevada.

Ben finds a better home for Zan but he can't keep it

Ben & Zan having their final goodbyes.

Courageous Acts

Ben standing up for Zan by being brave enough to talk to his dad about Zan.

Peter standing up to Richard for making him first Zan from Nevada.

Peter risking his job for Zan.

Ben's mom helping him sign Zan from Nevada.

Peter's mom standing up to Richard.

Types

Ben — Dad

Ben yelling at his dad for not giving care to Zan because Ben and his mom are doing all the work.

Ben's dad getting disappointed at him for smoking & jumping through fire

Ben getting mad at his dad for hitting Zan on the door because of his dad being protective of Ben's mom

Ben's dad getting mad at Ben & his mom for stealing Zan from Nevada.

Ben getting mad at his dad for having to take Zan back to Nevada.

Ben being proud of his dad for standing up for Zan and getting Zan a better home.

hug — more — Funny — Baby

(Dad) — (Ben)

are offered a variety of texts and can create a variety of texts, learning can be scaffolded in such a way that students begin to recognize that they can use some or all of the sources in their own work. Combining the use of a text set with open-ended tasks allows students to personalize their learning and select evidence that best supports their understanding.

Achievement has increased in both Andrea and Tammy's classes, which they believe, is partly due to high engagement with a variety of text formats and opportunities to personalize their learning.

Conclusion

By providing our students with diverse texts and materials, we provide scaffolding and support for all entry points to learning. When we offer students the opportunity to work across multiple texts, they have more ways into a topic and more opportunities to develop their critical thinking capacities.

We have come to realize there is no one-size-fits-all text. The benefits of text sets are many. Working across texts moves students away from regurgitation and toward synthesis. Working within a text set gives students the opportunity to apply and adapt learning strategies based on different text formats and attributes. Using a text set can introduce students to diverse perspectives on a topic, an issue, or a theme. Through the process of researching and acquiring text sets and using them with students, we have become much more responsive teachers and more culturally relevant teachers, but the most immediate result is increased student engagement. Working thematically, expanding our text repertoire to include visual literacy, and collaborating with colleagues, including teacher-librarians have created new pathways to learning for our students and ourselves.

Chapter 10

Creating Pathways through Writing

Educators Involved

Pamela Richardson: Instructor, Faculty of Education, UBC Okanagan, Kelowna, BC

Sheri Gurney: Classroom Teacher, SD 62, Sooke, BC

Laura Lancaster: Literacy Support Teacher, SD 62, Sooke, BC

When we think of writing teachers, Pamela Richardson comes to mind immediately. She is a writer who teaches and a teacher who writes. We need to be models for our students—taking the same risks and opening ourselves up in the same way that we ask of student writers. Pamela and Leyton work together at the University of British Columbia, Okanagan. They have a history of writing and reading together that stretches back to their days as graduate students in Vancouver. They have been working to integrate Pamela's Secondary English Language Arts Methods course with Leyton's Assessment for Learning and Middle School Methods courses. Their goal is to help their teacher candidates experience how these areas interconnect.

The Pleasure of Writing

These days, most of Pamela's thoughts about writing focus on helping beginning teachers with the art of teaching writing. By middle school, many students have long since decided whether or not they enjoy writing or are "good" at it. Not surprisingly, many beginning teachers, based on their own experiences in school, also either love or fear writing. Pamela helps teachers connect to the pleasure of writing so that they might better cultivate joy and engagement within their own students. Isn't that what it's all about, after all? Developing as a writer takes commitment and care. Without significant moments of enjoyment, our commitment weakens and our care stumbles.

When guiding student writing, we have to recognize the importance of all aspects of the process. Generating compelling ideas, developing and organizing these ideas, receiving and giving supportive feedback, communicating with an audience in mind, attending to details of tone and style—these are just some of the skills that go into making competent and confident writers. Writing is both technical and emotional. We enjoy the tasks that we're good at and that connect us to others in meaningful ways. Our feelings of enjoyment and success lead to deeper engagement, a sense of ownership, and an eagerness to share our work.

The following lessons on literary, personal, and informational writing offer ways in which all students can engage and develop as writers. In the section "Poetic Play Pays Off," Pamela offers two approaches to poetry that provide early success and leave students feeling surprised at what they can accomplish. In the section "A Pathway into Personal Writing," Linda shows us how personal writing, which brings to the surface the deeper meaning in students' lives, flows from shared movement, partner talk, and collaborative criteria-building. In the section "Writing through Inquiry with the 6+1 Traits," Sheri Gurney and Laura Lancaster focus on writing commentary (opinion pieces) as they share their collaboratively planned unit "Stand Up," based on a comprehensive approach to understanding what leads to powerful writing.

Poetic Play Pays Off

Lesson 1

Jeffrey Wilhelm and Bruce Novak, in their book *Teaching Literacy for Love and Wisdom: Being the Book and Being the Change* (2011), sing the praises of the following poem-writing activity adapted from Gabriele Rico's *Writing the Natural Way: Using Right-Brain Techniques to Release Your Expressive Powers* (2000). In her book, she focuses on the brainstorming process of "clustering" and its tendency to draw out the poetic imagination in short order, which impressed Wilhelm and Novak. Pamela agrees and recognizes that these seemingly magical results make sense when you understand how writing works.

The pressure of having to write a poem in three minutes produces results when students do pre-writing activities. Through word-association clusters, they create a bank of words and images to draw from so that the poem is already well on its way before the timer starts. Another key initial step is to begin the lesson with rich source material such as a short evocative poem on a theme relevant to what students are studying. These activities fuel the imagination and help foster connections.

Pamela is teaching in the Okanagan, and she likes to use a poem by Sharon Thesen, a local author, who speaks of the fire that ravaged the city in 2003. The poem evokes many memories and feelings in students who lived in the city at that time, and it connects well to themes of disaster, resilience, wilderness, community, and more. Poems written by local authors will often connect readily to the experiences of students from the region, but teachers can select any poem, from any time or place. Wilhelm and Novak suggest two-and-a-half minutes as the optimal amount of time for drafting the poem, but Pamela finds that three minutes has worked best for her. You decide for yourself.

Pre-Writing

- Choose a short poem connected to the unit theme, and give everyone a copy. Read the poem to the students once slowly, and then read it again. On the second reading, have students underline, on their copy, the words or phrases that they find interesting.
- Model on the board how to create a word association cluster, how to select one of the interesting words and make connections to related words—through the senses (the sounds, sights, tastes, smells, and touch evoked by the word); through memories and experiences (*What does the word remind me of?*); through the sound, meaning, or appearance of the word (*rhymes, assonance, synonyms, antonyms*) (Figure 10.1).
- Have students, in partners, draw a similar "sun" with eight spokes, then select a word or phrase to place at the centre of their "cluster." Ask them to share with a partner their thoughts about the word they chose and why.

Figure 10.1 Sample word association "cluster"

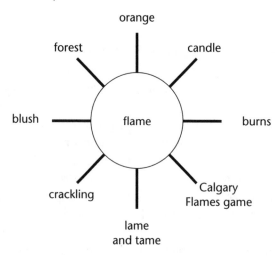

- To choose words and cluster them around their central word, suggest that students use the following hints:
  - ♦ Your senses: *What sounds, sights, tastes, touch, smells relate to this word or phrase?*
  - ♦ Your memories and experiences: *What does the word or phrase remind you of?*
  - ♦ Language: *What does it rhyme with? What does it sound like? What is its synonym? What is its antonym?*
- Ask students to discuss their clusters with their partner: *What connections did you make? Did you draw on senses? Memories? Language? Anything missing that you would like to add?*

Drafting

- Distribute copies of Figure 10.2 as a graphic organizer to support students in this activity.
- Set a timer for no longer than three minutes.
- Ask students to draft a poem based on their word cluster. They do not have to use all the words. They can repeat words and add new words. Don't think or plan, just GO!
- After the three minutes are up, invite students to share their poem with their partner and offer positive and supportive feedback.
- Invite students as a class to reflect on their experience of writing a poem in three minutes—including whether they already have ideas of what they would change.

Revising

- Offer suggestions to help students revise their poems for meaning and clarity.

- Students give their poem a title. *What is your poem about?*
- Students then draw an image about their poem. At the bottom of the drawing, they write a sentence that explains the image and how it connects to their poem.
- Model the following approach for students. Underline key words or phrases in the poem that connect with the drawing or the title. Circle key words or phrases they aren't sure about, and put a line through ones that don't connect at all.
- Then let students rewrite their poem, focusing on the words and phrases that are underlined or circled.
- They then share and discuss their revised poem with a partner and explain their thinking.

Lesson 2: A Collaborative Poem

This collaborative poem activity, adapted from Noreen Jeffrey and Bill Prentice (1997), is a low-risk way to engage in writing that helps build a sense of community. It also helps students learn about revising and editing as they collaboratively explore and discuss the impact of variations on poetic expression, such as word choice, grammar, and punctuation.

Pre-Writing

- Give students three minutes to do a quick-write poem on the prompt you give them.
- Have them re-read what they wrote, and highlight what they think is their most powerful or memorable phrase. Then, as partners, students discuss their quick-write and share their powerful phrases.
- Between the two of them, they decide on one phrase. They can combine their phrases or choose one or the other. It is up to them. The final phrase shouldn't be too long.
- They write it down.

Drafting

- Each pair reads their phrase aloud, and the teacher records the phrases on the board.
- Each phrase begins on its own line to give the shape of a poem.
- The teacher asks students how the phrase is punctuated, and so on, and takes care to write it exactly as the students dictate.
- When finished scribing, the teacher reads what is written on the board in an expressive voice, as one would when reading a poem to an audience.
- Discuss: *Is this a poem? Why? What makes it a poem? What doesn't make it a poem?*
- All students copy the "poem" onto a new sheet of paper.

Figure 10.2 Graphic organizer for student poetry activity

My 3-Minute Poem

_____

_____

_____

_____

_____

_____

_____

_____

_____

_____

My partner most enjoyed this about my poem:
My poem created this image in her or his mind:
My partner was surprised by or curious about this:
My thoughts about writing this poem:

Editing

- *How could we make it more like a poem?* On the board, model how you might edit the poem to make it more effective. Say: "*I am going to play with different possibilities to see what happens. Mine is just one approach. There are many ways you could rework this.*"
- Think aloud and explain your choices. Ask for student input. Involve students in creating new line breaks, reordering, deleting, or adding words, making changes to punctuation. When a student makes a suggestion, ask why she or he is making that choice.
- Students now revise their own copy of the original "poem."
- They share their new creation with a partner, and discuss the choices they made. Suggest a few students might volunteer to share with the whole class.

Reflecting

- Students write a few lines to explain their thinking as they revise their poem.

  "*What things did you do that made a difference to the poem? What questions do you have about your partner's poem?*"

Sharing

- Students share and discuss their questions with their partner.

Pamela believes that poetry can be a playful way to engage all students in exploring language, meaning, and self-expression. Poetry also helps students give voice to more personal and emotional topics.

A Pathway into Personal Writing

In Linda's lessons, she focuses on personal writing and how to engage students in transformative learning with regard to their own life experiences. This sequence uses movement to foster personal reflection in students. Students are prompted to consider sensory aspects of a personally significant memory. Guided movement activities can help students access and use emotion as well as concrete and sensory details to craft a narrative piece.

What came before?

Students had been making field book entries based on a collection of artifacts they brought to class. Modelling the process, Linda had begun the collection by bringing in three different artifacts which all related to her life as a teacher. They were small gifts that her students had given to her, and each one had a back story that she told to the class. Each story revealed a change that Linda had experienced as a teacher, a change through which she became more emotionally connected to her teaching practice. Each story helped her

See chapter 5 in Brownlie and Schnellert 2009

students create the criteria for their own stories (key events that produced change in their lives) and the artifacts attached to them.

Partner talk

Each time students write, partner talk is built into the process. Partners begin by describing their artifact and its significance. Linda shapes the way partners talk to one another to include a focus on active listening—in particular, highlighting significant words and phrases for their partners, such as "I heard you say your brother is courageous" or "I heard you say you will never forget the feeling of losing the game" or "I remember the best words were *uprooted*, *tournament*, and *friendship*."

Class-created criteria

Through listening to teacher modelling and partners' reporting out on their conversations to the whole group, the class creates criteria for a powerful field book entry. Generally, the criteria cover emotional impact, description and detail, a lesson learned, or a change in their lives. Because Linda has set up her modelling to reflect the criteria, students recognize and identify the criteria for a powerful field book entry.

As students begin to recognize the significant moments in their stories, the criteria develop. These lessons help them realize the growth and maturity they feel as they look back at the moments that have shaped who they are. Being sensitive to their process of discovery—some students begin to recognize their life's driving needs and how they get these needs met. There are often moments of self-actualization in this process.

Lesson 1

Warm-up must include working to become a "company." A company works together, like a community, to make decisions, create stories, and improvise together.

Connecting

With some music playing, introduce levels of movement (from stretching to walking to making gestures while walking) by modelling to the music what these movements look like. As students get warmed up and familiar with what is required of them, have them walk around the room in all directions. Then ask them to change the pace to faster or slower by creating a rating scale. *"Double the pace. Double it again, then halve it."* And so on. This helps them to understand the energy levels and pace required for the cacophony line later in the lesson.

Gradually release responsibility for the movement, energy, and gestures to the students so that they start and stop the movement without speaking, but as a company: *"Work together. Work from what feels right. Stay together. Work from your intuition."*

Processing

Prior to this lesson, scaffolded activities included artifact-related conversations and quick-writes in their field books.

See chapter 5 in Brownlie and Schnellert 2009

- Introduce how this lesson builds from previous lessons. "*Our next step as a class is to try to write for ten minutes about the major events in your life. Start at the beginning and try to hit on all the major events in your life, and keep writing until I ask you to stop. Later on, you will select from what you have to write about your life story.*"
- Model this by writing (on the board or a projected screen) at the front of the classroom as students write. Ask students to be prepared to share these events and work them into a group activity and a poetry-writing activity.
- Prompt students: "*Stop. Go over your writing and circle five words or phrases (not complete sentences) that stand out to you.*" Model this in front of the students. "*Create a physical gesture for each one. Don't worry about the transitions between each one.*"
- Model what this looks like for one of your own. Linda shares her first example "born on a farm" (a phrase from her writing), and pairs this with a gesture of a baby coming from the sky, then being cradled. "*Put them in an order you can present.*" Model this with the five items you chose from your list, and this time focus on how you get from one movement to the other (creating smooth transitions) so you are creating a movement sentence in five phrases. "*Rehearse them, learn them. You are creating a playlist*" "*Once you feel you know the order, add the word/phrase to the gesture, and practise putting it all together. Be prepared to present your gestures and words.*"

Transforming/Personalizing

Have students record their words/phrases with image, icon, or words to represent their gesture.

Lesson 2

Connecting

- Start the lesson with another warm-up to relax the class and to get them thinking with their bodies. Repeat the "company work" from the first activity and add more challenge for them to start/stop by having them simultaneously get down on the floor and up again with no cues or leader. Let them feel when the stop/start impulse begins and ends.
- Give them time to revisit their lines and gestures from lesson 1. When students are working together, divide the class into two or three groups (10 to 12 in each group).

Processing

Each group shares their gestures on a line facing their classmates. Instruct them to resist stepping forward, but to just make room for each other (cacophony line). The other groups observe them.

- *"You are all going to go through your playlist at the same time. Go neutral when you complete it."* To help them modulate the telling of the gesture story, ask them to share their playlist in parallel at a level 5; then ask for a 10 (i.e., really strong/powerful), then a 1 (close to the spine). This helps to develop performance and communication skills and awareness of energy and projection.
- Observers trade places with the storytellers. Repeat process.
- Then have groups go all at once; this time, encourage them to interact a bit with their neighbours to "let things affect you." Hold the last pose. (You might want to work more with levels of commitment to gestures and words.)
- Another variation is to go down the line one at a time like a wave, using only one gesture at a time to see how they might connect. This is a good bridge into the Poetry Circle.

Transforming/Personalizing

- Create two or more lines for each memory or life event.
- Share with a partner to decide on your best one.
- Share your line from your poem with a gesture to a small group.
- Move around and put yourself in an order to create a class poem. (Teacher facilitates.)
- *"Go back and adjust your poem based on what you did and heard. Write up the poem."*

Through movement, active listening, and illustrated poems, Linda created opportunities for students to re-live and re-create their life stories seeking deeper understanding of self and others. This sequence works well for developing personal histories as well. Finding and working with five key events/elements from one's own life and focusing on the emotional power and sensory information helps illuminate personal importance.

Writing Informational Texts through Inquiry

Sheri Gurney and Laura Lancaster, teachers in the Sooke School District, met to collaborate on a writing unit to co-teach in Sheri's middle years class at her school. As they talked about the kinds of writing they do, they realized that in their adult lives they had never written a short story, they did not write book reports, and they were not called upon in their careers to write five-paragraph essays. Laura recalled that when she started her master's project, she had to write a proposal, and having never written in that genre, she took the advice of two favourite authors Nancie Atwell (1998, 2002) and Katie Wood Ray (2006) to *read* texts in that genre.

In the following lessons, Sheri and Laura show us how a framework for assessment forms the foundation for inquiry into the reading and writing of informational texts. Students learn how to write commentaries (such as newspaper op-ed and opinion pieces) and show that they can stand up for what they believe.

Both teachers wanted their middle school students to see the possibilities for their writing—to know that they have a voice and can communicate with passion, persuasion, and authentic purpose. They also recognized that, like Laura, their students need opportunities to *read* powerful texts as models for writing. As they began to plan their unit of study, they articulated their guiding principles for teaching writing (Figure 10.3).

A Model: 6+1 Traits of Writing

When Laura first read *6+1 Traits of Writing* (Culham 2003), she remembered the spark of clarity that came when she saw what this model could do. It gave her a framework and a language to talk about writing with her students, and it became an anchor for teaching and assessing their writing. The 6+1 Traits model <educationnorthwest.org> emerged from a group of writing teachers who had examined thousands of papers and identified six common traits of good writing, across grade levels and genres:

- Ideas
- Voice
- Sentence Fluency
- Organization
- Word Choice
- Conventions

Figure 10.3 Guiding principles for teaching writing

Teachers should...	Students need...
• use what they know about their students' writing to guide their writing instruction • model and scaffold how to read like a writer • provide a range of topics and texts to accommodate the diverse interests and needs of students in the classroom • conference with students regularly (ask questions and offer timely feedback) about their writing when they are engaged in the writing process	• opportunities to write in real-world genres • some freedom to choose writing topics that they care about • time to read multiple examples of texts to develop awareness of writing style in that genre • time to talk with others about how a text is written • time to write in class • opportunities to develop their voice as writers • to learn how to support their ideas and opinions with relevant information • to become self-regulating, use writing strategies, and ask questions about the decisions they make as writers • to co-construct criteria and take ownership over their writing process and product • to set clear targets for their writing, to know what they are striving for, and what they need to do to get there

In applying the model to informational writing/commentary, Sheri and Laura learned that not every piece of student writing needs a summative assessment for all 6 traits. Working from a common model, teachers and students can communicate about writing traits and establish a common vision of what constitutes powerful writing. To focus their teaching and assessment, they thought it important to target one writing trait at a time, and to work with students to build criteria.

See Class Profile process in chapter 3.

From Sheri's assessment of her students' writing, she identified what they needed next as writers. When they had difficulty adding relevant details to support their ideas and opinions, she focused on the trait of Ideas. When she found her students' writing lacked personality and passion, she focused on the trait of Voice. Sheri and Laura always consider who their students are as learners when planning for writing instruction. Sheri knew her students were willing learners, albeit somewhat passive.

Sheri and Laura wanted to choose an inquiry question that would engage students and encourage them to speak up for something they felt strongly about. They decided the genre of "commentary" such as a newspaper op-ed piece could be a form that would allow students to express their opinions in their own voice. It would also require them to *support* their opinions with relevant information. They then planned that this piece of writing would be the summative assessment for the unit they called "Stand Up," and they worked with their students to establish the criteria for the writing piece, using the six traits to guide their student's thinking.

Immersion and Inquiry

Approaching writing as inquiry means that students must explore different options for how to write something. In teaching students how to write well in a particular genre, Atwell (1998) talks of having students "marinate themselves in a genre" (p. 100), and Ray (2006) suggests immersing students in reading within the genre with an eye toward writing in that style. Having students *read* real texts written in a particular genre hadn't been part of Sheri and Laura's previous writing classes, but they came to realize that *reading is part of a writer's work*. They wanted their assignment to mirror the way writing happens in the real world and be true to the *process* of writing. If students are to understand what is known about a particular topic, they need to simulate or recreate some of the inquiry by which the knowledge about that topic was created.

Writing Workshop

Sheri had established conditions for a writing workshop in her classroom, and the two teachers planned their teaching for the Stand Up unit within this structure. As Atwell suggests, students need to write for personal reasons and beliefs, so Sheri and Laura allowed the students to write about a cause that they passionately supported.

Figure 10.4 Class-created criteria for traits of good writing

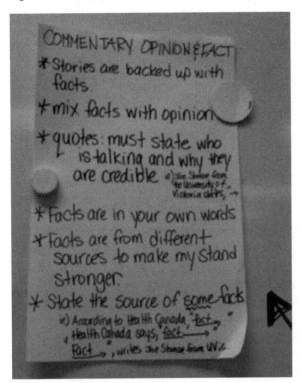

They began each writing class with a mini-lesson based on a targeted writing trait (Figure 10.4). For their later reference, students recorded ideas from the mini-lesson in their Writer's Notebook. Then, Laura and Sheri circulated to check in and conference with individual students while they engaged in independent writing for 25 to 30 minutes. At the end of each lesson, the teachers had the students engage in peer conferences in which they shared their writing and gave each other feedback. Then the whole class discussed the accomplishments or problems that emerged in their writing that day. This process served to nurture the community of writers in the classroom, and it gave Sheri and Laura information about where to go next in their teaching.

"CitizenKid" is a collection of books that aims to make complex global issues accessible. The collection covers topics such as water conservation, biodiversity, food security, micro-lending, citizenship, global awareness and more. Each book provides information and resources to inspire children to make a difference, both locally and globally.

Lesson sequences

Sheri and Laura's Stand Up unit was framed by the inquiry question *"Why should we stand up for what we believe?"* Sheri's class had been exploring the theme of global awareness, using picture books from the CitizenKid series, reading excerpts from novels and pieces of shorter texts, and viewing videos that highlighted children's rights. From the first lesson, the focus had been on engaging the students in commentary writing as a summative assessment activity for the unit. The teachers had encouraged the students to keep an ongoing list of possible writing topics as they worked their way through the unit.

Reading like a writer (approximately 5 lessons)

To scaffold students' ability to read text from the writer's point of view when inquiring into the genre of commentary, Sheri and Laura modelled a think-aloud as they read the text and talked out loud about how it was written, paying particular attention to the stand the author was taking, the evidence the writer used to support their stand, and how the writer conveyed passion (Figure 10.5).

- As a class, students noted the kinds of evidence (e.g., quotes, comparisons, data) that different authors used to support their opinion and coded them so they could start identifying the evidence in the subsequent texts.
- Sheri and Laura guided the students as they practised reading like writers. With each new piece of text, the students read and highlighted the evidence the author used to support their stand. The students then went back into the text to identify, using codes, what type of evidence was used. They talked about the impact that the different types of evidence had on the reader (Figure 10.6).
- Students used the graphic organizer to record their thinking about how the text was written. These responses were used to facilitate the discussion afterward and also as a record that would help guide them in their own writing when the time came.
- At the end of each class Sheri and Laura elicited from students what they noticed about how the commentary was written, what kind of evidence was used, and how much impact the author had in conveying his/her passion.
- Sheri and Laura deliberately chose examples of commentaries on different topics they thought would interest the students so as to expose them to possible topic ideas they may want to write about.

Inquiry Circles (approximately 5 lessons)

Sheri and Laura moved on to engage the students in Inquiry Circles where they participated in small-group discussions about the commentary they had chosen. The teachers began with a fishbowl, where they modelled an effective conversation about a piece of text. They asked the students to describe the key attributes of a successful conversation. Then, together they refined them into criteria on an anchor chart, which became a guide for students in subsequent Circle discussions.

- The teachers introduced six pieces of commentary and told their students that they were to choose three to read over the next three lessons. Each day they would read one piece of text and keep notes on their graphic organizer (Figure 10.7) to support them in their subsequent small-group discussion.

Figure 10.5 Graphic organizer for analyzing texts and videos

Why should we stand up for what we believe?

Think about the questions as you watch the video clip or read the text.

Video/Text: _____

Who is involved?	What do they believe?	Why do they believe it?	How are they standing up for what they believe?

Video/Text: _____

Who is involved?	What do they believe?	Why do they believe it?	How are they standing up for what they believe?

Why should we stand up for what we believe?

Reading from a writer's perspective

Text title: _____

Author: _____

Topic: _____

Before you read: What is your opinion on this topic?

_____

_____

_____

_____

_____

_____

_____

_____

During reading: As you read, highlight the evidence that supports the author's opinion.

_____

_____

_____

_____

_____

_____

_____

_____

After reading: What is your opinion on the topic after reading the piece?

If your opinion is different from before, what evidence caused you to rethink or question your initial opinion?

_____

_____

_____

_____

_____

_____

Figure 10.7 Graphic organizer for analyzing and coding opinion pieces

Why should we stand up for what we believe?

Reading from a writer's perspective

Stand the author is taking:	Intended **audience**:
Go back into the text and **code what kind of evidence the author used:** Examples: Ex Facts: F Comparisons: C Numbers: # Quote from a primary source: QPS Quote from a secondary source: QSS Can't find a code? Maybe we need to add to our list.	**Purpose** of the piece:
	What did you notice about how this piece is written, that is, its style?
	How does the author convey passion for their stand?

- Each Circle had a group of no more than six students (based on the commentary text they chose) to discuss what they noticed about the writing.
- While the inquiry groups were meeting, Sheri and Laura circulated around the room to listen in, observe, and facilitate where needed. They noted comments and commonalities within the conversations to bring forward to the full-class discussion.
- Each Inquiry Circle session wrapped up with a class discussion in which students shared notes about strengths and stretches in the writing, citing examples from their texts. Students began to build a shared vision of what strong commentary writing should include.

Writing a commentary using 6+1 Traits (approximately 5 lessons)

- The teachers began each lesson focused on a learning intention related to one of the 6 traits; for example: "I can write a lead that 'hooks' the reader so they want to read on." (Figure 10.8)
- Although their original writing focus was on the traits of Ideas and Voice, students noticed how the lead (introductory paragraph) hooked them (or not) and how the conclusion left the reader with a sense of the author's passion (or not). From this information, Sheri and Laura realized they needed to address the trait of Organization, specifically targeting leads and conclusions.

Figure 10.8 Class-created chart to focus students' writing

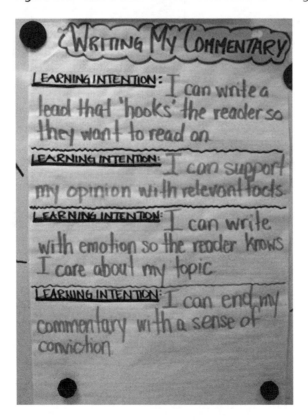

Class-created charts for writing good commentary

Figure 10.9

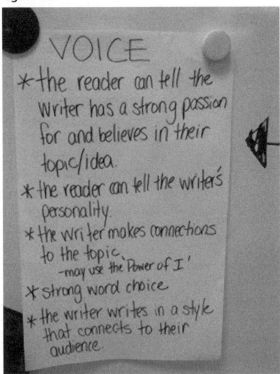

VOICE
* the reader can tell the writer has a strong passion for and believes in their topic/idea.
* the reader can tell the writer's personality.
* the writer makes connections to the topic.
    —may use the 'Power of I'
* strong word choice
* the writer writes in a style that connects to their audience.

Figure 10.10

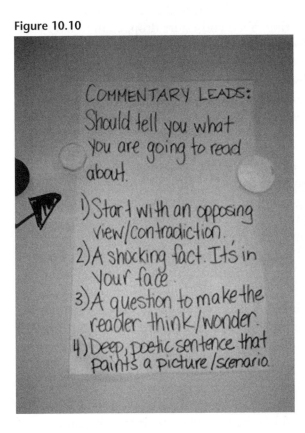

COMMENTARY LEADS:
Should tell you what you are going to read about.
1) Start with an opposing view/contradiction.
2) A shocking fact. It's in your face.
3) A question to make the reader think/wonder.
4) Deep, poetic sentence that paints a picture/scenario.

Figure 10.11

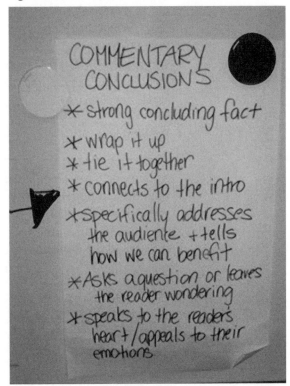

COMMENTARY CONCLUSIONS
* strong concluding fact
* wrap it up
* tie it together
* connects to the intro
* specifically addresses the audience + tells how we can benefit
* Asks a question or leaves the reader wondering
* speaks to the reader's heart/appeals to their emotions

- They planned mini-lessons focused on the traits their students needed:
  1. Ideas: supporting opinions with relevant facts (Figure 10.8)
  2. Voice: conveying a sense of emotion for a topic (Figure 10.9)
  3. Organization: leads that hook the reader (Figure 10.10)
  4. Conclusions: statement conveying conviction for a topic (Figure 10.11)
- For the lesson on each writing trait, students reviewed the commentary texts, noticing how different authors used that trait. For example, when looking at leads, students noticed some writers used a question or a shocking fact to make the reader think. Using these findings, the teachers created anchor charts for each trait. Students could refer to the charts as they considered how they would craft their own writing.
- While students were writing, Sheri and Laura dropped in to have short conferences—giving feedback based on the learning intention, and supporting students where they needed it. The learning intentions for the writing lessons helped give students the language of what it was they were trying to do in their writing, and therefore they could be specific in what they needed feedback on.

Building the Rubric

Together with the students, Laura and Sheri created the rubric to be used for the summative assessment (see Figure 10.12).

- Laura took the learning intentions for the writing lessons on the traits of ideas, voice, and organization and turned them into the language describing what "fully meeting" means.
- From there, Sheri and Laura elicited students' input to fill out the other columns in the rubric so students had a clear picture of what they needed to strive for.
- The final classes had students use the rubric to self-assess and peer-assess. Based on their self-assessments and peer feedback, students were given an opportunity to go back into their writing to make revisions.

Reflections

At the end of the unit, Sheri and Laura reflected on their teaching and student learning. Both agreed that the unit they created was far stronger than they could have created on their own. Each of them brought different strengths to the planning process, and with both of them looking for engaging resources, the planning was accomplished more efficiently and effectively than if they had done it on their own. Using the team-teaching model allowed for more authentic modelling and gave them the benefit of having another voice to confer with students.

Figure 10.12 Rubric for student self-evaluation

Part One: Take a few minutes to reread your commentary. Use a highlighter and highlight the phrases on the rubric that you think best describe your commentary. Your commentary will be evaluated using this rubric.

Writing Traits	Not There Yet	You're Getting There	You're There	Beyond There
Organization Lead Ending	There is no hook and/or the topic is not clear. There is no clear ending. The reader is left with a lot of unanswered questions.	My lead has a hook to introduce the topic but doesn't compel the reader. There is clearly an ending but it didn't wrap up the topic.	My lead hooks the reader so they want to read on. My writing ends with a sense of conviction about my topic. I've anticipated and answered the readers' questions.	My powerful lead is so compelling the reader does not or could not put it down. My ending leaves a lasting impression on the reader.
Ideas Opinion Evidence to support opinion	The reader cannot tell my opinion. My facts are not credible or are not there.	I have an opinion, but it is not always clear. I have some facts but more are needed to support my opinion.	My opinion is strong and clearly evident in my writing. I've used credible and relevant facts to support my opinion.	My opinion is unmistakable all through my writing. I've used a variety of credible and relevant facts that are well-placed to highlight my opinion.
Voice Passion/Emotion about topic	My voice is hidden. It could be anybody's writing; my personality does not come through.	My voice is soft. The reader gets a sense of who the writer is, but only glimpses.	My writing conveys passion and emotion, so the reader knows I care about my topic.	My voice is distinct and maturely conveys an undeniable passion about my topic

© Portage & Main Press, 2014, *It's All About Thinking: Creating Pathways for All Learnings in the Middle Years*, BLM, ISBN 978-1-55379-509-4

Figure 10.12 Part Two:

Write 3 to 4 sentences in response to each of the questions:

1. What are you most proud of in your commentary? Why?

_____

_____

_____

2. What part of your commentary do you think needs more work? Why?

_____

_____

_____

3. What might you do differently if you had a similar assignment again? Why?

_____

_____

_____

_____

Conclusion

Pamela, Linda, Sheri, and Laura have offered diverse approaches to teaching literary, personal, and informational writing. While each of them has unique methods as teachers, they also share common commitments. Students develop as writers when they engage in conversations at all stages of the writing process, share their thinking, and have opportunities to read, hear, and reflect on one another's work. Through reading high quality texts in the same genre, students learn to read like writers, to make better sense of and internalize the different styles of writing.

Assessment is an ongoing and fundamental aspect of the writing process. Students' understanding of what powerful writing is and their ability to create powerful work emerges from experiences as a reader and as a writer, both being paired with thoughtful reflection.

Writing is just one way of making our thinking visible. Multiple means of expression, such as drawing and movement are essential to engaging all students in discovering and sharing their ideas. Finally, to discover, develop, and express their writing self, students must go on a journey. May it be an enjoyable one with good companionship fueled by curiosity and with the confidence to explore unknown paths.

Chapter 11

Creating Pathways through Technology and New Literacies

Educators Involved

Mehjabeen Datoo: Classroom Teacher/Curriculum Consultant

Terry Taylor: District Principal of Learning, SD 10, Nakusp, BC

Lauren Smith: Classroom Teacher, SD 10, New Denver, BC

Larissa Sookro: Classroom Teacher, SD 8, South Slocan, BC

André Derais: Classroom Teacher, SD 8, Slocan City, BC

Patrick Kinghorn: Classroom Teacher, SD 8, Castlegar, BC

Tamara Malloff: Classroom Teacher, SD 8, South Slocan, BC

Janice Novakowski: Teacher-Librarian, SD 38, Richmond, BC

Karen Choo: Classroom Teacher, SD 38, Richmond, BC

Brooke Haller: Classroom Teacher, SD 74, Lytton, BC

Aislinn Mulholland: Classroom Teacher, SD 74, Cache Creek, BC

Errin Gregory: Classroom Teacher, SD 74, Lilloett, BC

For teachers, discussing technology as a teaching tool elicits responses ranging from enthusiasm to fear. We regularly face public pressure to ensure that our students are prepared for a future characterized by rapid change and the integration of technology into all parts of our lives. We have seen several shifts in the role that information and communication technologies can play in our learning environments. One significant shift is the recognition that learning and literacy are interactive processes not just between and among people but within different environments. Literacy skills such as decoding and inferring are still important, but our students must also learn to recognize that meaning is situated within particular contexts—what is inferred within one context may be different within another. One implicit but important message is that knowledge does not exist without context. Another implicit message is that knowledge is not a fixed element; rather it can be examined from many perspectives and built on within additional contexts.

The introduction and conclusion of this chapter were co-authored with Mehjabeen Datoo.

The tools that our students use become both the mechanisms and the places for negotiating meaning. Technologies and social media in all forms have become integrated into our everyday lives and work, which gives us another view of learning. Learning occurs within a complex interaction of people, tools, and representations engaged "in activity." Context is central because it defines the purpose of the learning. Such a view of learning comes from studies of people engaged in activities such as the members of a ship's crew, the members of a critical care medical staff, and even the members of a family on a grocery shopping expedition (Lave and Wenger 1991). Although these contexts seem removed from traditional concepts of "learning," they help us rethink "school." Too much teaching and learning are removed from the world. Learning must be experienced as purposeful and be applied to our world.

Research on learning recognizes that individuals can learn highly complex tasks within structures and environments that appear more informal but are, in fact, organized around networks, informal mentorships, and sophisticated tools. The learning in these environments is driven by a need to "do something." Learning becomes necessary to the activity rather than a precursor to it. Technology is integrated into this activity and provides support and mechanisms to hold and structure activity. It also helps us by "offloading"—more efficiently processing—certain tasks, which frees up our mind to engage in other parts of the task. Having computer programs graphically represent a map, calculate and represent temperature, wind speed, and ocean current helps the ship's crew members streamline their decision making. The necessary academic knowledge is not omitted from the learning process; rather, it is deeply contextualized within it.

In this chapter, teachers and students expand their learning contexts outside of the classroom and use tools to assist them in working across contexts. The learning patterns documented here demonstrate the connecting, processing, and transforming aspects of well-designed lessons. The texts, skills, tools, and interactions work together in a complex system—all focused on clearly defined but open-ended learning goals. Each of the examples engages students in inquiry—exploring something that matters in the world, that provides purpose and connection for them. Inquiry extends their notions of the world beyond their immediate contexts. These examples demonstrate the shift in our understanding of literacy and learning, not only as the development of an individual's mind and skills but also as the development of a collaborative learning community engaged in the co-construction of knowledge.

Making the World a Better Place Together

In this section, we describe the collaboration by three school districts, five teachers, and over 100 students. The dedicated team of teachers came from three West Kootenay school districts in British Columbia: School District 10 (Arrow Lakes), School District 8 (Kootenay Lakes), and School District 20 (Kootenay Columbia):

Terry Taylor, District Principal of Learning, SD 10

Lauren Smith, from Lucerne School in New Denver

Larissa Sookro, from Mt. Sentinel School in South Slocan

André Derais, from WE Graham in Slocan City

Patrick Kinghorn, from Stanley Humphries Secondary in Castlegar

Tamara Malloff, from Mt. Sentinel School in South Slocan

During a meeting at the beginning of June 2012, teachers in SD 10 and SD 8 asked "What would happen if we collaborated and connected our students across a range of curricular areas from Science to Language Arts and Social Studies with the overarching notion of making the world a better place?"

Science
The science teachers from the three schools connected via Skype to share ideas and plans to make the Water Unit in Science 8 relevant by personalizing it for their students. They produced three ideas and approaches:

1. Climb local glaciers and paddle Slocan Lake while studying the water cycle in a place-conscious experiential unit at Lucerne School.
2. Form a community–school partnership with the Slocan River Streamkeepers, a non-profit organization that protects and restores the aquatic and riparian ecosystems of the Slocan River <www.slocanriverstreamkeepers.com>.
3. Examine water quality at various points in the Slocan River drainage basin at Mt. Sentinel School.

Students posted their learning on a project blog. During the project, teachers also connected online.

English Language Arts

In the multi-grade English class at Lucerne School in New Denver, students created documentary films on the theme of their community as "A Place of Peace and Belonging." With the help of two professional filmmakers, the students pursued their inquiry into how their community had historically been a place of peace despite the larger global and national contexts of social injustice, racism, and war. They interviewed Doukhobor Elders who had been sent to residential school in the community; Japanese-Canadian Elders who had been interned there during WW II after Japan attacked the United States at Pearl Harbor in 1941; Vietnam War resisters who had moved to New Denver from the U.S. to find peace; and Aboriginal Elders who had strong traditions of peace in the valley. Some students created personal narratives about the peace they themselves had found upon moving to the community, and they shared their short films at community screenings.

Cross-District Online Literature Circles

A team of five teachers from three school districts and over a hundred students in grades 7 to 9 engaged together in Literature Circles. The teachers chose dystopic fiction and nonfiction as the catalyst for student thinking for several reasons:

- The theme of dystopia is predominant in our culture and particularly resonant with young people.
- Dystopic fiction grapples with real-world problems and issues that humans faced throughout the 20th century and still face now.
- Finally, the kernel of hope is inherent in the examination of dystopias.

They wanted their students to authentically discuss real-world problems, build their personal reservoirs of hope, and connect with one another to generate meaningful and actionable solutions.

Big ideas

- We as a society must pay attention to many real-world problems—issues of social justice and of environmental degradation are our responsibility.
- Although it's easy to become discouraged, it's within our grasp to take action and do something.
- Together, we can make a better world!

Tools to support learning

Teachers used VoiceThread to offer students a range of options to respond to text and share their thinking with peers in the four geographically dispersed classrooms. Students had these options: to record their own voice, to make a short video with their webcam and post it, or to write text in VoiceThread.

VoiceThread
<voicethread.com/>

Essential questions

- Is the world really a place of despair and disillusion?
- Is this young generation inheriting a world rife with problems and no solutions?
- How can we begin to shift the paradigm, to find hope, to take action—together?

Introductory Lesson

Teachers embedded a short YouTube text-based clip entitled "Lost Generation" into the online Moodle <moodle.org/> that students in all five communities could access. The text is a poem by Jonathan Reed, who created it in the form of a narrative palindrome (i.e., the same text makes sense being read forward line by line as it does being read backward). As the words appear on the screen and are read forward, the text suggests hopelessness and despair:

> View "Lost Generation" at: <m.youtube.com/watch?v=K6msKrqmN3w&desktop_uri=%2Fwatch%3Fv%3DK6msKrqmN3w>.

> I am part of a lost generation / and I refuse to believe that / I can change the world / I realize this may be a shock but / "Happiness comes from within" / is a lie and / "Money will make me happy."

Yet, as soon as the reader reads through to the end, the video reverses and, as the reader re-reads the lines from last to first, despair blossoms into strong, assertive hope.

> "Money will make me happy" / is a lie and / "Happiness comes from within" / I realize this may be a shock but / I can change the world / and I refuse to believe that / I am part of a lost generation."

The students' task was to view the video, reading and listening to the text, then to respond using the VoiceThread text box. Some students prepared a podcast to express their thinking. Although they could have chosen to prepare a video to share their ideas, no one did so.

The results

Student responses were rich and emphatic. They connected deeply with the text and with the underlying theme, and each student had something to add to the conversation. When students saw how others expressed their ideas, it helped to scaffold everyone's thinking. It was a terrific launch for the Literature Circle. Each teacher used the comments posted by other classes to highlight the richness of ideas and the range of thinking. These added to the classroom discussions and helped students better understand the notion of *dystopia*. They also recognized how real-world problems are connected to finding solutions and taking action. This cycled back to solidify the learning intentions both for the lesson and the unit—finding hope amid despair.

Offer Choice by Subtheme

Students chose their novels based on three subthemes:

1. the environment
2. societal criticism
3. human transformations

Essential questions

- What can we do about the environment?
- Why do some people treat others so unjustly? Are we capable of similar inhumanities?
- What choices do we have? Are we capable of changing things?
- What kernels of hope are within us all?

Online Teacher Collaboration in Planning

See Brownlie and Schnellert 2009, chapter 12.

The five teachers spent almost a month preparing the project for their students before the Literature Circle went live on the Moodle site. Lauren Smith, Larissa Sookro, Tamara Malloff, André Derais, and Patrick Kinghorn met face-to-face for training in using Moodle. They examined the frameworks of other Online Literature Circles that Terry Taylor, District Principal in SD 10, had done. Then they selected the books for their own Online Literature Circle, keeping their students in grades 7 to 9 in mind:

- *What were their students' interests and passions?*
- *What texts linked to the theme of dystopia, while also offering a range of reading levels and ways in which students could engage in thoughtful conversations, in their classroom as well as online?*
- *What books would inspire the joy of reading?*

Figure 11.1 Teacher's Lounge

They came up with three clusters of books and each teacher took the lead for one cluster.

In the next stage of planning, they developed thoughtful questions to spark students' reading and deep thinking during the Moodle discussion forums. Key to the planning phase—and used throughout the Circle—was an online Teachers' Lounge (Figure 11.1), a private discussion forum for the teachers to pose questions, seek input, and share ideas with one another.

Assessment Rubric

Lauren developed the rubric for the Online Literature Circle responses and discussions. She entwined key elements of the *BC Performance Standards in Reading, Writing, and Social Responsibility* into one rubric to be used for both formative and summative assessment. Teachers also used the rubric to frame their feedback to learners (Figure 11.2). They discussed the rubric with their students, who also used it to self-assess, to set their learning goals, and to guide their own feedback to peers.

Follow-Up Lesson Planning

From their assessments, teachers noted that many of their students had strengths as visual learners and oral learners. To assist the aural-oral students, Tamara, the technology guru on the learning team, scanned and reduced each book cover as a mini icon and linked the icon to the discussion forums within Moodle. At the same time, she read and recorded short VoiceThread <voicethread.com/> podcasts of the cover copy for each text. In this way, all students were able to preview the texts and choose one to read. Such universal design adaptations accessible to all students helped scaffold those whose learning benefited from visual and auditory cues.

The teachers developed a lesson for each of the three thematic clusters identified in the unit: Environment, Societal Criticism, and Human Transformation. Each lesson embedded four discussion forums—one for each book in each cluster, and had the discussions initiated by three or four questions to which the students could respond. They could also add their own thoughtful questions and reply to them or to other student-generated topics linked to the books. This stage of the unit of study took between four and five weeks—each school chose the length of time according to what worked best for their context.

Essential Question: *Can we make a difference for our planet?*

Theme One—The Environment

Text set focused on dystopic books connected to environmental destruction:

- *The Hunger Games* by Suzanne Collins
- *Ashes, Ashes* by Jo Treggiari
- *The Carbon Diaries 2015* by Saci Lloyd
- *H20 One Shot* by Grant Calof and Jeevan Kang

Theme Two—Societal Criticism

Text set focused on dystopic views that critique modern society:

- *Divergent* by Veronica Roth
- *Matched* by Ally Condie
- *The Giver* by Lois Lowry
- *The Wave* by Morton Rhue

Figure 11.2 Rubric for Literature Circle discussions of dystopic texts

Rubric for Literature Circle

Criteria	Not Yet within Expectations	Meets Expectations (Minimum Level)	Fully Meets Expectations	Exceeds Expectations
Communicating Response and analysis	Sometimes I have difficulty making connections to my own ideas or to the discussion questions. My reactions or judgments may be vague or have little supporting evidence.	The connections to my own ideas and to the discussion questions are fairly obvious. I offer reactions and judgments with some supporting evidence.	The connections I make to my own ideas/beliefs or themes in the novel make sense. My reactions or judgments are supported by solid reasons and examples.	I can support my opinions, judgments, and analysis with solid evidence from reliable and credible sources, including those from the novel. I offer creative ideas or insightful responses to the question prompts.
Respecting Solving problems in peaceful ways	In conflict situations, I often use put-downs, insults, or sarcasm. I often have trouble expressing my opinion clearly, and other people do not always understand what I am trying to say.	In conflict situations, I try to manage my feelings appropriately, listen respectfully to other points of view, express myself clearly, and always try to be fair.	In conflict situations, I usually manage anger appropriately, listen respectfully, and present logical arguments. I can paraphrase other peoples' viewpoints.	I am very respectful when working/talking with others, online and face-to-face. I understand and listen to other points of view. I show care and concern for others by including them in the conversation.
Sharing Making meaning	My explanations are usually short and I do not use examples to support my ideas. I stick to more general ideas and shy-away from using specific details. My reasoning is difficult to follow. I rarely begin conversations or participate in them.	My point of view is usually clearly presented. I try to add some relevant ideas, explanation, and/ or examples. I rarely begin a conversation, but might participate if someone else initiates it.	My point of view is original and clearly presented. I build on my position using details, examples, and explanations. I sometimes begin a conversation, ask a question, or encourage others.	My point of view is engaging and mature. I show individuality. I am able to convince others of the value of my position. I may use sophisticated strategies (e.g., irony). I often begin conversations, encourage others, and ask engaging questions.
Valuing Diversity and defending human rights	I am sometimes disrespectful. I may stereotype others. I may avoid people who are perceived as different in some way.	I am usually respectful. I try to support those who speak up or take action to support diversity and defend human rights.	I am respectful and fair. I am increasingly willing to speak up or take action to support diversity and defend human rights in my community.	I am respectful and ethical. I speak out and take action to support diversity and defend human rights, even when that may not be a popular stance.
Exercising Democratic rights and responsibilities	I tend to focus on my own perspective and do not try to imagine other people's perspectives and/or situations. I feel little sense of community or responsibility for others at this time.	I care about my community. Sometimes I join positive actions if someone else is organizing, but I do not like to commit in case I change my mind.	I care about my community/ world and feel a sense of responsibility. I am increasingly interested in taking action to improve the world.	I really care about improving my community/world, and I can describe, plan for, or show by my actions how to make a better world.

© Portage & Main Press, 2014, *It's All About Thinking: Creating Pathways for All Learnings in the Middle Years*, BLM, ISBN 978-1-55379-509-4

Theme Three—Human Transformation
Text set focused on how human beings transform or are transformed in disturbing ways:

- *The Chrysalids* by John Wyndham
- *Feed* by M. T. Anderson
- *SALT* by Maurice Gee
- *The Knife of Never Letting Go* by Patrick Ness

Tamara connected each book icon to its own set of discussion questions, with the expectation that the students reading that book would respond to the questions as they read. Some teachers in the Circle chose to have their students discuss their ideas in class in response to the questions, while others asked their students to write out their responses.

As in other versions of Literature Circles, students "have voice and choice" in selecting their text and in how they respond. All students were given the option of responding to the questions they chose in writing or by recording their response in podcast format. All the classroom discussions, whether by small groups of students reading the same text, or by reading other students' posts to the Moodle discussion forums—or in discussions with the teacher—helped scaffold and stretch student thinking. Each student was required to read at least one book in each theme, but they could also read more—and many did.

The results
Teachers reported that students really enjoyed this way of reading and responding to text. The wide range of books offered choices that engaged student interest. All students reported that their joy in reading increased with the Circle. Many shared their books with their parents, who also reported that they enjoyed the reading.

As a result of the project, the teacher team achieved their primary goal—to move students from despair to taking action, or at least feeling capable of taking action. Students reported that connecting with the community of online learners in the five schools gave them more ideas to discuss and share in their communities. They learned about how the issues they were reading about and discussing were often seen differently in the other communities.

Musqueam Inquiry—Using iPads

As part of her school's library program, Janice Novakowski, an educator in the Richmond School District, focuses on authentic inquiry with students. Using materials or images as a starting point allows students to notice details and discuss their observations—which leads to "I wonder" questions that students can then pursue or investigate by engaging with different text forms.

The school's Aboriginal Support Worker, a member of the Musqueam Nation, was invited to collaborate, but her scheduling did not allow her to become involved in the lesson planning. When Janice, a teacher not of Aboriginal descent, sought support in choosing materials and resources for this study, the teacher consultant for the Aboriginal Education Enhancement Agreement (AEEA) recommended a resource kit from the local Musqeuam Nation. As well, she collaborated with Janice as a "critical friend" to bounce ideas back and forth throughout the study. Janice's school district had only recently signed an AEEA with its local First Nation, and the agreement encouraged schools to help their students develop their knowledge of the Musqueam culture.

As part of a school-wide introduction, Janice worked with Karen Choo, a grade 5/6 teacher, to develop inquiry lessons that would also connect to the science curriculum focused on natural resources. Their overall goal for the inquiry was for students to investigate how the Musqueam traditionally used natural resources for food, shelter, clothing, and tools. Their guiding question was *"How did the Musqueam use the natural resources available to them?"* and they intended to look at both traditional and contemporary uses.

Museum Artifacts

Janice borrowed a Musqueam culture kit from a local museum (Figure 11.3). The kit had been developed in collaboration with the elders of the Musqueam nation. During the first lesson, the teachers introduced the kit (a box holding several museum artifacts), during which they learned that those who handled the artifacts had to wear conservation gloves. The gloved teacher placed one artifact on each table for students to observe and respond to the instruction: *"Describe the form and function of the artifact and what materials it is made of."* The students were highly engaged in examining the artifacts and noticing details of how the objects were made.

Janice and Karen ensured that the focus was on the Musqueam as a "living culture" and the artifacts reflected the changes and adaptations that the Musqueam nation made over time in the materials they used for tools, and the types of boats and materials they used for fishing. The students naturally began wondering aloud what the different items were and what they were made out of.

Janice asked the students to record the artifact at their table by drawing and including word labels describing observable features such as colour, texture, size, or material (Figure 11.4). Some students then shared their observations with the whole class. Janice asked students to consider

Figure 11.3 Kit holding artifacts of the Musqueam culture

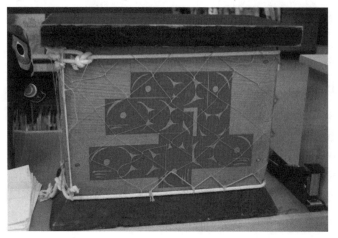

Figure 11.4 Students examine artifacts from the collection in the Musqueam kit

what they had observed and what they already knew about Aboriginal culture in order to make inferences about what the artifacts were and what they were made from. The students recorded their inferences under their drawings. Janice and Karen had planned for students to develop inquiry questions later in the unit, but students began asking "I wonder" questions as they observed the artifacts and inferred their purpose and material. These questions emerged naturally during the task and at the end of the lesson, Janice and Karen asked the students to record questions they had about the artifact or about Musqueam culture during the lesson. Janice explained that the students would have time to pursue some of their questions in a couple of weeks. One student recorded his thinking in three ways—imaging, inferencing, and wondering (Figure 11.5).

Historical Photographs

The following week, the students visited the library for the next lesson in the Musqueam inquiry process. Janice asked the students to discuss their exploration of the artifacts as she handed out copies of historical photographs

Figure 11.5 One student's observations, inferences, and wonders about the artifacts

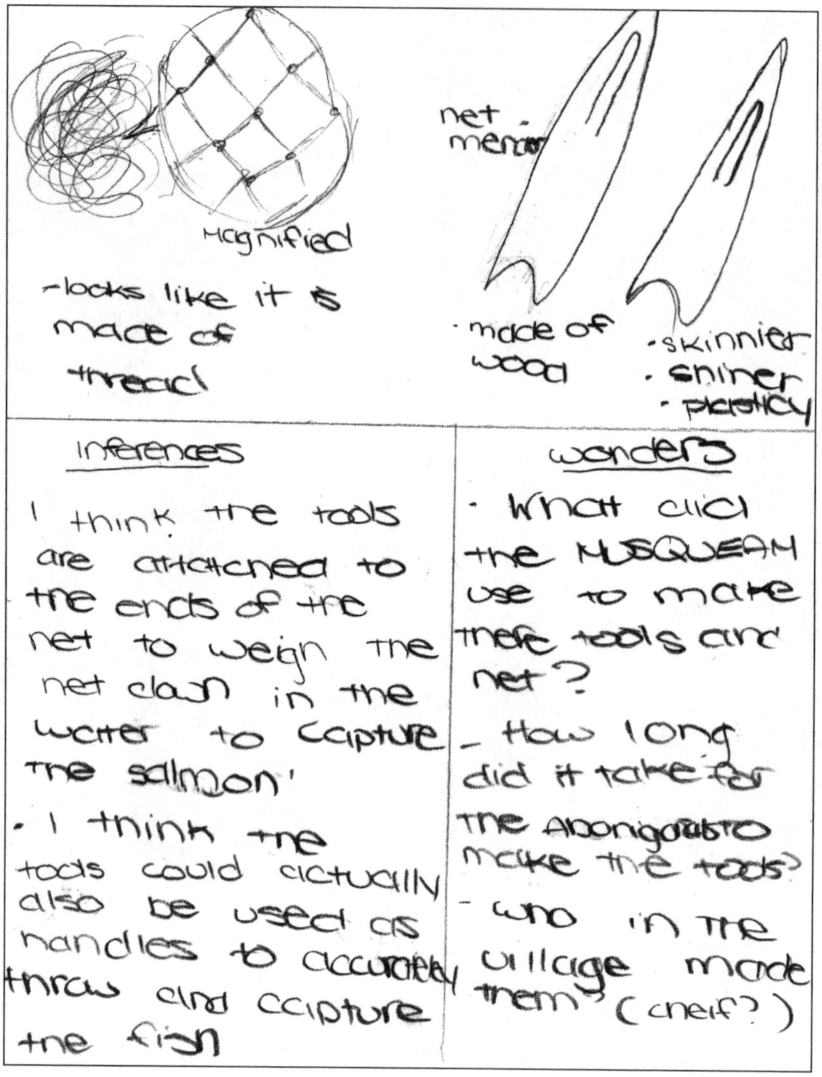

net.
mercar

Magnified

-looks like it is
made of
thread

· made of   ·skinnier
wood   · shiner
· plasticy

inferences	wonders
I think the tools are attatched to the ends of the net to weigh the net clown in the water to capture the salmon. · I think the tools could actually also be used as handles to accurately throw and capture the fish	· What did the MUSQUEAM use to make there tools and net? - How long did it take for the Aborigaribro make the tools? - who in the village made them? (cheif?)

from the museum kit. She told them that photographs are archived in museums because they are considered "primary source" documents that people can use to learn about cultures in the past. Then she asked the students to examine the black and white photographs to see what information they could "read" from them, by noticing details about the people, objects and events.

As the students looked at and discussed the photographs, Janice and Karen listened in, noting which students were making connections between the artifacts they had studied the previous week and the context of those artifacts in the photographs. While students were making inferences about when and where the photographs were taken, they also began asking for more specific information about the photographs. Janice asked the students to think about where they might go to find out more about the photographs.

Figure 11.6 Student sketch from historical photographs, with questions to research

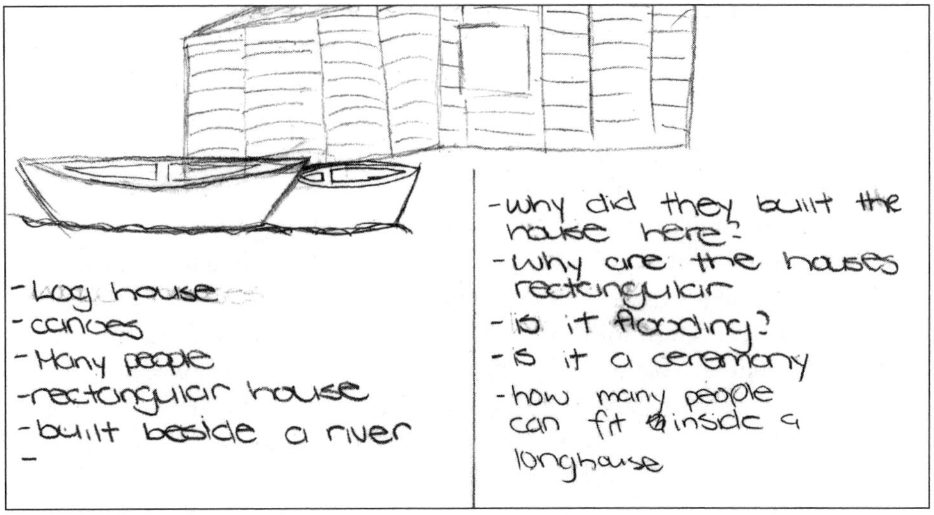

Students sketched details from photographs that interested them, then wrote out their questions about things they saw in the photographs (Figure 11.6). Some questions were not specific to the photograph, but the photograph became inspiration for further inquiry. Janice asked the students to share their questions with classmates at their table and to think about the different types of inquiry questions that they were asking. She explained that the next week they would investigate one of their questions—either a question from their observations about the artifacts, or about one of the historical photographs, or about an aspect of Musqueam culture that they wanted to know more about. Both teachers reminded the students that their inquiry questions should be "researchable" because they would use online sources for the next stage of their research.

Pursuing Inquiry Questions

Janice and Karen's school emphasized two goals—digital literacy and citizenship—that they believed could be combined with their students' increasing awareness of how to find information online. For this third class, students learned about researching online using iPads provided in the library-resource centre. Janice asked the students to choose one of their inquiry questions they had recorded during previous lessons while she got the iPads ready for distribution. With the goal of developing their digital literacy, Karen asked the students how they would know whether or not a website was reliable and the information valid. The students discussed the topic for a few minutes at their tables, then shared their thinking with Karen.

After she had given an iPad to each student, Janice had them load the student version of World Book online <www.worldbookonline.com>. The students knew from previous experience that the author of each article on this website was an expert in the topic. When Janice asked the students to enter "Musqueam" in the search field, the students were surprised that no article showed up, just a map of Vancouver with the Musqueam reserve located on it. When Janice asked what they could do to refine the search, one student noted that they needed to broaden the search. When they tried the term "Coast Salish," the students were glad to find a short article on the Coast Salish peoples of British Columbia.

Janice had thought the World Book site would provide a good start, but its information was obviously too general to provide answers to the students' questions. She then suggested they explore the website developed by the Musqueam First Nation for more specific information about their history, culture, and fishing. Together, they discussed the importance of seeking authentic sources for reliable information. Both teachers looked at the site with the students and noticed the specific tabs to help locate information and navigate the site. Janice and Karen asked the students to think about where on the site they would start reading for specific information about their question, and gave them half an hour to read and take notes. As Janice and Karen circulated, they noted some students were not really sure where to start their research so they provided direct support, helping them to navigate the website.

Musqueam First Nation website <musqueam.bc.ca>

Karen commented how engaged the students were overall. Both teachers thought their students' motivation came from having developed their own questions because of their interest in seeking answers to those questions, not just doing general research.

Sources of information

During the students' next two research classes, Janice reviewed the different ways to use a search engine such as Google to find specific information. With such support in framing searches, that is, in using keywords and structuring their questions, the students were able to search more independently. Janice reminded them to question the reliability of websites, and stressed the importance of recording the date and source for any information they wanted to use. She also introduced students to the concept of triangulation and the importance of using multiple sources to cross-check their information. Both teachers also pointed out the reference books and other text materials available throughout the library for student use as they investigated their inquiry questions.

Representing what we've learned

When the students had compiled notes from more than one source, Janice asked them to choose from iPad apps which one they would use to represent their question and answer. She showed the students four apps to choose from: Drawing Box, Doodle Buddy, Writers Studio, and Notability. It was interesting to watch which students spent their time drawing detailed pictures to illustrate their information and which others used text-based formats to convey their message. However, most of their writing was in short, succinct responses to their questions.

Assessment

Throughout the Musqueam inquiry, Janice and Karen noted students' ability to share and discuss their observations, inferences, and inquiry questions. At each stage of the inquiry, both teachers shared their expectations with the students, and worked with them to develop the criteria for the research and their final representation. The rubric in Figure 11.7 shows the teachers' criteria for "fully meeting expectations," which they used as the basis for developing—with the students—similar descriptions for the other levels of achievement.

Reflections

Janice and Karen noted the high engagement of the students during the inquiry process. They believed that starting the unit with observation of "real" artifacts and examination of historical photographs gave their students a stronger sense of the study's authenticity, and stimulated their curiosity enough so that their inquiry questions were genuinely meaningful to them. They also noted that their students could be both engaged and distracted while working on the iPads. They needed time to navigate websites and to read for information; the school's allotted block of time ended the work sessions too soon. Helping their students figure out how to use particular apps, how to create images, change fonts, and become generally familiar with the use of the technology took longer than Janice and Karen had planned. This was the first year their students had iPads to use at school, and the teachers needed more time in their own schedule to help students become familiar with the applications available.

Janice and Karen also noted that most of the students didn't actually write very much as part of their response to their inquiry question. Although writing a succinct response is an important skill, they saw that they might include "adding details" and "expanding ideas" as future writing goals for students. Karen was satisfied with the curricular connections the students made throughout the study. She felt that they had an increased awareness of Aboriginal uses of natural resources and had begun to understand the Musqueam as a living culture.

Students became highly engaged when the Musqueam Nation faced the issue of a building developer who was excavating Marpole Midden, the land of a traditional burial site. The students were far more connected to this issue and passionate about the social injustice of it than they would have been before this study introduced them to Musqueam culture. Overall, throughout the inquiry, Karen and Janice felt they had modelled the spirit of inquiry themselves and that their students would be able to apply the stages of an inquiry process in other contexts.

Figure 11.7 Partial rubric for student research project, showing "fully meeting" criteria

Start of rubric for student research project

	Not yet meeting expectations	Meeting expectations	Fully meeting expectations	Exceeding expectations
Observations, connections, and inferences			Notices details and materials Makes personal connections and relates objects and events to personal experiences Makes inferences based on both acquired knowledge and personal experiences	
Development of inquiry questions			Creates open-ended, investigable questions related to the topic	
Online research			Utilizes reading for information strategies Assesses online sites as reliable sources of information	
Question and answer representation			Representation includes question, full response, supporting image and sources of information referenced	

Creating Pathways with New Technologies

Teachers Brooke Haller, Aislinn Mulholland, and Errin Gregory work together as part of the Connected Classrooms Project in SD 74 (Gold Trail, a rural school district). This project merges their three geographically distant classrooms of grade 4 through grade 7 students (roughly aged between 9 and 13) by using technology and collaborative instruction. The three teachers and their classes used daily videoconferencing, online collaborative work by both teachers and students, and shared resources, including student-created multimedia content. Collaboration lies at the core of the project, which is one of many district initiatives that respond to declining student enrolment, very small student peer groups, and rural isolation. The project also helps strengthen their ability to work within a team in a variety of interactive ways—creating a community of learners among both the students and the teachers.

> Various technologies and software make Connected Classrooms possible by bridging the geographical distances between the classroom sites. The technologies in the classrooms, both Bridgit and online spaces, help connect the learners within the project.

Over the past few years, the learning has been jointly organized by teachers Brooke, Aislinn, and Errin who co-plan on a daily, weekly, and monthly basis. The teachers model the collaborative process that they promote among their students. Each teacher focuses on their area of expertise and their passions to sculpt lessons and activities that they then facilitate in a weekly videoconference and manage the online forum that complements the topic. The nature of the videoconferences is reciprocal. The students engage in project-based activities that require cooperation, creativity, and critical thinking. The learners and the teacher-facilitators interact during the videoconferencing and share SMART board work via Bridgit and participating in online forums and discussions.

> Bridgit is a desktop sharing software that allows multiple classrooms to see what the teachers and students are sharing during connections. Bridgit conferencing software enables both home and distant sites to collaborate on projects, share what students create on the SMART board, and effortlessly exchange ideas. It is an extremely user-friendly software that helps classrooms share voice, video, and data over the Internet <www.smarttech.com/bridgited>.

Moodle, too, has become a powerful communication and sharing tool—students frequently message each other and their teachers, and engage deeply in discussion forums. Throughout the course of the project, the teachers witnessed new and exciting learning relationships and partnerships between students, as well as increased engagement and motivation to learn. The shared Moodle site has provided an authentic audience for students' work, and is a venue for students to use peer-assessment and self-assessment to reflect critically on their own learning.

Project Goals

The project has several key goals for exploring the value of new technologies:

1. to enhance digital literacy and the ability of students to collaborate through the seamless use of transformative technology
2. to create project-based learning experiences that are interdisciplinary in nature and to promote student collaboration, creativity, and critical thinking
3. to broaden the learning community of geographically distant students
4. to focus on improving literacy skills for students who are constantly challenged to respond critically to text, to media, and to the world around them
5. to improve reading, writing, and inquiry skills within the majority of lessons

This section focuses on the lessons that laid the foundation for the student work online and created the momentum of the project. The lesson sequence was aimed at enriching students' written responses to questions and activities within the Moodle forum.

A digital space is the perfect way to connect students in both synchronous and asynchronous ways. At the elementary level, students connect via a district Moodle site. Students respond to weekly forums, receive messages from teachers and other students, participate in Online Literature Circles and engage in chats with learners across the district. Moodle is a password-protected e-learning platform that serves as a central hub for the classrooms within the project <moodle.org/>.

The students engaged in a great deal of learning and communicating with peers through Moodle, and the teachers recognized the importance of setting and maintaining an academic tone for the discussions. Although student engagement in online forums was high, teachers found their written responses began at the basic level. The following examples show how the teachers worked on extending students' ability to think critically and to craft compelling written responses online. Throughout the year, they consistently guided students to deepen their responses by providing details that clarified their reasoning, and by reflecting on their thinking process.

The teachers developed a series of video-conferencing lessons and drew on the principles of assessment for learning, of modelling and guided practice, and of peer collaboration within their Moodle forum.

Interactive Lessons via Videoconference

Although the sequencing differed from activity to activity, most lessons followed the structure of "connect— process—transform" with ample time for students to talk and participate in groups, exemplifying the connective nature of learning. Teachers modelled the challenges and rewards of working together, and students engaged in group projects and peer collaboration daily. In every lesson, they expected and encouraged their students to draw on the insights of their peers and share their own insights. While combining their varied ideas, the students began to recognize that their thoughts were valued, and they became more capable constructors of their own learning.

Online Collaborative Work on Moodle

Within the project, students engaged in weekly thematic Moodle forums, discussions about the selected texts for their Online Literature Circles. Each teacher was responsible for leading and moderating a Moodle forum. Aislinn moderated a Reading Forum, Errin one on Photography, and Brooke another on Current Events—forums that linked directly to each teacher's special interest. Students responded to a variety of prompts and media, ranging from probing questions, photos or videos, to academic articles. The teachers' ultimate goal was to guide their students in writing strong responses that showed evidence of their thinking by connecting, inferring, and synthesizing their thoughts and by reflecting on their own writing.

Current events forum

Brooke gave students a prompt for exploring a news topic and posed a question that required some research and intense thought and reflection. The core idea was that real-world problems captured students' interest and provoked serious thinking as they acquired and applied new knowledge in a problem-solving context.

Reading forum

Aislinn developed "essential questions" and "inquiry questions" for their students to encourage critical and creative thinking as well as inferencing from the research data they collected. Students could reply to the question with their own thoughts and opinions or they could take the discussion further by asking their own related questions. Students were engaged through the online conversation, and the practice strengthened their ability to reason their way through a question or problem. By combining these skills with other skills developed while working through collaborative activities to resolve problems, the students began to apply them to other areas of their learning.

Photography forum

Students responded to a photo of the week, a photo through which they explored their emotions and reactions along with the principles and elements of design. They responded in weekly videoconferences, with their observations and inferences about the photos.

Formative assessment

Teacher facilitators provided frequent formative assessment within Moodle forums, and offered their students descriptive feedback on their responses and Moodle messages; their students offered similar descriptive feedback to one another. The students engaged in continual self-assessment and peer-assessment, and took ownership of their learning by co-developing and then trying to follow the criteria for assessing their projects and Moodle responses. The critical part of this process began in September when teachers guided their students in co-creating and learning to use the criteria to improve their writing and their ability to craft strong responses in weekly Moodle forums and online Information Circles. Throughout the year, Moodle provided all students with a larger and authentic audience—students in the other classrooms—to respond to their writing, which made all contributions and critiques more meaningful.

Essential question

Aislinn launched the journey into Moodle for Connected Classrooms with the intention of establishing a safe and respectful online community while also improving the quality of written responses. She began the year with a videoconference aimed at fostering student ownership of their Moodle coursework (Figure 11.8). Classrooms at all three sites, connected via videoconferencing, received two essential questions *What worries you about sharing online?* and *What makes a Moodle response powerful?*

Connecting

The connecting screen and the questions were left on in the background as students at all three sites were encouraged to engage with a partner and brainstorm responses. At the beginning of the school year, many students were new to the world of Moodle, but they were not new to online venues. They could draw on their experience with a variety of social media platforms, and were able to activate that background knowledge, drawing on both negative and positive online experiences.

After small-group discussion, the students reported out from their individual classes and shared collective thoughts. Their comments ranged from concerns about online bullying to how to manage their time in an online environment. Each class then shared their contributions among the three classrooms, creating a single list of concerns and responses via Brigit. Students were keen to hear about online experiences and related contributions from the variety of students involved in the project. The opportunity to draw on

Figure 11.8 One of the classrooms involved in the Connected Classrooms project

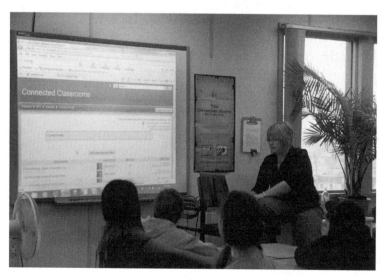

their own reflections as well as the advice from a much larger group of students provided a rich collection of responses to the essential question.

Processing

In each classroom/community, students crafted categories that combined to describe a "powerful Moodle response," based on content, writing style, and evidence of each student's understanding and reflection. Using these categories, students drafted a set of performance standards to use when evaluating their own written Moodle responses over the year. The fact that students created the criteria meant that they had become invested in the process. If students could internalize the assessment methods, it would mean that self-assessment could become an on-going process in the classrooms.

Transforming/Personalizing

Aislinn's next lesson was an activity that used student exemplars to show the progression in meeting performance levels on the student-created rubric of criteria (Figure 11.9). During the videoconference, she asked students to respond, as individuals, to a question that required some thought. The students at all three school sites were to respond with individual quick-writes and, after they had written their initial response, they were to tuck it away for later reference. Then the teacher produced responses by students in the previous year's Moodle as exemplars. At each school site, groups of current students received one of these student exemplar responses and were asked to score it using the categories and levels on the rubric they had created, and to give reasons why they made their decision.

When finished, representatives of the groups at each site shared their decisions with the other students via the wireless microphones. Each exemplar was read out, and the group from that exemplar thoroughly defended their assessment decisions. Having each group look deeply into one response and discuss it together helped all students begin to clearly see and explain the differences between posts—those that did not yet meet expectations, or met them minimally, fully, or exceedingly. Having such a rich variety of responses from many different students via the technology that brought those responses into their virtual space made the students' discussion about assessing quality more comprehensive than otherwise possible.

For the final transformative piece in this lesson, teachers asked the students to refer to their initial response, and score it with the same rubric. Then they shared how the lesson had helped them see areas for improvement in their own writing. The students found it much easier to self-assess after they had seen and discussed exemplars from other students and weighed where they fit on the performance standards. Students who thought they had written a strong initial response realized that the response was lacking in one or more category. Teachers asked the students to write goals for their future posts based on the criteria in the rubric. Throughout the year, their goals shifted and evolved as their writing progressed.

Figure 11.9 Student-created criteria for online Moodle responses

Not Yet Meeting Expectations 1	Minimally Meeting Expectations 2	Fully Meeting Expectations 3	Exceeding Expectations 4
• 1–2 sentence answer • Not on topic • No thoughts • Few details • No description • Lacks proofreading • No evidence to support answer • Unrelated to developing discussion thread	• Response is less than one paragraph in length • On topic • Many errors • Some of own thoughts and opinions • Little evidence to support answer • Some connections • Shows awareness of developing discussion thread	• Response is 1 paragraph in length • Well-developed, and stays on topic • Few errors in spelling or grammar • Lots of detail • Uses descriptions • Uses descriptive vocabulary • Interesting to read • Clear • Evidence of editing • Reasons given to support answers • Includes own thoughts and opinions • References to developing discussion thread	• Response is several (2-3) well developed paragraphs • Stays on topic • Proper paragraph structure • Has no errors in spelling/grammar • Evidence of editing • Includes lots of details • Use of descriptive vocabulary • Good connections • Deep thinking • Amazing descriptions • Uses evidence from the book to support answer • Includes own thoughts/ opinion • Relates to and draws from developing discussion thread

Deepening Moodle Responses

Connecting with media

The biggest concern over the next few weeks on Moodle continued to be the depth and level of detail found in students' posts. This was particularly evident in the area of connecting to current events. Although the current events forums were highly popular, and students themselves had created the assessment criteria, many of their responses had remained at the basic, literal level. In their follow-up discussions, the teachers found that, when students were asked to respond without having an opportunity for talk time, connecting, questioning and contemplating, most responses fell into the "minimally meeting" category. In contrast, when they integrated the forum questions into more structured learning activities, the students' written responses were stronger. Consequently, the teaching team used formative assessment to direct their lesson-planning.

From week to week, they would review students' Moodle posts for trends in their writing, then use this evidence to relate each writing lesson to the type of prompt given, and offer strategies for improving writing skills. Brooke designed a series of lessons aimed at supplementing her current events forum and to guide her students in responding to different types of prompts. She also presented varied strategies for accessing difficult texts in current event materials and for responding effectively with supporting details.

Connecting

Students' initial Moodle posts had indicated that they were struggling, in isolation, to activate background knowledge and connect to the topics under discussion. Brooke began her writing lesson by asking students at all three sites to share their thoughts as they recalled their collaborative work on *"What makes for a powerful response?"* The students were quick to share the successful posts by other students that had impressed them. It was exciting and motivating for students to hear positive comments about their individual responses from students in another community because it confirmed that their posts had meaning and were being viewed and enjoyed by the larger connected community. Peer assessment was alive and well and showed that, if they could evaluate what made the writing of their peers "powerful," they would benefit from activities designed to transfer those skills to critiquing their own writing.

During these current events sessions, Brooke led an activity on the Occupy Movement which was reaching its peak at that time and seemed to consume the news. During a visit to Vancouver, she had stayed at a hotel directly across from the Occupy camp, and decided to visit the camp and take videos of the Occupy protesters, their posters, and other signs or messages that could offer good discussion points for her students.

Before delving deeply into the topic, Brooke planned to first have the students activate whatever background knowledge they might have about the purpose of the movement. She asked the three classes to discuss separately what the students in each class knew about Occupy Vancouver, and to prepare a presentation for the others. The students at each site worked in stages—from individual quick-writes to partner talk to whole-class share-out. Then the three classes took turns presenting their notes to the other class sites. Being able to collect so much information from diverse groups of students in different communities and contexts—made possible by the virtual connections—gave the students a rich, divergent collection of background information to share.

Processing

When Brooke then showed the film she had compiled from her videos, the students became fully engaged. Her inside view of the camp was something new to them, and the topic was real and current. Knowing that the person delivering both the video and the lesson gave the students an even stronger connection to the topic—and a primary source of information. The posters and signs created by the campers contained proverbs, slogans, messages, and pleas about their concerns, adding the human and emotional element.

The teaching team asked their students at each site to record their thoughts and reactions while the images played. Some responded on paper and some in online messages. The students in Brooke's home class responded in real time on their net books in a back chat while the film played (Figure 11.10). Brooke had also created a virtual meeting space on Today's Meet <todaysmeet.com/>, and some students were responding online with their reactions to the film. Their instantaneous conversations also documented the students' perspectives on the varied emotions and reactions in their own classrooms, and how those reactions shifted over the course of the film. The teachers at each classroom site collected the notes on how the students thought and felt as they responded to the images, and again shared these responses via videoconferencing.

Transforming/Personalizing

The teachers at all three sites made multiple copies of each photo in the film, and they assigned students to choose the single most powerful image, in their opinion, and write a reflective response about it. Students were not asked to agree or disagree with the Occupy movement, but to write a single response about one aspect of it.

Students crafted their work as a Moodle response, explaining how the image made them feel, their reactions to the camp and the movement, and the message they thought the author of the sign in their photo was trying to send. They also described their feelings about the message, and explained why they felt that way. Students went on to post a digital copy of their chosen image and their written response on Moodle. As the teachers at each site monitored their students' work, they found that the responses were not just crafted much better but also showed all the writing skills of connecting, inferring, and transforming—finally supporting their responses with relevant details. The responses on Moodle were now much more "fully meeting expectations" or "exceeding expectations" through using the videoconferencing technology to draw on the insights of many more

Figure 11.10 Students respond online with their reactions to the film, in partners or individually

students, and use this input to refine their thoughts. They had become a "community of practice" (Wenger 1998).

This lesson structure had produced much better responses than a single essential question on the Moodle forum about the Occupy camp. The multimedia images and collaborative discussions they participated in during the videoconference made a major difference. Students were eager to view the completed posts by their classmates and their accompanying images on Moodle, which showed a deeper understanding about different perspectives on the Occupy messages.

Marking Text for Accessibility

The topics the teaching team chose for the current events forum reflected real events happening locally or globally at the time, quite often related to environmental issues and stewardship. In one lesson, Brooke presented an article about a recent study on everyday household pollutants that find their way into the ocean, mentioning the toxicity levels of the waters off the BC coast. The topic immediately resonated with students, but when they clicked on the links, they were confronted by articles that most could only scan and some really struggled to comprehend—the text of most articles was lengthy and written at a higher reading level than that of most middle level students.

Connecting

In response to their concern, the teachers first asked students to engage in table talk about household chemicals and pollutants in their own area, then share out to the larger Connected Classrooms to compile an extensive list of connections and prior knowledge. They also invited the students to revisit the work they had done on describing criteria for powerful responses. When the students reviewed their criteria, they did so from the perspective of responding to an informational article. The students at all three sites constructed their ideas specifically referencing such text, finding evidence in the literature to support their opinions, and sharing them in the early stages of the videoconference.

Processing

The teaching team also decided to prepare lessons to introduce "marking text" as a reading strategy for dense informational text. They chunked the solid page of text in the article into shorter pieces and encouraged students to write on (mark) the text as much as they could and make use of margins and spaces between lines—as they dissected the text. They then asked their students to visually represent what they understood from each piece of text. On the read-through of the first chunk, the teachers asked their students to draw an illustration in the margin to represent a concept for that small chunk. On the read-through of the second chunk, they were asked to write a personal connection to that small chunk. On the read-through of the third chunk, they were asked to write any questions they had.

By reading the text in small chunks several times, the task of thinking about and taking several actions within each small chunk helped the students gain a greater understanding of the text. When this process was coupled with intermittent sharing of illustrations, connections, and questions with and from other students between every chunk, the students gained twenty new connections and questions for every one they made by the time they were done with the article.

Transforming/Personalizing

Brooke had her own students submit their marked articles, and she took a digital image of each. To show students the benefits of learning from each other, she opened each image in Photoshop, increased its transparency, and added one on top of the other into a single layer while her students watched. As the image grew from a single sheet of student paper to one with a plethora of illustrations, connections, and questions, the message was clear—that it represented the collective contributions and understandings of the whole class. When reflecting on that final layered image, one student remarked how cool it was to see into twenty different brains on a single page.

After the students shared their thoughts and understandings online, they gathered responses to the article and responded in the current events forum. The sharing of final responses at the end of the videoconference was meaningful when students could see how their contribution helped other students learn. As a closing activity, students were asked to assess their work, using the criteria they had established, and to set a new goal for their next Moodle post.

Adding Detail and Evidence to Support Writing

The next facet of students' writing and responding that the teaching team wanted to develop was the level of detail and evidence they incorporated in writing their opinions or responses. Students did not often explain their reactions to and insights about the weekly photo. During this lesson sequence, Leyton co-taught the three classes from Brooke's classroom. Brooke and Leyton provided a photographic analysis process for students to use and apply to their weekly Moodle posts.

Connecting

Using Brigit, Brooke shared her desktop with the three classes and sent students the initial prompt—an image of a young boy, sitting alone in rubble with his hands covering his face. The question for students was "Why is this boy covering his eyes?" The students had to draft an individual written response, then share out their idea of why the boy was covering his eyes. Most preliminary responses were emotional, noting that the boy might be sad, alone, or in a war zone, but they gave no details, and many did not explain their thinking.

Processing

Leyton and Brooke introduced the strategy of photo analysis, and broke up the work between sites, asking each class to focus on a different aspect of the photo and examine that single aspect thoroughly. The idea was to create class experts who would deeply examine their given aspect.

Students worked in small groups at each site to brainstorm possibilities for their assigned aspect of the photo. Aislinn's class engaged in a deep analysis of the other people and objects in the photo. They compiled a list of everyone and everything they saw in the photo and left no corner of the image unexplored. Errin's class tackled the setting and activities in the photo. They used what they observed to infer the location and context, and they created a profile of the setting and action in the image. Leyton and Brooke's class examined the invisible—or inferred—relationships in the photo. Students paid close attention to the cues of how the people in the background might be related to the boy, for example, and they explained details of how they came to their conclusions, based on evidence from the photo.

Each class drew on the work of their whole group, examining the aspect they had been given in great detail. As each site shared, participants were keen to record the thoughts and details from other sites about the photo. By the time the sharing was done, the students not only had insight into their particular aspect of the photo, but they had acquired a strong understanding of every aspect of the photo, and had been exposed to possibilities and scenarios they hadn't initially considered.

Transforming/Personalizing

After the share-out, students revisited the photo and the initial question. Armed with the knowledge acquired from their peers, they prepared a final response to post on Moodle. Some elaborated on their initial answer, and some went in an entirely different direction after hearing the insights from other classes. These responses showed a much greater level of detail, and nearly all used detailed evidence from the photo to support their assumptions about why the boy was covering his eyes. They had gone much deeper into the photo than initially.

They then debated who had made the "correct" assumptions about the photo, and demanded to know the real story behind it. Students read through posts from others, and engaged in multiple discussion threads about the photo, debating whether or not they were correct in their conclusions, and how they justified those conclusions in their posts based on the evidence in the photo. By examining multiple perspectives from multiple students via videoconferencing, the photo was brought to life and students found ways to add detail and evidence to their posts. Peer assessment was evident in the way they compared posts to analyze who had made the better case. This led to lengthy discussions about how to write powerful Moodle posts that compel the reader to see it from their perspectives. While students again assessed their Moodle response on the performance standards, the value of using the posts of others to encourage students to step up their own writing was evident.

Reflection

Connected Classrooms is about human beings working together through technology and being connected in a meaningful way. Through the Connected Classrooms Project, students have been provided with valuable opportunities to collaborate and learn from one another. This use of technology created a new kind of interactive school environment, contributed new learning, and shifted the assessment process within the three classrooms.

Opportunities for self- and peer-assessment were created for students through Moodle participation; students often note that they discovered new ideas by reading the work of other students. Having a larger but authentic audience also provides greater accountability and creates an awareness that they are writing for a purpose. It makes students more aware of the written work they post. They respond to each other's online submissions, and they know that it will be read by someone other than their teacher. Through technology, collective idea-creating and sharing, students are able to approach topics from a variety of angles and perspectives.

Videoconferencing and Moodle allowed the teachers to combine their classrooms and create a richer, more diverse learning environment. For an explanation of research foundations, project goals, and student/teacher feedback on the project, visit <prezi.com/vozxkyo7q0q8/connected-classrooms-in-sd74/>.

Conclusion

The examples shared in this chapter address the importance of integrating technology into the classroom. With technology, and the access it provides to people in other communities, we will always have new literacies to discover and learn. With the rapid evolution of technological devices and software, the definition of new literacies is always changing. We, as educators, must recognize that all learners still need guidance in developing the knowledge and skills that will support them in using new technologies appropriately and effectively in various facets of their lives.

As we help build our students' success, we notice positive student engagement and motivation to learn. Collaborating with others and feeling free to express oneself through technological media are essential elements of learners' development in the 21st century. As educators we hope to encourage participation in new literacies and emerging technologies to expand learning and broaden thinking.

References

Aboriginal Education Enhancement Agreement (AEEA). <www.bced.gov.bc.ca/abed/agreements/>.

Achor, Shawn. 2011. *The happiness advantage: The seven principles of positive psychology that fuel success and performance at work.* New York, NY: Crown Business, A Division of Random House.

Apple Inc. 2012. *Challenge-Based Learning: A Classroom Guide.* <www.challengebasedlearning.org>.

ArtsLink Project. 2012. Residential School Artists. <www.edonline.sk.ca/bbcswebdav/library/materials/ArtsLink/main_pages/about-us.html>.

Association for Middle Level Education (AMLE). 2010. *This we believe: Keys to educating young adolescents,* editor John H. Lounsbury. Westerville, OH: Association for Middle Level Education. <www.amle.org/>.

Atwell, Nancie. 1998. *In the middle: New understandings about writing, reading, and learning.* Portsmouth, NH: Heinemann.

Atwell, Nancie. 2002. *Lessons that change writers.* Portsmouth, NH: Firsthand/Heinemann.

Bay-Williams, Jennifer M., and Sherri L. Martinie. 2004. *Math and literature: Grades 6–8.* Sausalito, CA: Math Solutions Publications.

Bennett, Barrie Brent, and Noreen Carol Rolheiser-Bennett. 2001. *Beyond Monet: The artful science of instructional integration.* Toronto, ON: Bookation.

Birchak, B., C. Connor, K. M. Crawford, L. H. Kahn, S. Kaser, and K. G. Short. 1998. *Teacher study groups: Building community through dialogue and reflection.* Urbana, IL: National Council of Teachers of English.

Black, Paul, and Dylan Wiliam. 1998. "Assessment and classroom learning." *Assessment in Education* 5 (1): 7–74. Assessment Research Group, 2002: British Columbia Ministry of Education.

Black, Paul, Chris Harrison, Clara Lee, Bethan Marshall, and Dylan Wiliam. 2003. *Assessment for learning: Putting it into practice.* Maidenhead, UK: Open University Press/McGraw-Hill Education International.

Bond, L. A., and A. M. Carmola-Hauf. 2004. "Taking stock and putting stock in primary prevention: Characteristics of effective programs." *The Journal of Primary Prevention* 24 (3): 199–221.

Booth, David. 2005. *Story drama: Creating stories through role-playing, improvising, and reading aloud,* 2nd ed. Markham, ON: Pembroke Publishers.

Booth, David, and Charles Lundy. 1985. *Improvisation: Learning through drama.* Toronto, ON: Harcourt, Brace, Jovanovitch.

Booth, David, and Kathleen Gould Lundy. 2007. *In graphic detail: Using graphic novels in the classroom.* 2007. Oakville, ON: Rubicon Publishing.

British Columbia Ministry of Education. *Dance: K–7.* 2010. Victoria, BC: British Columbia Ministry of Education. <www.bced.gov.bc.ca/irp/subject. php?lang=en&subject=Dance>.

British Columbia Ministry of Education. *BC Performance Standards: Reading Literature, Reading for Information; Writing, Numeracy.* Revisions 2009 and ongoing. Victoria, BC: Student Assessment and Program Evaluation Branch. <www.bced.gov.bc.ca/perf_stands/reading.htm>.

British Columbia Teacher-Librarians' Association. 2010. *The points of inquiry.* <bctf.ca/bctla/pub/documents/Points%20of%20Inquiry/PointsofInquiry.pdf>.

Brownlie, Faye. 2005. *Grand conversations, thoughtful responses: A unique approach to literature circles.* Winnipeg, MB: Portage & Main Press.

Brownlie, Faye, Susan Close, and Linda Wingren. 1988, 1991. *Reaching for higher thought: Reading, writing, thinking strategies.* Edmonton, AB: Arnold Publishing.

Brownlie, Faye, and Catherine Feniak. 1998. *Student diversity: Addressing the needs of all learners in inclusive classrooms.* Markham, ON: Pembroke Publishers.

Brownlie, Faye, Catherine Feniak, and Leyton Schnellert. 2006. *Student diversity: Classroom strategies to meet the learning needs of all students,* 2nd ed. Markham, ON. Pembroke Publishers.

Brownlie, Faye, and Leyton Schnellert. 2009. *It's all about thinking: Collaborating to support all learners—in English, social studies, and humanities.* Winnipeg, MB: Portage & Main Press.

Brownlie, Faye, Carole Fullerton, and Leyton Schnellert. 2011. *It's all about thinking: Collaborating to support all learners—in mathematics and science.* Winnipeg, MB: Portage & Main Press.

Brownlie, Faye, and Judith King. 2011. *Learning in safe schools,* 2nd ed. Markham, ON: Pembroke Publishers.

Buehl, Doug. 2014. *Classroom strategies for interactive learning.* Newark, DE: International Reading Association.

Butler, Deborah L, and Leyton Schnellert. 2008. "Bridging the research-to-practice divide: Improving outcomes for students." *Education Canada* 48 (5): 36–40.

Butler, Deborah L., and Leyton Schnellert. 2012. "Collaborative inquiry in teacher professional development." *Teaching and Teacher Education* 28: 1206–1220.

Bybee, Rodger W. et al. 1989. *Science and technology education for the elementary years.* Washington, DC: National Center for Improving Science Education.

Bybee, Rodger W., J. A. Taylor, A. Gardner, P. Van Scotter, J. Carlson, A. Westbrook, and N. Landes. 1997, 2006. *The BSCS 5E instructional model: Learning cycle: Origins and effectiveness.* Colorado Springs, CO: Biological Sciences Curriculum Study.

Campbell, Brian, and Lori Fulton. 2003. *Science notebooks: Writing about inquiry.* Portsmouth, NH: Heinemann.

Campbell, Linda, Bruce Campbell, and Dee Dickinson. 2004. *Teaching and learning through multiple intelligences.* Boston, MA: Allyn and Bacon/Pearson.

Carmichael, Allan, William Shaw, Kirsten Farquhar, Sarah Marshall, and Joy Reid. 2006. *BC Science Probe 8.* Toronto, ON: Nelson Education.

Challenge-based learning: A classroom guide. 2012. Apple Inc. <www.challengebasedlearning.org/public/toolkit_resource/02/0e/0df4_af4e.pdf?c=f479>.

Chancer, Joni, and Gina Rester-Zodrow. 1997. *Moon journals: Writing, art, and inquiry through focused nature study.* Portsmouth, NH: Heinemann.

Christensen, Linda. 2000. *Reading, writing, and rising up.* Milwaukee, WI: Rethinking Schools Publications.

Close, Susan. 2014. GOSSIP (Go out and selectively seek important points). Smart Learning. <www.smartreading.ca/smart_learning_founder.shtml>.

Cohen, Jonathan. 2001. "Caring classrooms/intelligent schools: The social emotional education of young children." *Social and Emotional Learning 2.* New York, NY: Teachers College Press.

Collaborative for Academic, Social, and Emotional Learning (CASEL). 2013. *Effective social and emotional learning programs: Preschool and elementary school edition*, p. 9. <www.casel.org/>.

Confucius.1956. *Confucian Analects (The Analects 551–479 BCE).* London, UK: P. Owen.

Connected Classrooms Project. 2012–2015. *Achievement contract: A three-year plan.* <www.sd74.bc.ca/Pdf/District/2011/AchieveCont11-14FINAL.pdf>.

Costello, Bob, Joshua Wachtel, and Ted Wachtel. 2013. (e-book). *Restorative circles in schools: Building community and enhancing learning.* Bethlehem Books.

Culham, Ruth. 2003. *6+1 Traits of writing: The complete guide, grades 3 and up.* Markham, ON: Scholastic Publishing, Canada.

Cumming-Potvin, W. 2007. "Scaffolding, multiliteracies, and reading circles." *Canadian Journal of Education* 30 (2): 483–507.

Cutting, Robert. 2007. *The 10 most revolutionary inventions.* The 10 Series, editor Jeffrey D. Wilhelm. Markham, ON: Franklin Watts/Scholastic Publishing, Canada.

D'Adamo, Francesco, and Ann Leonori. 2003. *Iqbal* (English translation). New York, NY: Atheneum Books for Young Readers.

Daniels, Harvey, and Steven Zemelman. 2004. *Subjects matter: Every teacher's guide to content-area reading.* Portsmouth, NH: Heinemann.

Darby, Jaye, and James Catterall. 1994. "The fourth R: The arts and learning." *The Teachers College Record* 96 (2): 299–328.

Davies, Anne, Caren Cameron, and Kathleen Gregory. 2011. *Setting and using criteria,* 2nd ed. Knowing what counts Series. Winnipeg, MB: Portage & Main Press.

Dils, Ann. 2007. "Why dance literacy?" *Journal of the Canadian Association for Curriculum Studies* 5 (2): 95–113.

Donovan, M. Suzanne, John D. Bransford, and James W. Pellegrino, eds. 1999. *How people learn: Bridging research and practice*. Washington, DC: National Academies Press.

Duffy, T. M., and D. J. Cunningham. 1996. "Constructivism: Implications for the design and delivery of instruction." In *Handbook of research for educational communications and technology* 170–98, edited by D. J. Jonassen. New York, NY: Macmillan Library Reference.

Easton, Lois Brown. 2008. *Powerful designs for professional learning*, 2nd ed. Oxford, OH: National Staff Development Council.

Ebbers, Margaretha. 2002. "Science text sets. Using various genres to promote literacy and inquiry." *Language Arts* 80 (1): 40–50.

Ekdahl, M., M. Farquharson, J. Robinson, and L. Turner. 2010. *The points of inquiry: A framework for in-formation literacy and the 21st-century learner*. Vancouver, BC: British Columbia Teacher-Librarians' Association (BCTLA).

Elias, Maurice J., and Harriett Arnold, eds. 2006. *The educator's guide to emotional intelligence and academic achievement: Social-emotional learning in the classroom*. Thousand Oaks, CA: Corwin Press.

Ellis, Deborah. 2006. *I Am a Taxi*. Toronto, ON: House of Anansi.

Gaga, Lady, J. B. Laursen, D. W. Shadow, F. Garibay, and RedOne. 2011. "Born this way." Streamline/Interscope/KonLive/Cherrytree.

Gardner, Howard. 1999. *Intelligence reframed: Multiple intelligences for the 21st century*. New York, NY: Basic Books.

Gardner, Howard. 2006. *Multiple intelligences: New horizons in theory and practice*. New York, NY: Basic Books.

Gay, Geneva. 2002. "Preparing for culturally responsive teaching." *Journal of Teacher Education* 53 (2): 106–116.

Gay, Geneva. 2010. *Culturally responsive teaching: Theory, research, and practice*, 2nd ed. New York, NY: Teachers College Press.

Goatly, Andrew P. 2000. *Critical reading and writing: An introductory coursebook*. Oxford, UK: Routledge/Taylor and Francis Group.

Gross, Jonathan. 2011. *Two sides to every story 2*. Dayton, Ohio: Teaching and Learning Co.

Gross, Jonathan; illustr. Jeff Richards. 2012. *Two sides to every story 2: An examination of ethics, dilemmas, and points of view through discussion, writing, and improvisation*. Dayton, OH: Teaching and Learning Co./Lorenz Educational Press.

Hales, Jennifer. 2010. *Learning about homelessness in British Columbia: A guide for senior high-school teachers*. Vancouver, BC: Simon Fraser University.

Harper, Maddie, illustrator Carlos Freire. 1993. *Mush-Hole*. Toronto: Sister Vision Press.

Harvey, Stephanie, and Anne Goudvis. 2007. *Strategies that work: Teaching comprehension for understanding and engagement*, 2nd ed., chapter 7. Portland, ME: Stenhouse Publishers.

Hawkins, J. D., B. H. Smith, and R. F. Catalano. 2004. "Social development and social and emotional learning." In *Building academic success on social emotional learning: What does the research say?* 135–150, by editors J. E. Zins, R. P. Weissberg, M. C. Wang, and H. J. Walberg. New York, NY: Teachers College Press.

Heink, Jill, and William Farnau. 2008. "Learning through the arts in Lexington's Catholic schools." *Momentum* 39 (2).

Henkin, Roxanne, Janis Harmon, Elizabeth Pate, and Honor Moorman. 2009. "Editors' message: Service-Learning: The intersection of civic and academic engagement." *Voices from the Middle* 17 (1): NCTE. <www.ncte.org/journals/vm/issues/v17-1>.

Hong, Lily Toy, author and illustrator. 1993. *Two of Everything*. Judith Matthews, ed. Park Ridge, IL: Albert Whitman & Company.

Hong, Tina. 2000. "Developing dance literacy in the postmodern: An approach to curriculum." Paper presented at Dancing in the Millennium, international conference in Washington DC, July 2000.

hooks, bell. 1994. *Teaching to transgress: Education as the practice of freedom*. New York, NY: Routledge.

hooks, bell. 2003. *Teaching community: A pedagogy of hope*. New York, NY: Routledge.

Hyde, Arthur A. 2006. *Comprehending math: Adapting reading strategies to teach mathematics*. Portsmouth, NH: Heinemann.

Jeffrey, Noreen, and William Keith Prentice. 1997. *Writing in the middle and secondary classrooms: Theory into practice*. Toronto, ON: ITP Nelson

Kelner, Lenore Blank, and Rosalind M. Flynn. 2006. *A dramatic approach to reading comprehension: Strategies and activities for classroom teachers*. Portsmouth, NH: Heinemann.

Lave, Jean, and Etienne Wenger. 1991. *Situated learning: Legitimate peripheral participation*. Cambridge, UK: Cambridge University Press.

Levine, Melvin D. 2002. *A mind at a time*. New York, NY: Simon & Schuster.

Lounsbury, John H. 2010. "This we believe: Keys to educating young adolescents." *Middle School Journal* 41 (3): 52–53.

Lyubomirsky, Sonja, Laura King, and Ed Diener. 2005. "The benefits of frequent positive affect: Does happiness lead to success?" *Psychological Bulletin* 131 (6): 803.

Lyubomirsky, Sonja, Chris Tkach, and M. Robin DiMatteo. 2006. "What are the differences between happiness and self-esteem?" *Social Indicators Research*, 78, 363–404.

Martinez, Joseph G. R., and Nancy C. Martinez. 2001. *Reading and writing to learn mathematics*. Boston, MA: Allyn and Bacon.

Marzano, Robert J. 2010. "Developing expert teachers." In *On excellence in teaching*, editor R. J. Marzano. Bloomington, IN: Solution Tree Press.

Monnin, Katie. 2009. *Teaching graphic novels: Practical strategies for the secondary ELA Classroom*. (e-book). N. Mankato, MN: Maupin House.

Morgan, Norah, and Juliana Saxton. 2006. *Asking better questions*, 2nd ed. Markham, ON: Pembroke Publishers.

Nation, M., C. Crusto, A. Wandersman, K. L. Kumpfer, D. Seybolt, E. Morrissey-Kane, and K. Davino. 2003. "What works in prevention." *American Psychologist* 58: 449–456.

National Council of Teachers of English (NCTE). 2007. *Adolescent literacy: A policy research brief, 1–8*. Urbana, IL: James R. Squire Office of Policy Research. <www.ncte.org.ezproxy.library.ubc.ca/library/NCTEFiles/Resources/PolicyResearch/AdolLitResearchBrief.pdf>.

Newbald, Jill, and Prue Goodwin. 2004. "Dance and the literacy curriculum." In *Literacy through creativity: Informing teaching*, editor Prue Goodwin, 105–111. New York, NY: David Fulton Publishers.

Ngeow, Karen Yeok-Hwa. 1998. *Enhancing student thinking through collaborative learning*. ERIC Clearinghouse on Reading, English, and Communication. Bloomington, IN: Indiana University Press.

Olsen, Sylvia. 2001. *No time to say goodbye: Children's stories of Kuper Island Residential School*. Winlaw, BC: Sono Nis Press.

O'Neill, C. 1995. *Drama worlds: A framework for process drama*. Portsmouth, NH: Heinemann.

Palmer, Parker J. 2007. *The courage to teach: Exploring the inner landscape of a teacher's life*. 10th anniversary edition. San Francisco, CA: Jossey-Bass.

Pearson, P. David, and Margaret C. Gallagher. 1983. "The instruction of reading comprehension." *Contemporary Educational Psychology* 8 (3): 317–344.

Perry, Bruce D., and Maia Szalavitz. 2010. *Born for love: Why empathy is essential—and endangered*. New York, NY: HarperCollins Publishers.

Physical and Health Education Canada. 2013. <www.phecanada.ca/programs/dance-education>.

Ray, Katie Wood. 2006. *Study driven. A framework for planning units of study in the writing workshop*. Portsmouth, NH. Heinemann.

Reid, Carrie, and Flora Cook. 2000. *Duck soup for the Aboriginal soul*. Vol.1. Vancouver Island North, BC: First Nations Programs, School District #85.

Respress, Trinetia, and Ghazwan Lutfi. 2006. "Whole brain learning: The fine arts with students at risk." *Reclaiming Children and Youth* 15 (1): 24.

Rico, Gabriele Lusser. 2000. *Writing the natural way. Using right-brain techniques to release your expressive powers*. Penguin Random House Company: Tarcher/Putnam.

Riestenberg, Nancy. 2012. *Circle in the square: Building community and repairing harm in school*. St. Paul, MN: Living Justice Press.

Schnellert, Leyton, Mehjabeen Datoo, Krista Ediger, and Joanne Panas. 2009. *Pulling together: How to integrate inquiry, assessment, and instruction in today's English classroom*. Markham, ON: Pembroke Publishers.

Seligman, Martin E. P. 2011. *Flourish: A visionary new understanding of happiness and well-being*. New York, NY: Free Press.

Shakespeare, William. *A midsummer night's dream*. 1918 Series: The Yale Shakespeare, editor W. H. Durham. New Haven, CT: Yale University Press.

Shea, Pegi Deitz, and Leane Morin. 2006. *The carpet boy's gift*, 2nd ed. Gardiner, ME: Tilbury House.

Small, Marian. 2012. *Good questions. Great ways to differentiate mathematics instruction*, 2nd ed. New York, NY: Teachers College Press.

Smith, Michael W., and Jeff D. Wilhelm. 2006. *Going with the flow: How to engage boys (and girls) in their literacy learning*. Portsmouth, NH: Heinemann.

Stiggins, Rick. 2005. "From formative assessment to assessment for learning: A path to success in standards-based schools." *Phi Delta Kappan*, 324–328.

Tarlington, Carole, and Wendy Michaels. 1995. *Building plays: Simple playbuilding techniques at work.* Portsmouth, NH: Heinemann.

Truth and Reconciliation Commission of Canada. 2008.<www.trc.ca/websites/trcinstitution/index.php?p=10>.

Urban Aboriginal Peoples Study. 2010. *Urban Aboriginal Peoples Study: Main report.* Ottawa, ON: Environics Institute. <www.uaps.ca/wp-content/uploads/2010/03/UAPS-Main-Report_Dec.pdf>.

Weare, Katherine, and Melanie Nind. 2011. "Promoting mental health of children and adolescents through schools and school-based interventions: Evidence outcomes; School-based interventions." Southampton, UK: School of Education, University of Southampton.

Wenger, Etienne. 1998. *Communities of practice: Learning, meaning, and identity.* Cambridge, UK: Cambridge University Press.

Western and Northern Canadian Protocol (WNCP) for collaboration in education. 2006. *Common Curriculum Framework for K–9 Mathematics.* <www.wncp.ca/>.

Wiederhold, C. W., in consultation with Spencer Kagan. 1998. *Cooperative learning and higher level thinking: The Q-matrix.* San Clemente, CA: Kagan Publishing.

Wiggins, Grant, and Jay McTighe. 2005. *Understanding by Design*, expanded 2nd ed. Alexandria, VA: ASCD.

Wilcox, Kristen Campbell, and Janet I. Angelis. 2007. *What makes middle schools work.* Albany, NY: University at Albany SUNY, Institute for Research in Education.

Wilhelm, Jeffrey D. 2001. *Improving comprehension with think-aloud strategies.* New York, NY: Scholastic Professional Books.

Wilhelm, Jeffrey D. 2002. *Action strategies for deepening comprehension.* New York, NY: Scholastic Professional Books.

Wilhelm, Jeffrey D. 2007. *Engaging readers and writers with inquiry.* New York, NY: Scholastic Professional Books.

Wilhelm, Jeffrey D., Tanya Baker, and Julie Dube. 2001. *Strategic reading: Guiding students to lifelong literacy, 6–12.* Portsmouth, NH: Heinemann.

Wilhelm, Jeffrey D., and Bruce Novak. 2011. *Teaching literacy for love and wisdom: Being the book and being the change.* Language and Literacy Series, Teachers College Press <www.tcpress.com/>.

Willms, J. Douglas, Sharon Friesen, and Penny Milton. 2009. *What did you do in school today? Transforming classrooms through social, academic, and intellectual engagement.* First National Report. Toronto, ON: Canadian Education Association.

Zimmerman, Barry J., and Dale H. Schunk. 2011. *Handbook of self-regulation of learning and performance.* New York, NY: Taylor & Francis/Routledge.

Zins, J., R. Weissberg, M. Wang, and H. J. Walberg, eds. 2004. *Building academic success on social and emotional learning: What does the research say?* New York, NY: Teachers College Press.

Index of Frameworks, Approaches, or Strategies